Agatha Christie

AND ARCHAEOLOGY

Edited by Charlotte Trümpler

THE BRITISH MUSEUM PRESS

© 1999 Ruhrlandmuseum Essen and Scherz Verlag Bern,
München, Wien
English edition and translation
© 2001 The British Museum Company Ltd

First published in Great Britain in 2001 by
The British Museum Press
A division of The British Museum Company Ltd
46 Bloomsbury Street, London WC1B 3QQ

Translated from the German by Anthea Bell in association with
First Edition Translations Ltd, Cambridge, UK

A catalogue record for this book is available from the British Library
ISBN 0 7141 1148 1

Printed in Slovenia

FRONTISPIECE
Agatha Christie in front of the head of Ramesses II, in the Ramesseum at Thebes,
Egypt 1931 or 1933 (photo: Max Mallowan)

Contents

8   **Acknowledgements**

10   **Foreword**
Mathew Prichard

11   **Introduction**
Charlotte Trümpler

Biography

19   **Agatha Christie** (1890–1976)
Janet Morgan

39   **Max Mallowan** (1904–78)
Henrietta McCall

Archaeology: The Excavations

55   **Ur of the Chaldees**
Hans J. Nissen

73   **Nineveh**
Renate Gut

89   **Arpachiyah**
Stuart Campbell

Chagar Bazar   105
Augusta McMahon

Tell Brak   121
David and Joan Oates

Nimrud   137
John Curtis

Life on Site

'*Le camping* **begins**':   163
Life on an Archaeological Site in the 1930s
Charlotte Trümpler

Agatha Christie, Nimrud and Baghdad   205
Joan Oates

'**A dark-room has been allotted to me …**':   229
Photography and Filming by Agatha Christie on the Excavation Sites
Charlotte Trümpler

Travelling

From Orient Express to Desert Bus: 258
Agatha Christie's Travels in the Near East
Axel Heimsoth

Traces of Agatha Christie in Syria and Turkey: 287
An Oriental Journey Seventy Years afterwards
Tom Stern

Agatha's Arabs: 303
Agatha Christie in the Tradition of British Oriental Travellers
Reinhold Schiffer

Detective Novels

335 **'The Glamour of the East':**
Some Reflections on Agatha Christie's *Murder in Mesopotamia*
Nadja Cholidis

351 **Agatha Christie and her Use of Ancient Egyptian Sources**
Waltraud Guglielmi

391 **The Detective and the Archaeologist**
Barbara Patzek, Regina Hauses and Andreas Dudde

411 **Rules of the Game:**
Agatha Christie's Construction of the Detective Story
Ulrich Suerbaum

425 **The Archaeology of Murder**
Volker Neuhaus

Films

437 **The West Films the East:**
Agatha Christie, the Cinema and Archaeology
Tom Stern

466 Map of Travel Routes and Excavation Sites

468 Glossary

471 Works by Agatha Christie

473 Picture Credits

Acknowledgements

The exhibition and book would not have happened without the great help of Rosalind and Anthony Hicks. Agatha Christie's daughter and her husband supported the project not only with loans but also by providing contacts with other friends and relatives of the Mallowans. On various occasions I was able to enjoy the generous hospitality and warm-hearted atmosphere of their house in Devon and take part in many discussions about Agatha Christie's love of the Orient. John Mallowan and his wife Frances put Max Mallowan's entire photographic records at my disposal and were also extremely helpful in other ways. My heart-felt thanks are also due to Mathew Prichard – Agatha Christie's grandson – who supported the project in many ways.

I owe a special thanks to the exhibition's biggest contributor, the British Museum, particularly John Curtis of the Ancient Near East Department. From the start he and Julian Reade tirelessly opened all stores and archives, which were a real goldmine for this project.

We thank the following institutions and private lenders for placing exhibits at our disposal or supporting the exhibition in other ways. Unfortunately we are unable to list the names of everybody who helped with the exhibition, and great thanks are also due to those who have not been named:

Hans-Dieter Abring, *Essen*
Ägyptisches Museum und Papryrussammlung, *Berlin*
Agatha Christie Limited, *London*
Agatha Christie Society, *London*
Angels and Bermans, *London*
Sabine Böhme, *Istanbul*
British Film Institute, *London*
The British Museum, *London*
Compagnie Internationale des Wagons-Lits et du Tourisme, *Paris*
Michel Cozic, *Paris*
Fouad Debbas, *Beirut*
Deutsches Archäologisches Institut, *Damascus*
Deutsches Archäologisches Institut, *Istanbul*

Deutsche Botschaft, *Damascus*
Deutsche Botschaft, *Istanbul*
Deutsches Filmmuseum, *Frankfurt*
Enzio und Sebastian Edschmid, *Frankfurt*
Rolf Ehlert, *Heidelberg*
Georg Gerster, *Zumikon*
Pierre de Gigord, *Paris*
HarperCollins Publishers, *London*
Hughes Massie Limited, *London*
Wahid Khayata, *Aleppo*
Jürgen Klein, *Mönchengladbach*
Library of Congress, *Washington*
London Weekend Television
Sally Mazloumian, *Aleppo*
The Metropolitan Museum of Art, *New York*
Ministry of Information, *Damascus*
Michel Mulders, *Wageningen*
Sultan Muhesen, *Damascus*
National Portrait Gallery, *London*
Jaques Normand, *Rambouillet*
Joan and David Oates, *Cambridge*
Anthony Powell, *London*
Wolfgang Röllig, *Tübingen*
Odile Schaeffer, *St Germain en Laye*
Lord Snowdon, *London*
Werner Sölch, *Munich*
Christine Strube, *Heidelberg*
Syrian Embassy, *Bonn*
Thomas Cook Archives, *Peterborough*
Türkisches Konsulat, *Essen*
The University Museum, *University of Tokyo*
Verein der Freunde und Förderer der Archäologischen Sammlung Essen e.V.
Vintage Museum, *London*
Louis Vuitton, *Paris*
Donald Wiseman, *Tadworth*

Foreword

Mathew Prichard

I am so pleased that an exhibition that links my grandmother Agatha Christie with archaeology and the Middle East has finally been mounted. Like many really good ideas, it is quite simple, and one is left wondering why it has not happened before!

Nearly seventy years ago a shy but successful authoress, Agatha Christie, met a young enthusiastic archaeologist, Max Mallowan. Their marriage, which lasted nearly fifty years, was a very happy and successful one, and during it both archaeology and detective fiction were huge beneficiaries. There were important finds in northern Iraq, which were enshrined in the magnificent book *Nimrud and its Remains*, not to mention countless articles, lectures and exhibitions that my grandfather wrote and supervised. And, of course, there were over sixty detective novels, plays and short stories, some of the most famous of which used settings in the Middle East that Agatha knew so well from her visits there. There can be few marriages that have been so productive in terms of both scholarship and pure entertainment.

This exhibition is a living memorial to those achievements and to the other talents that Agatha and Max encouraged and surrounded themselves with in both their professions. To give but one example, I consider the covers designed by Robin Macartney for *Death on the Nile*, *Appointment with Death* and *Murder in Mesopotamia* among the most appropriate and evocative as any in detective fiction. And Macartney was an architect assisting Max in his investigations of archaeological mounds – some cross-fertilization.

But for me personally there is something even more important that this exhibition represents. From the ruins of a broken-down first marriage, Agatha's exposure to Max's unbridled enthusiasm for his profession and his life rejuvenated her, allowing her to regain her confidence in herself and plunge herself with renewed energy into her own writing. For their partnership we are all the richer, but particularly my mother and I!

My congratulations to Charlotte Trümpler and her colleagues on a brilliant idea brilliantly executed.

Introduction

Charlotte Trümpler

Last but not least, I am happy to mention the great debt I owe to my wife who has been an indefatigable and stimulating helper, and has accompanied me in the field, both on excavation and on survey, for more than thirty years.[1]

The original German title for this book was 'Agatha Christie and the Orient'. This might have seemed a contradiction in terms if we associate Agatha Christie with her fussy but psychologically astute character, Miss Marple, the spinster lady who can detect human wickedness, however well concealed, and solves murders against the rural background of English villages and market towns. But, if we turn to the settings in which Hercule Poirot operates, the subject becomes more relevant, for Poirot moves in a cosmopolitan atmosphere. He does investigate cases of murder in English country houses, but he also visits Syria, travels on the Orient Express, exposes a murderer on a dig in Iraq and tries (not very successfully) to relax on a Nile steamer in Egypt.

While Hercule Poirot's field of activity is internationally famous, few readers know much about the diversity and variety of places where his creator herself lived and worked. Who remembers Agatha Christie as the wife of the English archaeologist Max Mallowan, who was knighted for his achievements? She spent years accompanying her husband and helping on his digs in Iraq and Syria, where she wrote many of her detective stories. Who remembers that the Mallowans' visits to other archaeological sites, before and after these excavations, were the inspiration for her world-famous crime novels *Murder on the Orient Express*, *Death on the Nile* and *Appointment with Death*? 'Agatha Christie and the Orient' is a wide and fascinating theme, and many of its more unexpected aspects have only come to light in the course of intensive study.

The idea for this exhibition was conceived at a seminar on the subject conducted in 1991 by Barbara Patzek of the Faculty of Ancient History at Essen University. Turning theoretical concepts into an exhibition, however, called for a process of almost criminological exactitude. As if in a crime story by Agatha Christie herself, the first approach was to search for clues in places far distant in space and now in time as well, and to interview any contemporary eyewitnesses still alive (cf. Tom Stern's essay 'Traces of Agatha Christie in Syria and Turkey' in this volume). Agatha Christie spent a great deal of time in the Orient between 1928 and 1958, which meant there was a period of thirty years to be studied and rescued from oblivion. While personal encounters with relations, friends and archaeologists called primarily for a psychological approach – in the true spirit of Miss Marple and Hercule Poirot – it was more appropriate to use archaeological methods for delving into the archives and studying accounts of excavations. The search for clues paid off. An increasingly clear picture of the crime writer and her life in the Orient emerged as time went on, just as it might in a criminal case or an archaeological dig – not least through the new photographic material which has been found.

While my own impression at the beginning of this project was overwhelmingly one of great respect for Agatha Christie's achievements on the site of archaeological excavations, with time another and equally important factor came to influence my view of her life in the Orient: the deep happiness she found living and travelling in eastern countries, a happiness expressed in the few extant photographs and in her autobiographical memoirs.

Agatha Christie's services to archaeology are not well known, and since she was not and never claimed to be an archaeologist herself, this area of her life has been largely neglected. After her marriage to Max Mallowan in September 1930, she regularly spent three or four months a year taking part in her husband's digs in Syria and Iraq, although 'taking part' is not quite the way to put it. Already internationally famous for her detective stories, Agatha Christie was of invaluable assistance to the archaeological team. At first she developed all the photographs taken on the excavations, and then in 1937 she began photographing the digs and the archaeological finds herself. She helped with the restoration of ancient vessels and the labelling of exhibits, and after the war she also worked on the cleaning and conservation of ivory pieces which had been buried in large numbers (cf. the essays by Charlotte Trümpler, 'Le camping begins', and Joan Oates, 'Agatha Christie, Nimrud and Baghdad'). She wrote in her autobiography:

> Many years ago, when I was once saying sadly to Max it was a pity I couldn't have taken up archaeology when I was a girl, so as to be more knowledgeable on the subject, he said, 'Don't you realise that at this moment you know more about prehistoric pottery than almost any woman in England?'[2]

In spite of her hard work on the sites, she paid for her own board and lodging and her travel expenses, and she also supported the excavations as an anonymous sponsor. In Nimrud she made financial contributions to the team's food, and she paid for her colleagues' holiday excursions. Sometimes she donated the rights of a detective story to the excavations. Even at the age of sixty-eight she was still sleeping in one of the expedition's tents, like any other archaeologist on a dig, and she endured the frequent trials of living on archaeological excavations without a murmur.

Thanks to her inexhaustibly fertile imagination, she could withdraw into a world of her own while she was spending months on end in the desert with three archaeologists. After the war, when excavating teams grew larger, she derived inspiration from the atmosphere and from conversations in which she was principally a listener, although she immediately turned them into dialogue for her books in her head.

Life on an archaeological dig is an important aspect of the exhibition and of this book on *Agatha Christie and Archaeology*. The excavations on which Max Mallowan worked, either as one of a team or as the leader, are presented here in chronological order. The first was Ur, Abraham's birthplace, where a gigantic cemetery containing over 6,000 tombs was uncovered in the 1920s. Its sensational finds attracted a great deal of attention in both archaeological circles and the media. In Nineveh (1931–2) Mallowan cut a trench 27 metres deep in order to be the first archaeologist of his day to establish the chronology of the early civilizations of Assyria. He took a great interest in the earliest sixth-century ceramics found on the Tell Arpachiyah settlement mound, which he studied in Iraq in 1933; he discovered unique ceramics of very high quality in a potter's kiln, and his scientific studies of these items are still highly regarded today. His interest in prehistoric civilizations led to his investigation in 1934–8 of two further settlement mounds, Chagar Bazar and Tell Brak in Syria. On the basis of these excavations he established an archaeological framework in a very important but then unknown district of northern Mesopotamia. After the war he was granted his greatest wish: to excavate Nimrud in Iraq, the Assyrian capital. The first digs here had begun a hundred years earlier, bringing to light huge stone statues, relief slabs and ivory carvings; Max Mallowan resumed work on these excavations, which had lain abandoned for seventy years, and his uncovering of many temples and other buildings, together with the finds discovered in them – in particular some spectacular ivories and cuneiform tablets – made a great contribution to our modern understanding of the history and art of Assyria.

Agatha Christie's novel *Murder in Mesopotamia* (1936), which refers to the Ur excavations, their director and his wife and is set in a building probably modelled on the expedition house in Uruk, gives a good impression of life on a dig and the procedures carried out by archaeologists (cf. the essay by Nadja Cholidis, 'The Glamour of the East'). It also shows that even in these early years Agatha Christie had already acquired a sound knowledge of archaeology.

Two films made by Agatha Christie herself in 1938 in Syria and 1952/7 in Iraq, but never shown, give a unique insight into the countries and peoples of the Middle East, as well as everyday life on a dig at the time (cf. the essay by Charlotte Trümpler, 'A dark-room has been allotted to me …'). They bring what is now the distant past to life before our eyes, with affectionate irony and much humour. It is clear both here and in her autobiographical works that Agatha Christie found the indigenous population fascinating, and took a great interest in the different ethnic groups. Sad to say, these documents are also unique in that they present the co-existence of peoples and religions in a way that has become unimaginable today.

It is not least because of her great interest in human nature that these travels were among the most enjoyable and intensely felt experiences of Agatha Christie's life. Many of her detective stories set in trains, ships and hotels bear witness to this passion of hers. She dedicated *Destination Unknown* (1954) to her son-in-law: 'To Anthony, who likes foreign travel as much as I do'. Several passages in her memoirs illustrate her love of trains, especially the Orient Express, on which the Mallowans always used to travel to their archaeological sites before the war. In 1934 an adventure of her own inspired her to write *Murder on the Orient Express*, set in the train itself (cf. Axel Heimsoth's essay 'From Orient Express to Desert Bus'). An original sleeping compartment complete with wash-basin from a 1930s Orient Express train, original luggage by Louis Vuitton of Paris, and costumes from the film introduce visitors to the exhibition to the film version of this novel, while posters, leaflets, postcards and items from trains of the period present a seductive picture of the fascinating atmosphere of travel in the 1920s and 1930s.

Those books marked by Agatha Christie's personal experience or based on incidents in the Orient are integrated into the biographical section of the exhibition. Interestingly, or perhaps understandably, she never uses ancient Mesopotamia as the scene of a crime. *Murder in Mesopotamia* and *Appointment with Death* are set in the twentieth century, and her references to archaeologists in other crime novels are confined to the same period. She probably felt too much respect for the civilizations that were part of her husband's professional field to use them, and it seems likely that Max, as a serious scholar, could not or would not have conceived a murder story with an ancient Mesopotamian background. She had also hesitated at first to choose ancient Egypt as a setting, but eventually, after intensive and lengthy research, she wrote the detective story *Death Comes as the End* and her play *Akhnaton*, both of them set in ancient Egypt with characters based in part on historical figures. Analysis of their texts provides clear evidence of Agatha Christie's thorough and scientific attitude to her archaeological sources, and shows how seriously she took them. She integrated extant textual sources of the time with her own work outstandingly well, although doing so was a considerable linguistic challenge. The play *Akhnaton* is redolent of the literary and cultural ambience of the 1920s and 1930s, which saw the Pharaoh as the founder of a monotheistic religion anticipating Christianity (cf. the two essays by Waltraud Guglielmi in 'Agatha Christie and her Use of Ancient Egyptian Sources'). Since the play was never actually performed, it is represented in the exhibition by a small stage with model figures.

The detective story *Death on the Nile*, to which archaeological sites and the Orient are only a backdrop, is particularly interesting because here Agatha Christie allows Hercule Poirot, in conversation with another character, to point up the very close parallels between detective investigations and archaeological procedures (cf. Barbara Patzek's essay 'The Detective and the Archaeologist'). The passage shows her making a close comparison between archaeology and criminology, with an astute analysis of their comparable methods. It also explains just what it was about archaeology that so fascinated Agatha Christie, and why her marriage was a unique partnership with her husband professionally as well as personally.

The contributions to this book, however, go beyond biographical analysis of Agatha Christie works. Ulrich Suerbaum (cf. his essay 'Rules of the Game') studies the question of why Agatha Christie is still the most widely read of all women writers, and why her books have been translated into forty-four languages and sold in a hundred and three countries. In his view, which is based on close study of her works, her success rests principally on the outstanding qualities of construction so essential to the detective story, a field where none of her rivals has surpassed her. A cultural and developmental survey of the history of the detective story from its first emergence in 1863 to the present day is presented in Volker Neuhaus's essay 'The Archaeology of Murder'. He believes that the metaphorical and methodical analogy between the crime novel and archaeology is evident even in the earliest examples of the genre, but in his view it was Agatha Christie who first succeeded in establishing a real connection between archaeology and detection.

Attracted by the myth of the Orient, Agatha Christie first visited Baghdad as a tourist. She found happiness there in her second marriage and a second career in her work on her husband's excavations. In the tradition of other British travellers to the Orient she made a close study of the land, its people and its mythology. Unlike many of her countrymen, however, she avoided a moralizing attitude and the perpetuation of deep-rooted prejudices (cf. Reinhold Schiffer's contribution 'Agatha's Arabs').

Fascinated at first by the myth, she became an oriental myth in her own right and a tourist attraction for those who visited Nimrud mainly because of her. Despite the increasingly high regard in which she was personally held, she remained an unpretentious and modest woman who fitted in easily with the rest of the archaeological team. A passage at the end of her *Autobiography* of 1977 shows how dear to her heart these archaeological excavations were and how much she identified with them. She began the book in Nimrud, and wrote, of the work they had done there:

> We have scarred it with our bull-dozers … Here was once Calah, that great City. Then Calah slept … Here came Layard to disturb its peace. And again Calah-Nimrud slept … Here came Max Mallowan and his wife. Now again Calah sleeps …
> Who shall disturb it next?
> We do not know.[3]

Despite her reserved nature and Victorian upbringing, it mattered to her to link herself with her husband in this context. She either thought her contribution to archaeology significant enough to be worth mentioning or wanted their work in Nimrud to be seen as a joint achievement.

But independently of archaeology itself and her work on the excavations, she felt deeply bound to the Orient. She was happy there – anything strange and foreign fascinated her, and at the same time she was able to approach the local people without preconceived inhibitions. She wrote:

> How much I have loved that part of the world.
> I love it still, and always shall.[4]

NOTES

1   M.E.L. Mallowan, *Nimrud and its Remains*, London 1966, vol. 1, p. 19.
2   A. Christie, *An Autobiography*, 1981, p. 546.
3   Ibid.
4   Ibid., p. 548.

Indonesian translation of *Murder on the Orient Express*

78.104

Agatha Christie
Pembunuhan di Orient Express

Biography

Agatha Christie (1890–1976)

Janet Morgan

A gatha Christie's life began again when she was forty. Her marriage to Max Mallowan took her to distant lands and ancient civilizations, and brought her new friends and new interests. She shared the frustration and excitement of scholarly research and found pleasure in working as one of a team. Above all, she had by her side a kind, thoughtful, amusing confidant; our lives, she said to Max, moved 'on a nice parallel track'.

As a child, Agatha had once before known just such an easy, companionable domestic life. She was born at the end of Victoria's reign, on 15 September 1890, in the soft sea air of Torquay on the south Devon coast. Her father, Frederick Alvah Miller, an amiable American, lived on income from a trust fund; her mother, Clarissa ('Clara') Margaret Boehmer, Frederick's cousin from his father's second marriage, was light-hearted, affectionate and impulsive. The family and their servants lived comfortably and hospitably at Ashfield, a large villa with extensive gardens, an orchard, conservatories, and a tennis and croquet lawn, surroundings that were to provide the backdrop to many of Agatha's later stories of apparently secure upper middle-class lives shockingly disrupted by murder.

Agatha spent much of her childhood with adults: nurse, cook and two solid presences, her Grannie B (Clara's mother) and Auntie-Grannie (Clara's aunt and Frederick's stepmother). The elderly ladies, dispensing bon-bons and hushed gossip, were each, years later, to contribute to Agatha's picture of Miss Marple.

Monty, Agatha's wayward brother, and her sister Madge, a spirited girl who loved play-acting and dressing-up, were sent away to school but her own formal education was minimal: dancing, singing and piano classes, a few untaxing lessons when she was fourteen, various well-intentioned finishing

Agatha Christie as a child

Agatha Christie with her father and her first dog

schools in France. She taught herself from her father's library, stocked with complete editions of nineteenth-century novels, long runs of magazines, the articles and essays interspersed with word and number games, which, like algebra, Agatha loved. She was a self-contained and secretive child, inhabiting imaginary worlds with imaginary friends: 'I don't like parting with information', she once announced, quoting a self-important grown-up.

When Agatha was eleven, her father died of heart disease. His affairs had been mishandled and, short of money, Clara struggled to keep Ashfield. For Agatha's first season, her mother took her to Cairo, less expensive than London but with dances, polo, the races and, perhaps, suitors. Agatha was

Agatha Christie in Paris, 1906

attractive and energetic, tall, with thick, long, blonde hair and a pleasant voice. She was, however, paralysingly shy. Her nervousness in public had led her to abandon thoughts of a career as a singer or pianist; a cruel partner told Clara that, while her daughter danced beautifully, she should learn to talk. Instead, Agatha wrote sentimental verse, stories about visions and seances, and a novel, scrutinised by a kind neighbour, a writer, and sent to his literary agent, who sent it back.

Agatha was neither ambitious nor anxious about her future. When war came in 1914, she worked first with the Voluntary Aid Detachment in a local hospital and then, like the title of a poem she wrote when fascinated by poisons, 'In a Dispensary'. Challenged by Madge, Agatha now embarked on a detective story; her investigator, inspired by the refugees she saw in Torquay, was a retired Belgian police officer, Hercule Poirot. The structure of her story, the accumulation of complication with a neat and surprising resolution, was to become her favourite device. *The Mysterious Affair at Styles* was eventually published in America in 1920 and in England in 1921, the publisher taking an option on five more books.

The typescript had been submitted under Agatha's new name; in a rush, during his first leave at Christmas 1914, she had married Archibald Christie, a young officer in the Royal Flying Corps. When the war ended, Archie was, at twenty-nine, a colonel, with decorations for bravery and a job in the Air Ministry, at which he found it difficult to settle. Agatha's success, however, was just beginning. Terms were meagre but her books and stories were popular; when in 1922 she accompanied Archie on an overseas mission, to which he had been appointed Secretary, to drum up support for the forthcoming British Empire Exhibition, Agatha found she had almost as many

Agatha Christie in Egypt, 1931 or 1933 (photo: Max Mallowan)

admiring readers abroad as at home. She moved to a more appreciative publisher; her first book for Collins, *The Murder of Roger Ackroyd*, published in 1926, daringly broke the conventions of crime writing at that time and triumphantly tricked her readers.

The book caused a fuss; the sensation came six months later, in December. Miserable after her mother's death, exhausted by the strain of clearing Ashfield, lonely – Archie was preoccupied by his job in the City and by golf – Agatha grew increasingly distressed. When Archie revealed that he had fallen in love with Nancy Neele, a golfing partner, Agatha broke down and, leaving her daughter Rosalind now seven years old, fled from her home. Police searched the country, attended by bloodhounds and newspapermen. Colonel Christie was suspected of murder, Mrs Christie of seeking publicity. Ten days later, Agatha was found at the Hydropathic Hotel in Harrogate.

She remembered little of her flight. Doctors and neurologists concluded that a mental breakdown had brought about a temporary loss of awareness of her own identity; she never recovered a complete memory of that time. Agatha was appalled by the attention her flight had caused; those who knew her well were amazed by the absurdity of the unceasing speculation about the motives for and manner of her disappearance. Sensibly, Agatha tried to put the episode behind her. Her autobiography does not mention it but an oblique picture of the dissolution of the Christies' marriage may be found in *Unfinished Portrait* (1933), one of six novels Agatha wrote as 'Mary Westmacott'. The Christies were divorced in 1928; from that time Agatha, a devout Christian, felt unable to take Communion.

Free now to go where she pleased, in the autumn of that year she booked a ticket on the Orient Express. From Baghdad Agatha travelled on to Ur, to Leonard Woolley's excavations, widely publicised in England at that time. Vistors to Woolley's dig were discouraged but Mrs Christie was warmly received, the formidable Katharine Woolley being an admirer of her books. Agatha was entranced by the beauty of the desert and the life of the camp and took up Katharine's invitation to return early in 1930. Max Mallowan, one of Woolley's team, who had been absent the year before, was now instructed by Katharine to escort Agatha on a tour of local sights on the way back to Baghdad and, when she had to return home urgently to Rosalind, who was ill, Max travelled with her to England.

They kept in touch, Max came to stay in Devon, and in the spring of 1930 he asked Agatha to marry him. She hesitated: Max was fifteen years younger than she was and, as he was a Roman Catholic, his marriage to a divorced woman would not be recognized. (Furious, he left his faith.) Agatha was wary of another close commitment. After a month she said yes. Did she mind, Max asked, that his profession was 'digging up the dead'? Not at all, she

told him, 'I adore corpses and stiffs.' (What she never said was that one of the pleasures of being married to an archaeologist was that the older you became, the more interesting you were to him, a quip first made by a newspaperman in the *Gothenburg Trade and Fishing Journal*.)

Life with Max took Agatha to worlds she had not known and her notebooks and letters show how stimulating she found these new experiences. Of her books she always said that, while her characters were fictitious, the settings were real. Her plots and people were, none the less, inspired by things seen and overheard deftly and imaginatively utilized. In December 1931, for example, after travelling home from Nineveh, where Max was working with Campbell Thompson, she sent her husband a long letter describing her journey on a train that broke down in the snow; here were the origins of *Murder on the Orient Express* (1933). *Murder in Mesopotamia* (1936) depicts the excavations in Ur, where Max assisted between 1925 and 1930; *Death on the Nile* (1937), in which the layout of the Nile steamer SS *Karnak* is crucial to the plot, originated in a voyage the Mallowans took with Rosalind in 1933; and *Appointment with Death* (1938) is set in Petra, which Max and Agatha had visited on a journey home. Wicked people, Agatha believed, can be found in any setting; greed, jealousy and vengefulness disturb any group of human beings. The personalities and motives of the people in these books might be found anywhere; the atmosphere – of an archaeological camp, a Nile steamer, the gorge confining the rose-red city – is based on specific observation.

Agatha's reading, always eager, was enlarged by her husband and his colleagues. She was not a rigorous thinker, although she liked to discuss ideas

Left Agatha Christie with Max Mallowan outside the front of Greenway House, Devon, January 1946

Below Agatha Christie and Max Mallowan in the park at Greenway, January 1946

Above Agatha Christie, 1946

Left Agatha Christie with her grandson Mathew

Agatha Christie and Max Mallowan in Greenway House, Devon, January 1946

with Max, but her intellectual exploration influenced her writing. Her play *Akhnaton* (1937) proved too difficult and expensive to stage; *Death Comes as the End* (1945) was more successful. She began this story after reading about the Hekanakhte Papers, found in a rock tomb near Luxor in the early 1920s and discussed in a book she borrowed from Stephen Glanville, the Egyptologist and a friend of Max since the 1920s. Max, worried that Agatha might be ridiculed, wrote anxiously from Tripolitania, where he was stationed at the end of the war. Glanville reassured him:

> No archaeological apparatus was to be imported that was not essential ... At the same time there had to be enough implicit Egyptian feeling to make it impossible for the layman to feel that this particular story could have happened in Pimlico, and to make the Egyptologist feel that there was no reason why it shouldn't have happened in Thebes. It was an extraordinarily difficult thing to do, and she's brought it off.

Agatha had dedicated *Murder in Mesopotamia* to 'my many archaeological friends in Iraq and Syria'; she enjoyed sharing Max's wide circle of colleagues and students and they remained friends for life. Robin Macartney, who worked with Max at Chagar Bazar, designed covers for the Crime Club edi-

Agatha Christie, 1949 (photo: Angus McBean)

tions of four of her books, and Louis Osman, assisting at Tell Brak, built
Agatha a squash court at Winterbrook, the house by the Thames she acquired
in 1934. Four years later, when Agatha bought Greenway House on the banks
of the Dart in Devon, it was rearranged by Guilford Bell, architect to the Tell
Brak excavation. Barbara Parker, epigraphist and photographer, nursed
Agatha in her old age.

Agatha loved houses and gardens and had a gift for making things
agreeable. She liked the simplicity of desert life in the open air but the Mal-

Agatha Christie in Syria, 1930s

lowans' camps were always comfortable, for she organized the supply of much of the provisions and furniture, descending on the bazaars for lamps, ornaments, cushions and rugs, and supervised the cook. Compared with other expeditions, Max said, they lived 'like fighting cocks', for Agatha ensured that fresh local produce was used whenever possible and herself devised ingenious recipes: eclairs with cream from water buffalo, walnut or hot chocolate soufflés cooked in a tin box.

Agatha Christie at Balawat, with Max Mallowan examining the newly discovered bronze gates, 1956

Like her companions in Syria, Agatha slept in the expedition house. Each season she would plan and write her books, often more than one, happy in the intimacy and rhythm of camp life. She was glad to miss the worst of English winters; the clean desert air and absence of distraction, allied to her strong constitution and remarkable stamina, helped her remain physically and intellectually resilient. She described the time in Syria in *Come, Tell Me How You Live* (1946), a charming volume of autobiography.

Anxious to return to the Near East, in 1947 Agatha asked Edmund Cork, her literary agent, how sterling funds might be released. He had no difficulty in arranging a business allowance for her and, while Max negotiated with the authorities in Baghdad, she worked first at the Hotel Zia and then, sitting on a balcony overlooking the river, at their rented house, Karradet Mariam 17 – both depicted in *They Came to Baghdad* (1951). The improbable plot horrified Agatha's publisher, but its sales outstripped those of any of her earlier books.

The site Max chose to excavate was Nimrud, a lovely place, first investigated by Layard a century before. 'A very peaceful and happy life', Agatha told Cork. Nor was it spartan. The airmail copy of *The Times* was delivered via Mosul by arrangement and Cork forwarded post from home. At Nimrud, as everywhere, the Mallowans changed for dinner. Agatha dressed in the desert as she did in England, in tweed, silk and cashmere, her hat tied on with

Alfresco breakfast near Baghdad, 1950s

a scarf, handbag always by her side. In the digging season the camp was home, the team part of the Mallowans' family. Each member was commemorated by one of Agatha's 'Cautionary Verses for Archaeologists', and birthdays and other celebrations were marked by 'Nimrud Odes'. Many of these verses appear in her husband's memoirs.

Max's expeditions were small and economical and Agatha was an

Agatha Christie at the Acropolis, 31 August 1958

important member of the team. The photographic record of the finds was largely her responsibility and in 1951 she asked her American agent to find her a special camera, complete with flash. With her favourite tools, orange sticks and Innoxa face cleansing milk, she removed dust and dirt from ivory fragments. Max dug at Nimrud from 1949 to 1958, making wonderful discoveries. Agatha was thrilled by the finding of the Nimrud treasure and delighted by

Max's professional success. In 1947 he was appointed to the first chair in Western Asiatic Archaeology at the Institute of Archaeology in the University of London, moving in 1962 to a Fellowship at All Souls' College, Oxford, where he was able to concentrate on the preparation of *Nimrud and its Remains* (1966). In 1968 he was knighted; visitors were often surprised to discover, later on, that the unassuming Lady Mallowan whom they had met at college gatherings was Agatha Christie, the world-famous writer.

By the early 1970s Agatha had published more than eighty crime novels, eleven books of short stories, fifteen plays, among them *The Mousetrap*, first produced in 1948 and still running more than fifty years later. Her detective novels were intriguing puzzles, their characters deployed like chessmen, but from book to book she experimented, playing games with ambigu-

Agatha Christie and Max Mallowan in the south of France while staying with Claude and Odile Schaeffer, 1972

ities of speech, with memory, timing or motive, or with tricks of light or mirrors. Her situations, like her characters, were archetypes. Critics described her work as formulaic; that, however, made her work adaptable. Her books were translated into more than a hundred languages, a hard task, for her lan-

Agatha Christie, about 1965

guage is precise and written to deceive. Self-contained and self-controlled, she manipulates her audience, her timing unerring. Unlike great writers, she was unable to depict the depth and complexity of human relationships. Her readers must be satisfied by narratives that make a clear distinction between good

Oskar Kokoschka painting Agatha Christie's portrait in 1969

and evil, reflecting Agatha's own beliefs. Her fiction is cathartic: harmony is disturbed, evil surmounted, order restored.

Habit and the pleasure of achievement underlay her extraordinary assiduity, and also anxiety about money. From the late 1930s she had been entangled in litigation over tax assessments on her copyrights, uncertainties that took thirty years to resolve. 'Poirot is rather insufferable', she had told Cork in 1938 but, although two years later, in *Curtain*, she gave him his last case, it remained unpublished until 1975, for, she explained, she could not kill 'my chief source of income'.

In 1971, her eightieth year, she became Dame Agatha. Success was pleasing, celebrity unwelcome. 'Writers should write', she said, shunning radio, television and the press. She remained modest to the end, living quietly and privately, enjoying books, music, flowers, her houses and their gardens, and her friends. She died on 12 January 1976 at Winterbrook, just after luncheon, and was buried in the churchyard at Cholsey, nearby. 'It left me', Max wrote, 'with a feeling of emptiness after forty-five years of a loving and merry companionship.'

BIBLIOGRAPHY

Autobiography and biography
Agatha Christie, *Come, Tell Me How You Live*, London 1946
Agatha Christie, *An Autobiography*, London 1977
Max Mallowan, *Mallowan's Memoirs*, London 1977
Janet Morgan, *Agatha Christie: A Biography*, London 1984

Detective novels, books and plays by Agatha Christie
The Mysterious Affair at Styles, London 1921
The Murder of Roger Ackroyd, London 1926
As Mary Westmacott: *Unfinished Portrait*, London 1933
Murder on the Orient Express, London 1934
Murder in Mesopotamia, London 1936
Death on the Nile, London 1937
Akhnaten, London 1937
Appointment with Death, London 1938
Death Comes as the End, London 1945
The Mousetrap, London 1948
They Came to Baghdad, London 1951
Curtain, London 1975

Max Mallowan (1904–78)

Henrietta McCall

M ax Mallowan was born in central London on 6 May 1904 and named after his grandfather, another Max Mallowan, who was of Slav origin but whose home (appropriately enough for the grandson he never knew) had been in Syria. Max's father Frederick was Austrian by birth, but went to London in his thirties and died there in 1959. His mother was Parisian, the daughter of a well-known opera singer of the time.

Max had two brothers, Cecil and Philip. The family moved to a house in Kensington in 1908 and it was there that Max showed early inclinations of becoming an archaeologist. Aged four, he dug up some Victorian china sherds, which were then properly recorded and photographed, presumably with help. In 1912 the family moved again, to Wimbledon, to a large house with a tennis court. Max was enrolled at a nearby school called Rokeby where he began to learn Greek under the aegis of a Miss Vines, who wore a straw hat appropriately decorated with grapes. This was the start of his lifelong fascination with antiquity.

At Lancing, his public school, Mallowan found a more sophisticated successor to Miss Vines in J.F. Roxburgh, a brilliant classicist who also bullied his pupils into writing elegantly and precisely, something for which Mallowan was always grateful.

Mallowan left school and entered Oxford University in 1921, where at New College, he read Classical Greats. By his own admission he was no great scholar, though he found his tutors, H.W.B. Joseph, Stanley Casson and particularly Percy Gardner, stimulating. They rekindled his childish interest in archaeology, so much so that, after he had finished his final examinations in the summer of 1925, he seized the opportunity of an interview with Leonard Woolley, who had written to the Keeper of the Ashmolean Museum, D.G.

Max Mallowan, about 1930

Hogarth, asking if he could recommend a likely young man to work at the site of Ur. Mallowan went to see Woolley and was duly engaged to start the following October.

This was Woolley's third season at Ur. With the somewhat euphemistic title of general field assistant, Mallowan was given the tasks of filing field records and registering finds, identifying possible dig-spots, and making tentative chronological sequences based on careful dissection of stratification levels. It is likely, however, that Woolley himself did much of the technical work, as he was rigorous in his attention to detail. He was an exacting instructor and set a compelling example of leadership. Mallowan's role could perhaps be described as general organizer. He had to show visitors around, keep the pay-book for some 200 men, learn Arabic and act as medical adviser. His most demanding patient was Lady Woolley herself, who required to have leeches applied to her forehead from time to time to alleviate the pain of migraines.

Mallowan might well have remained at Ur had not fate stepped in, in the guise of love. In 1930 one of the visitors that Max was asked to show round the site was the celebrated crime novelist, Agatha Christie. Like many others, Agatha was fascinated by the magnificent discoveries at Ur that had been regularly featured in the popular press, and at a dinner party in London she had met Katharine Woolley, who had read and greatly admired *The Murder of Roger Ackroyd*. Katharine invited Agatha to come out to Mesopotamia. On Agatha's first visit to Ur Max was absent on sick leave – with appendicitis – but on her return the following year Max was back, and Katharine commanded him to show Agatha something of the surrounding area. Agatha, always self-effacing, felt this was a great imposition on a young man of twenty-five who doubtless had many more exciting things to do, but Katharine insisted.

What happened next surprised them both. There was a trip to nearby Nippur, from where they went on to Karbala. Here, after the excitement of walking round the terrifyingly high battlements of the castle of Ukhaidir hand in hand, they decided to take an impromptu bathe in a nearby salt lake to cool down, Agatha wearing a pink silk vest and a double pair of knickers. At this inopportune moment their car broke down leaving them marooned in the desert, after which the only accommodation they could find was two adjoining police cells at the local constabulary. Following these adventures Max decided that Agatha was the only woman he could possibly spend the rest of his life with, and after various vicissitudes, including her reservations about the fourteen-year age gap, they were married quietly in Edinburgh on 11 September 1930.

Max Mallowan with Sheikh Hamoudi at Ur, 1920s

Above Max Mallowan in Egypt, 1931 or 1933 (photo: Agatha Christie)

Left Max Mallowan on the roof of the expedition house at Ur, 1920s
(C.L. Woolley, *Digging up the Past*, London 1930)

Mallowan parted company with the Woolleys and Ur at the end of the 1930–31 season. Katharine had made it clear that other wives were not welcome. So when R. Campbell Thompson asked them both to join him at Nineveh, they accepted with enthusiasm. Campbell Thompson was a very different man from Woolley. He was an epigraphist by training and, according to Mallowan, had no high regard for archaeology, being chiefly interested in the acquisition of clay tablets. Max made his own particular task the digging of a deep sounding right through the huge *tell* (settlement mound). The deeper they dug, the more lethal the shaft became, and it was characteristic of Max that he was the only man prepared to descend to the bottom.

Max Mallowan, the excavation architect Guilford Bell and Agatha Christie in Syria, 1930s

Mallowan had one season with Campbell Thompson at Nineveh, after which, at twenty-eight, he felt ready to conduct an expedition of his own. The great sounding at Nineveh had revealed examples of a decorated pottery called Halaf ware, but it was uncertain how it fitted into the pottery sequence of southern Mesopotamia. He needed to find more accessible Halaf levels. To this end, he decided on the small mound of Tepe Rashwa near the modern village of Arpachiyah, about 5 kilometres to the north of Nineveh. The expedition began in spring 1933 but tense relations with the Iraqi government, mainly over division of finds, persuaded Mallowan he should move north-eastwards into Syria.

He selected for his first venture the Khabur valley, which had sites with some similarities to those with which he was familiar. The first few weeks were spent making a rapid survey of the area, but it was a trial sounding at the site of Chagar Bazar that promised to be most fruitful. And so it proved: Mallowan dug a deep sounding in the north-west corner of the mound and found five levels of Halaf ware sandwiched between fragments of painted Samarra ware and a new type they called Khabur ware.

The house they had rented near the excavations was overrun by mice and fleas so for the next season they built their own out of mud-brick, to a design by Robin Macartney. It had a central domed hall and a big common room, as well as a darkroom and proper kitchen. Besides various household activities, Agatha also found time to write: at Chagar Bazar in 1935 she produced *Murder in Mesopotamia*, in which an archaeologist's wife (bearing an uncanny resemblance to Katharine Woolley) is murdered in the excavation house. As well as all this, she helped Max with the photographing, cleaning and recording of finds.

The third and last season at the site was marked by the discovery in a burnt-out palace of about seventy cuneiform tablets, dating to the reign of Shamshi-Adad. The tablets confirmed the dating of the painted Khabur pottery, for they rested on fragments of it. They revealed much about daily life and the personal names on them gave interesting insights into the ethnic background of the population.

Mallowan now turned his attention to the large mound of Tell Brak, which had exercised a certain fascination ever since he first came to Syria. He conducted his first of three campaigns of excavation there in the spring of 1937, followed by two more in the spring and autumn of 1938. They lived in a large empty *khan* (inn) with ten main rooms plus kitchen and so on, as well as

Max Mallowan assessing the finds. Still from the film made by Agatha Christie at Tell Brak in 1938

Above Agatha Christie and Max Mallowan outside Greenway House, Devon, 1961

Left Agatha Christie and Max Mallowan at home – Winterbrook House – in Wallingford, 1950

a large courtyard into which the expedition lorry could drive to unload. Mallowan described their three seasons' work as of extraordinary interest archaeologically, historically and artistically. He concentrated on two major structures, both of which demonstrated links with southern Mesopotamia: the Agade palace, where bricks inscribed with the name of Naram-Sin were found, and the Eye Temple, so-called because of the hundreds of little eye idols of black and white alabaster that lay all over the floors.

The full excavation of Tell Brak needed several decades, and time was then running out. Not only were there distant rumblings of war but, more immediately, Mallowan found it hard to work with the local landowners. He decided to move about 160 kilometres westwards into the Balikh Valley, remote marshy country on the Syrian-Turkish border. Five mounds were the

Above Max Mallowan, Robert Hamilton and Mahmoud at Nimrud, 1949

Above right Max Mallowan uncovering cuneiform tablets in Nimrud, 1949

object of his interest. They lay in a tract of territory bordered at the sides by the Balikh and Euphrates rivers, the city of Harran to the north and the town of Raqqa to the south. A lightning six-week survey showed Mallowan that there was rich potential for the establishment of early prehistoric sequences and for comparison with other contemporary and neighbouring sites.

Mallowan was at an archaeological conference in Berlin in summer 1939 when war was declared. The conference came to an unscheduled conclusion and he hurried home. Too old to be called up, a disappointed Mallowan settled down at Greenway House to write up his seasons at Chagar Bazar and Brak, and the Balikh Valley expedition. He joined the Brixham Home Guard. Early in 1940 he was invited to run the Anglo-Turkish Relief Committee, apparently with some success, because a year later its president, Lord Lloyd, managed to get Max into the Intelligence Department of the RAF, something that had hitherto not been possible because Max's father was Austrian and therefore an alien. His first year was enjoyably spent at the Air Ministry in Whitehall where he walked from the flat in Hampstead that Agatha had rented. Then he was posted to Cairo as liaison officer.

In 1943 Mallowan went to North Africa as assistant to the senior civil affairs officer of the Western Province whose headquarters were at Sabratha, an ancient Phoenician settlement rich in Roman remains. It was a relaxing interlude: the duties of the day over, he browsed happily in the library. Six months later, he was put in charge of a lonely oasis called Hon in the Eastern Province, then moved to the coastal town of Misurata and was eventually promoted to Adviser on Arab Affairs in Tripolitania with the rank of Wing Com-

Left Max Mallowan in front of the stele of Ashurnasirpal II at the British Museum in 1952

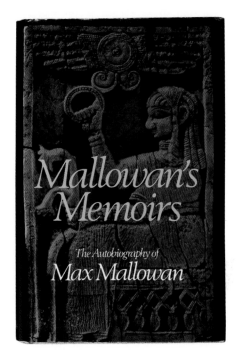

Left Max Mallowan and Agatha Christie during the division of finds at Nimrud, 1950s

Below left Donald Wiseman, Agatha Christie, Max Mallowan and Neville Chittick at Nimrud, 1950

Right Cover of Max Mallowan's autobiography, published by HarperCollins, 1977

mander. Mallowan had done his duty: now he longed for home and Agatha. On a May morning in 1944 he landed at Swindon and staggered back to Hampstead under the weight of his kit. Agatha, who was not expecting him, was just embarking on a kipper that they proceeded to share. 'We experienced the matchless joy of being reunited again,' wrote Max.

Mallowan retired to Greenway and took up again the recording of his seasons at Chagar Bazar and Tell Brak. Friends set about finding him an academic post and in 1947 he was appointed as the first professor of Western Asiatic Archaeology at the Institute of Archaelogy in the University of London, a post he held until 1960. The Institute was then at Bute House in Regent's Park; it became famous for its colourful triumvirate of Mallowan at Nimrud, Kathleen Kenyon at Jericho and Mortimer Wheeler at Mohenjo Daro. From now on Mallowan's time was divided between teaching and writing in England, and excavation in Iraq, where he had decided on the site of Nimrud. In 1949 Mallowan was appointed the first Director of the British School of Archaeology, a post he retained until his retirement from Nimrud in 1958. He was the School's Chairman from 1966 to 1970.

To Mallowan Nimrud was the most beautiful mound in Assyria. The tell and the ziggurat tower over the surrounding plain, some of it fertile and in the spring dotted with sheep and scarlet ranunculus. Little had changed in the

Max Mallowan and Agatha Christie, about 1970

preceding ten years except that the local workforce was more expensive, and a record was now kept in Arabic as well as in English. Some of the workers had been at Nineveh and Arpachiyah and referred to Agatha as their aunt.

Mallowan's dig at Nimrud lasted until 1958, when his leadership was taken over by a younger colleague, David Oates. The accumulated results over the years in terms of treasure (particularly the ivories), texts and records of architecture were of incalculable value. Mallowan's personal success was described as a happy combination of academic teaching and research with practical training of archaeologists and fruitful co-operation with Iraqi and foreign colleagues. To young colleagues, working with Max and Agatha was an unforgettable experience: he was a fund of knowledge and anecdote, she of personal kindness, encouragement and advice. Together they maintained harmony and to a certain extent hilarity.

After Mallowan's retirement from the field he turned his energies to finishing his best-known work, *Nimrud and its Remains*, and to founding the British Institute of Persian Studies. In 1962 his contribution to Assyriology was rewarded with his election to a fellowship of All Soul's College, Oxford. Mallowan was delighted and deeply honoured by his election; he felt it redeemed a somewhat undistinguished academic beginning. He had been appointed CBE in 1960 and in 1968 he was knighted. In 1973 he was appointed a Trustee of the British Museum. In 1974, to commemorate his seventieth birthday, the whole of the annual journal of the British School of Archaeology in Iraq was dedicated to him, with a wide range of articles and tributes by friends and colleagues. In 1977 he published his autobiography *Mallowan's Memoirs*, which recorded in an epilogue how, as he was writing the last few words, his beloved Agatha had died. Shortly afterwards, he married again. His second wife was Barbara Parker, on old and close friend, who had been Secretrary/Librarian of the British School of Archaeology in Baghdad from 1949 to 1961 and had worked with the Mallowans as epigraphist at Nimrud. She had been particularly kind in helping to look after Agatha in her final illness and had been devoted to Max – and he to her – for many years.

Max Mallowan died on 19 August the following year. Obituaries linked him with another great British archaeologist, Sir Henry Layard, a comparison with which Mallowan would have been pleased. Like Layard, Mallowan was at his best as a field archaeologist. Mallowan was always grateful to Woolley for his early training: he dug systematically to ensure comparison with finds at complementary sites both geographically and chronologically. He was responsible for our wider understanding of early civilization. He was a natural organizer of people and things and a man of energy and of great presence. He wrote up, and published, his own discoveries without delay and encouraged all who worked with him to do the same. His large corpus of published work is a testimony to this colossus of Western Asiatic archaeology.

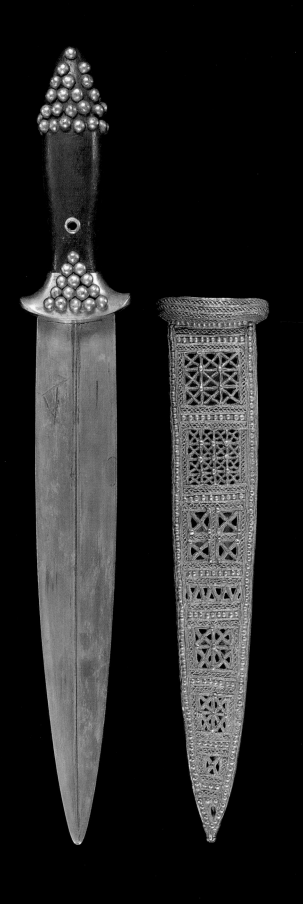

Archaeology: The Excavations

Ur of the Chaldees

Hans J. Nissen

s with many other cities of the ancient Near East, the name of Ur had been known for much longer than the remains of the city itself. It had always been familiar from the Old Testament as Abraham's place of origin, 'Ur of the Chaldees', but its archaeological remains were not located until the nineteenth century.

In the 1840s the English geologist William Kenneth Loftus visited the eastern part of the Ottoman Empire to determine its precise border with Persia, a subject that had aroused controversy almost verging on violence not

Above The ziggurat of Ur, about 1853, drawing by W.K. Loftus (W.K. Loftus, *Travels and Researches in Chaldaea and Susiana*, London 1857)

Left Dagger with sheath from Ur, gold and lapis lazuli (copy in the British Museum, London; original in the Iraq Museum, Baghdad)

Above Katharine and Leonard Woolley excavating Grave 789 at Ur, 1927–8 (photo: Max Mallowan)

Previous double page Aerial photograph of the excavations at Ur (photo: Georg Gerster)
Below The ziggurat of the moon god Nanna at Ur, *c.*2250–2233 BC (photo: Max Mallowan)

Reconstruction of the ziggurat of the moon god Nanna at Ur, isometric projection for the period around 2300 BC, 1937 (British Museum, London)

long before. In 1849 he set out to reconnoitre the country south of Baghdad and visit the ruins of the great cities of antiquity there. It was on this journey that he saw the ruins known as Tell Muqqayar, and wrote an enthusiastic account of the possibilities they might present.

The British consul in Basra of the time, J.E. Taylor, was asked by the British Museum to pay special attention to the place described by Loftus as the 'pitch-built hill', a literal translation of its Arabic name. Excavations there brought to light little worth mentioning apart from some tablets of the kind found as inscribed plaques on buildings in ancient Mesopotamia. After enumerating the titles of the person who had commissioned the building, usually a king, these inscriptions generally mentioned its name, the god to whom it was consecrated and above all the name of the place where it stood. Cuneiform script had recently been deciphered, and there could be no doubt that the ruins were the site of the ancient city of Ur. At a time when the identification of places mentioned in the Bible was a subject of special interest it soon became clear that this settlement could be identified with Ur in the Chaldees.

From that time British archaeologists held the licence to dig on the site, although it was not until the later years of the First World War that work could be resumed there. In fact the situation then was particularly propitious, since Ur was near the Indo-British army camp stationed in the region in the last years of the war, close to the modern town of Nasiriyah. But, as Leonard

Woolley, the archaeologist who later excavated the site, dryly remarked, lack of cash soon brought any digging to an end.

In 1922, however, matters changed when the Museum of the University of Pennsylvania offered to go into partnership with the British Museum and supply the necessary financial means to resume excavations. Ur was the target site, and Leonard Woolley was appointed director of operations. He had already worked for the British Museum in Nubia some years earlier, and in 1912–14 had successfully uncovered architectural remains in the Late Hittite royal residence of Carchemish.

Easily the most intriguing part of the remains of Ur was the temple tower, or ziggurat, to give it its name in antiquity. The point of this structure was obviously for the temple standing on it to reach as great a height as possible. To achieve this end, two or three mighty rectangular brickwork terraces were built on top of each other. The dimensions of the ziggurat were impressive: the structure measured some 60 metres at the base, and the first platform was 11 metres high. However, it was notable not just for its dimensions and its height, but also for its central position in an area which itself stood several metres above the surrounding city. In addition, the stairways up the building were visible from afar. They comprised a flight of steps leading to the centre of the lower platform and two further flights at the sides, placed at an angle such that all three flights met at a point in the middle of this first platform.

Buildings of similar design had already been discovered in Nippur and Uruk, and others were found in the course of later excavations. Obviously all these structures were related, and further research showed that in most cases they had been commissioned by Ur-Nammu, first ruler of the Third Dynasty of Ur. In all probability the ziggurat of Ur was the prototype of this architectural form, and once it had been designed Ur-Nammu had similar buildings erected in all the large cities of his realm, which at the time covered the entire Babylonian plain.

This ziggurat, built by Ur-Nammu shortly before 2000 BC and last renovated and embellished by Nabonidus around the middle of the sixth century BC, was built of fired brick, but over the centuries the weather had taken a severe toll of the building, with the result that the original masonry emerged only here and there from a gigantic pile of rubble. Further excavations showed that the ziggurat lay within a narrow courtyard reached through an entrance flanked by towers, leading off a courtyard in front of it. We know from the inscriptions that this was the sanctuary of the moon god, the patron deity of Ur.

Leonard Woolley with workers on the excavations at Ur, 1920s (photo: Max Mallowan)

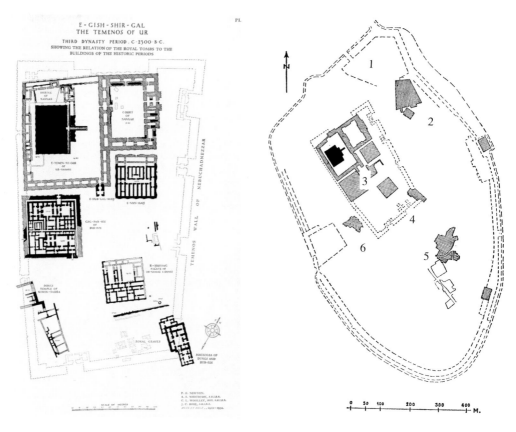

Above left Plan of the central area of Ur with the ziggurat (E-temen-ni-gur), the surrounding buildings and royal tombs (C.L. Woolley, *Ur Excavations* II, 1934)

Above right Plan of the city of Ur: (1) harbour, (2) palace of the sixth century BC, (3) central area, (4) the Royal Cemetery and (5–6) residential districts

However, there were other buildings within their own enclosure wall, separating them from the rest of the city, which lay on a lower level. The character of these buildings shows that they were not only inhabited by religious dignitaries but were also the repositories of rich treasures. To the south-east of the ziggurat, for instance, stood a large square building with a strong wall round it, which turned out, again according to the building inscriptions, to be the residence of the high priestesses of the moon god. It contained the rooms in which the priestesses actually lived as well as two smaller sacred precincts, obviously for private use. Next to it is a building which at first appears unusual because of the division of its interior into many long and narrow rooms, although its function is clear from its traditional name of the 'Great Barn', which shows that it was a storage area. We may conclude from its central position that items of great value were kept here; it may even have been the

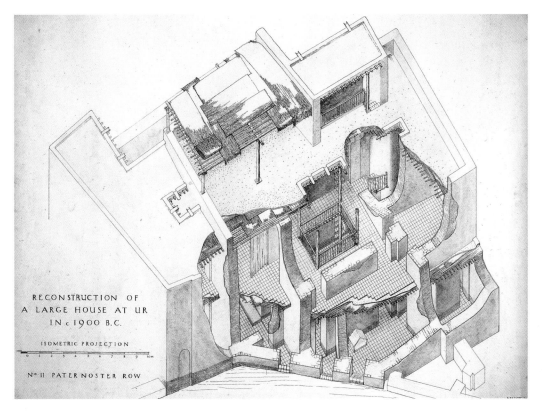

RECONSTRUCTION OF
A LARGE HOUSE AT UR
IN c 1900 B.C.

ISOMETRIC PROJECTION

Nº 11 PATER NOSTER ROW

Reconstruction of a large house of around 1900 BC at Ur, isometric projection, 1933
(British Museum, London)

state treasury. Finally, and further to the south-east, there are the remains of
a building which can be identified from an inscription as the palace of Shulgi,
second ruler of the Third Dynasty of Ur and the son of Ur-Nammu, mentioned above.

The city itself, surrounded by a wall pierced by gateways, was densely
crammed with houses, as we know from a series of excavations in the residential districts. They give us some idea of the typical dwelling house of the
period around 1800 BC, which consisted of rooms grouped around a central
courtyard. Access from the street was through a small room with doorways
set opposite each other in such a way that no one could see straight into the
courtyard from the street. A stairway led to the rooftop, where people probably slept on hot summer nights as they still frequently do today, to catch the
faintest breath of wind. There may also have been one or two rooms directly
under the roof, although it seems unlikely that a house of this kind had an
entire second storey.

Workers excavating Grave PG 1054 in the Royal Cemetery of Ur, 1927–8

It is interesting to compare the different quarters of the city because they show that in one district the average size of the buildings might be considerably larger than in another, a difference that can perhaps be ascribed to differences of social status and wealth. There are also differences in the layout of the streets. While the streets in one district intersect almost at right angles, another area shows the kind of layout that exists to this day in the 'old town' centres of large Near Eastern cities: major traffic arteries wind their way through the quarter, with smaller streets running off them and providing access to small blind alleys, which lead just to the dwelling houses. Unfortunately not nearly as much as one could wish is known about the internal organization of cities of the time, but the assumption that certain residential areas were inhabited by groups of different social or tribal origin has been confirmed by the observations described above.

While these discoveries and buildings mark crucial milestones in our knowledge of the history and culture of ancient Babylonia, to the public in general the name of the city of Ur is connected with another excavation area known as the Royal Cemetery of Ur.

During his first season in 1922–3 and while tracing the course of the enclosure wall to the south-east of the central area, Woolley had come upon tombs just beneath the surface. They contained gold jewellery as well as grave goods such as bronze weapons and metal and pottery vessels. A large quantity of gold beads made him suspect that even richer tombs might lie further down and that their excavation would be a task beyond his still inexperienced workmen. In his usual dry manner Woolley describes the way in which gold beads were found when the foremen or one of the archaeologists happened to be present; none, apparently, came to light when the workmen were left unsupervised. One Saturday he let it be known that he would pay three times the usual price offered by the local goldsmith for gold beads. Next Monday he was presented with lavish quantities of the beads, which the men had bought back from the goldsmith on their Sunday off. After these initial exciting finds Woolley stopped work on the tombs to concentrate for several years on excavating the large buildings of the city, those described above. He returned to the site of the cemetery only in the winter of 1926–7, when he had gained more experience.

Over the next six winter digging seasons almost 2,000 tombs preserved intact with their grave goods were brought to light, while the soil between them was full of countless other objects from about 4,000 other tombs no longer extant. In time, however, and most important of all, many major funerary complexes with walled vaults emerged. Most of them had already been robbed in antiquity, but one such vault still in a good state of preservation and the remains of others suggested that they had been extraordinarily richly furnished. It was from these tombs that the whole precinct gained its name of the Royal Cemetery.

Despite this enormous wealth and diversity of information, a number of questions remain unanswered, since no one has succeeded in linking these finds with contemporary textual records. This is particularly regrettable because evidence repeatedly found shows that it was usual for up to eighty individuals to accompany the occupant of the tomb on his or her journey into the underworld. Since there are around fourteen complexes of this nature, no doubt used over several generations, such a retinue was obviously an established custom and not anything out of the ordinary. However, the custom must have been abandoned before the time from which the first texts of any length date, for they contain not the slightest reference to it.

The discovery of one of these funerary complexes in 1927–8 attracted particular attention. It had not, like the others, been robbed, and the archaeologists were therefore able to marvel at its extensive and rich furnishings. The general situation became clear when a large number of human skeletons richly equipped with weapons and jewellery were found on a level which first sloped and then ran horizontally. They were carefully arranged in rows, but none was distinguished from the others in such a way as to identify it as the principal occupant of the tomb.

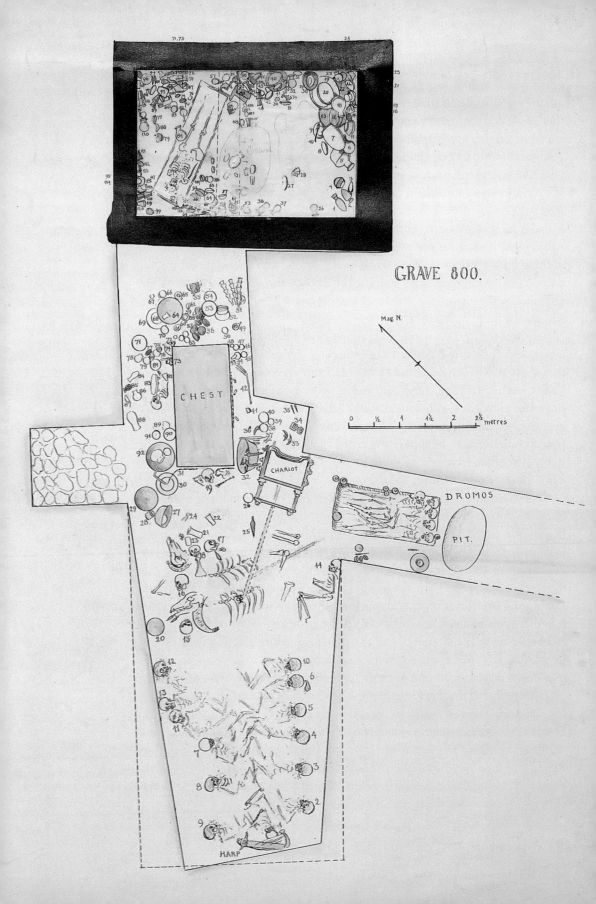

GRAVE 800.

CHEST

CHARIOT

DROMOS

PIT.

Mag. N.

0 ½ 1 1½ 2 2½ metres

HARP

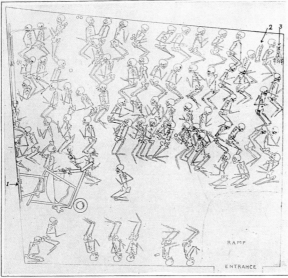

Above Plan and excavation of burial shaft 1237 at Ur; seventy-four members of a dead person's retinue, including musicians with lyres and harps, were buried here (*Illustrated London News*, 26 January 1929)

Left Plan of Grave 800 at Ur, the burial place of Queen Pu-abi with her retinue and two oxen which pulled a vehicle (British Museum, London)

Drawing of the golden lyre from burial shaft 1237 at Ur (C.L. Woolley, *Ur Excavations* II, 1934)

The remains of a lyre were found on the same level, its wooden parts now decayed, but once covered with rolled gold. The front of the soundbox was ornamented with mosaic work in lapis lazuli, cornelian and shell, and ended in a golden bull's head with the eyes and beard also made of lapis lazuli. Above these remains lay the skeleton of a harpist crowned with a golden diadem. The skeletons of two oxen lay beside this find, one on each side of a pole leading to a lavishly ornamented vehicle. A ring was once mounted on this pole and bore two eyelets, through which reins from the body of the cart or sleigh ran to the animals pulling it. The ring was a little work of art in itself, being surmounted by the expressive statue of a small golden donkey. The skeletons of the ox drivers lay in front of the animal bones. Although this burial cannot have comprised the entire court at the disposal of the living ruler, it must contain what was regarded as an adequate selection.

Countless implements and vessels made of gold, silver and coloured

Reconstruction drawing of the burial shaft, showing the queen's retinue and the ox drivers, 1928 (British Museum, London)

semi-precious stones were found on the same level, as well as a wooden board for games, with the playing areas inlaid with precious materials. Games counters similarly ornamented lay beside it.

The grave chamber here was so close to an older chamber that their floors were on the same level, and they were clearly closely connected. Objects made of gold, silver, bronze and precious stones far surpassing anything previously found were not the only grave goods discovered in this second chamber; most important of all was a seal made of costly lapis lazuli, with an inscription telling us the name of the occupant of the burial complex, Queen Pu-abi. Unfortunately she is not known to us from any other written sources, but that is not surprising, for these royal graves date from just before the time when it first became possible to record historical accounts of any length in writing (roughly around 2600 BC).

These archaeological finds, and study of the thousands of clay tablets found in Ur, have added a great deal to our knowledge of ancient oriental art and culture, principally owing to the purposeful energy shown by the archaeologist Leonard Woolley and his sensitive restoration of works of art, many

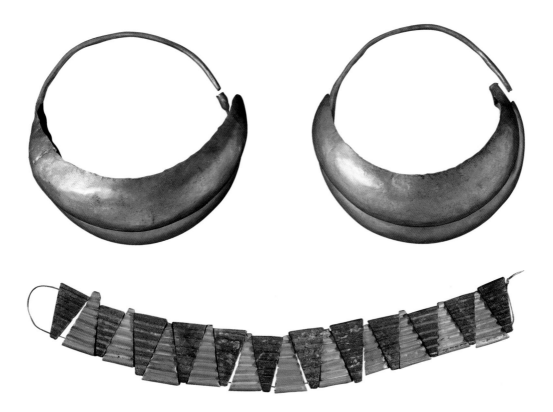

Top Pair of boat-shaped earrings from Ur, gold, *c.*2600 BC (British Museum, London)

Above Necklace from Ur, gold and lapis lazuli, *c.*2600 BC (British Museum, London)

Above left Necklace from Ur, gold and lapis lazuli, *c.*2600 BC (British Museum, London)

Left Wreath with leaves from Ur, gold, lapis lazuli and cornelian, *c.*2600 BC (British Museum, London)

of which were found in a dilapidated condition. His archaeological assistant Max Mallowan also made a considerable contribution. Mallowan worked with Woolley for six years, until he fell in love with a woman visiting the dig, married her and after a certain interval left the Ur expedition in order to work on sites where he and his new wife could be together. The woman's name was Agatha Christie.

BIBLIOGRAPHY

C.L. Woolley and P.R.S. Moorey, *Ur 'of the Chaldees'*, New York 1982
C.L. Woolley, *Ur Excavations*, 10 vols, London 1927–76
H.J. Nissen, *Grundzüge einer Geschichte des Vorderen Orients*, 3rd edn, Darmstadt 1995

Nineveh

Renate Gut

I n the summer of 1930, after becoming engaged to Agatha Christie, Max
Mallowan decided that the next excavation season at Ur in ancient southern
Mesopotamia should be his last. He intended to look around for a different
archaeological site where Agatha could participate in his work. By chance, an
opportunity soon came up. Reginald Campbell Thompson was looking for an
assistant on the excavations he planned to carry out in the winter of 1931–2 at
Nineveh, the capital of the late Assyrian or Neo-Assyrian empire, situated in
the north of modern Iraq.[1] Mallowan was interested, and after his return from

Left Felix Jones's map of Assyria, 1852, detail (British Museum, London)

Below The restored gateway of Shamash at Nineveh (J. Curtis, ed., *Art and Empire*, London 1995)

Tell Nebi Yunus, early 1930s

Ur finally agreed to join the party. He was thus laying the ground for almost thirty years of archaeological work in northern Iraq and the north of Syria, and for many crime stories written in the places where the Mallowans stayed on these expeditions.

Nineveh, like Ur, was known from the Bible and was equally famous. The story of the prophet Jonah had long appealed to the imagination of travellers and scholars: sent by God to warn Nineveh of impending doom, Jonah put to sea in the Mediterranean to avoid doing his duty, was then swallowed by a giant fish and only obeyed God's commandment when freed from its belly. Nineveh is described in the Bible as 'an exceeding great city of three days' journey … wherein are more than six score thousand persons that cannot discern between their right hand and their left hand, and also much cattle'.[2] Until the destruction of their empire by the Medes and Babylonians in 612 BC, the Assyrians were powerful enemies of the kingdom of Judah and their capital was one of the greatest cities of its time.

As early as the twelfth century AD Benjamin of Tudela had identified the ruinous mounds of Kuyunjik and Nebi Yunus (grave of the prophet Jonah) directly opposite Mosul as the ancient city of Nineveh. He noted that the city had disappeared entirely beneath ruins, but was so large that many villages were then scattered around what had once been the area it covered. At the end of the seventeenth century Pietro della Valle gives a very precise description of the course of the city wall, then still clearly visible on the site, as an irregular rectangle 'with four sides, but not of the same length, nor is it square'. Neither man doubted that this was Jonah's 'exceeding great city of three days' journey'. The city wall enclosed an area of 750 hectares. Nineveh was thus one and a half times as large as its rival Babylon, and about twice as large as ancient Rome when that city was at its largest. A complex system of canals, reservoirs and aqueducts brought water from the eastern mountains. Together with the river Khosr which flowed through the middle of the ancient city, this system ensured its water supply and the irrigation of the many parks and gardens for which Nineveh was famous.

The archaeological excavations concentrated mainly on Kuyunjik, with its royal palaces and temples. Nebi Yunus, the smaller mound, with a mosque and the tomb of the prophet Jonah, was sacred Islamic territory and beyond the reach of archaeologists. In 1847 Henry Austen Layard, the most famous excavator of Nineveh, had discovered the palace of King Sennacherib (704–681 BC) in Kuyunjik.[3] It was Sennacherib who made Nineveh his new capital and expanded it into a city more magnificent than anything previously known. His palace contained over seventy-three rooms, and their walls were covered with stone slabs decorated with reliefs of religious, hunting or battle scenes. Layard's work marked the beginning of almost a century of

Dying lion, relief from the north palace in Nineveh, c.645–640 BC, height 16.5 cm (British Museum, London)

excavations at Nineveh under the aegis of the British Museum, lasting until the time of Campbell Thompson. World-famous finds from these excavations include the lion-hunting scenes on the walls of the palace of King Ashurbanipal (668–c.631 BC), and reliefs showing the siege and capture of the Judaean city of Lachish. In addition, over 30,000 fragments of clay tablets that were once part of Ashurbanipal's library were found, including such literary texts as the Gilgamesh epic, inscribed on twelve tablets and containing the story of the Deluge.

The Mallowans agreed with Campbell Thompson that Max would go to Nineveh at the end of September, and Agatha would follow at the end of October.[3] Agatha paid her own way on the dig. According to the contract drawn up with Campbell Thompson, she was charged a pound a week for bed and board, and met her expenses for travelling and other items of personal use. Since she was a writer, it was expressly stipulated that she was not to write any account of the finds made at Nineveh without reference to Campbell Thompson.

Before the excavations, Campbell Thompson tested the ability of the new members of his team to stand up to the rigours of the Orient. Both Agatha and Max describe his methods with amusement in their memoirs.[5] He invited them to his home on a wet weekend, took them walking across country for hours on end, and observed what kind of shoes they wore and how resolute they were. Agatha, who liked walking and had often been out and about on Dartmoor, passed this 'cross-country scramble' test with flying colours. The weekend was also designed to show whether she was fussy about her food, and once again Campbell Thompson was able to set his mind at rest. He decided that she would 'fit in well enough' at Nineveh.

Agatha spent October in Rhodes, writing, and travelled on from there. She planned to go to Iskenderun by ship and then travel on in three daily stages to Mosul. However, the weather was too bad for her ship to put in at Iskenderun, and it had to go on to Beirut. Agatha then had a sixteen-hour train journey to Aleppo, where she boarded the Orient Express for Nisibin, at that time the terminus of the Baghdad Railway. Violent rain further delayed her journey, since the dry tracks had turned to torrential streams.[6] On arriving in Mosul she found Max standing at the place where they had agreed to meet. 'Weren't you terribly worried when I didn't arrive three days ago?' she asked. 'Oh no,' he said. 'It often happens.'[7]

Nineveh was 2½ kilometres away from Mosul, on the opposite bank of the Tigris. There was a fine view from the highest point of the ruins, the mound of Kuyunjik. No greater contrast can be imagined than that between the desert steppes around Ur, with their wind-blown sandy dunes, and the fertile agricultural plains of northern Mesopotamia. To the west ran the deeply carved riverbed of the Tigris, with the minarets and domes of the mosques of

publication,) but these should be discussed with Dr Thompson
and Mr Mallowan together before publication: providing that
the English members of the expedirion, and any benefactor
are duly mentioned by name, with credit here it is due.
8.,,, with the exception of the first lecture , to be given
by Dr Thompson, there shall be no limit to the lecturing
either by him or Mr Mallowan separately. If Mr Mallowan is
available, and suall so wish, he shall share the first
lecture (and title) by speaking of his pottery or prehistory.
Mr Mallowan shall be at liberty to write scientific articles
on his pottery or prehistory, or tomlecture thereon, once
the joint article is published, under his own name alone,
with the proviso as aforesaid that he shall mention the names
of the English members and any benefactor. In doing this
he may rely on the goodwill of the expedition to do its best
to further such publications.
9.— The British Museum shall have first right to buy any
antiquity offered to Mr Mallowan or Dr Thompson while on
the expedition.
10.Mr. Mallowan shall be insured against sickness by arrange
ment.
11. Mrs Mallowan will be a welcome guest at the expediton's
house for the last month of the expedition: she paying
her own expenses, travelling and otherwise, and one pound
weekly for service, board and lodging to the expeditionary
funds while in the house. The expedition shall not otherwise
be responsible to her: She will not publish locally or elsewhere
here any account of things found , without reference to Dr
Thompson.

M. E. L. Mallowan. 29. VI. 31.

R Campbell Thompson
29 June 1931

Part of the contract of 29 July 1931 between R. Campbell Thompson and Max Mallowan, agreeing terms
for work on the excavations at Nineveh in 1931–2 and mentioning that Mrs Mallowan (Agatha Christie)
may take part in the dig for the last month (British Museum, London)

NINEVEH · VOL · 2 ·

P 25

If lost please return to

M. E. L Mallowan.

c/o · BRITISH MUSEUM

LONDON.

[FINDER WILL BE REWARDED]

Left Excavation journal kept by Max Mallowan at Nineveh in 1931–2 (British Museum, London)

Previous double page Aerial view of Nineveh (photo: Georg Gerster)

Nineveh.

Menu.

Right Menu card with picture of Nineveh, early 1930 (British Museum, London)

Mosul beyond it. Far to the north rose the blue band of the Turkish mountains. In the east one could see the snow-covered peaks of the Maqlub mountains and the foothills of the Zagros range dividing Assyria from the Iranian highlands. Directly south lay Nebi Yunus, and beyond it was Yarimjah, a mound later to give its name to the archaeological site in *Murder in Mesopotamia*. By comparison with Ur, their new surroundings seemed paradise to Agatha and Max.[8]

A small house surrounded by a garden at the foot of Nebi Yunus acted as the expedition's base. Agatha liked it very much. It had a flat roof, a stone porch and a tower room that was occupied by the Mallowans. There were rose bushes all around the house, but to Agatha's regret the flowers were picked early every morning to make valuable attar of roses.[9] Life on the dig was very harmonious, which had not always been the case in Ur. Campbell Thompson

The 90' pit looking E.
Men passing up baskets

View of the deep pit dug by Max Mallowan at Nineveh, 1931–2

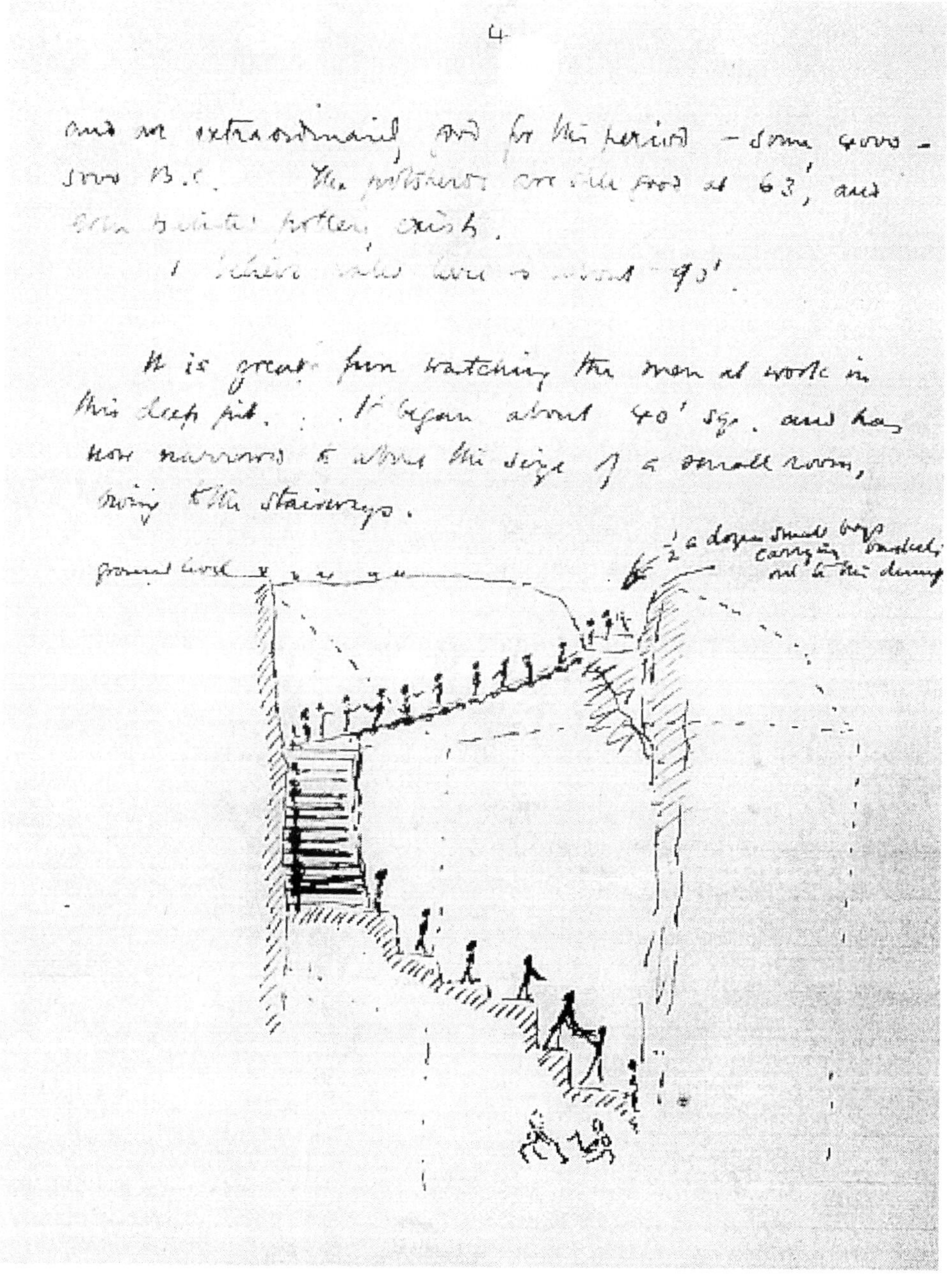

4

and an extraordinary *and for the period* — *some 4000 – 5000 B.C.* The *potteries are all good at 63',* and *even white potters exist.*

I believe also have a most 90'.

It is great fun watching the men at work in this deep pit. It began about 40' sq. and has now narrowed to about the size of a small room, owing to the stairways.

ground level

a dozen small boys carrying baskets out to the dump

Sketch of the deep pit by R. Campbell Thompson, with the men in a chain passing up baskets containing soil and archaeological finds (British Museum, London)

was extrovert, cordial and unconventional, his wife Barbara charming, kindly and selfless.[10] Only Campbell Thompson's very thrifty streak sometimes led to farcical moments. The furnishings of the house, for instance, were spartan, consisting almost entirely of empty orange boxes, and when Agatha went to the Mosul bazaar and bought herself a solid table on which she could work at her typewriter, Campbell Thompson considered the expense a wicked extravagance. Although she had paid for it herself, he could not understand why she needed it.[11] At this table she wrote *Lord Edgware Dies*.[12]

Digging began at five every morning. Since some of the workers came from a considerable distance away, a decision on whether the day's weather was good enough for the excavations had to be taken before sunrise. A lantern signal from the flat roof of the expedition house conveyed this decision to a look-out up on Kuyunjik, and he then passed it on to the surrounding villages. After this ritual Campbell Thompson and Max set off for Kuyunjik.[13] Campbell Thompson had bought Max the cheapest horse to be obtained in the bazaar at Mosul, a small and refractory pony. Max had ridden only twice in his life before, and was lucky that he was not watched by Campbell Thompson when he mounted the pony and rode up the mound, and that he never fell off, which would have lost him the respect of the local workmen.[14] Barbara Campbell Thompson and Agatha followed at eight o'clock to have breakfast with them, a meal of hard-boiled eggs, tea and native bread. Then the women returned to the house, and walked up Kuyunjik a second time later on, for lunch.

Campbell Thompson had first dug at Nineveh under L.W. King in 1904–5, and had continued his work there since 1927. The winter of 1931–2 was to be his last digging season. The site of his excavations lay between the Assyrian royal palaces, and he hoped to bring to light two temples consecrated to the deities Nabu and Ishtar. Unlike Woolley and Mallowan, Campbell Thompson was first and foremost an epigraphist whose overriding interest was in written texts, chiefly clay tablets in cuneiform script or other objects bearing inscriptions. He was less enthusiastic about the archaeological side of a dig, but he had an outstanding knowledge of Assyrian history and many other talents.[15]

Mallowan was responsible for the pottery and prehistoric finds that came to light. His chief task was to supervise the digging of a deep pit that was expected to provide information about the extent and origins of the prehistoric settlement of Nineveh. It was a task he was happy to undertake, since he had already helped Woolley to excavate levels from the period around 3000 BC in the Flood Pit at Ur. Furthermore, these early periods were largely uncharted territory where there was still a great deal to discover. As Agatha described it: 'It was endlessly interesting. Although it was so old – it was *new!*'[16]

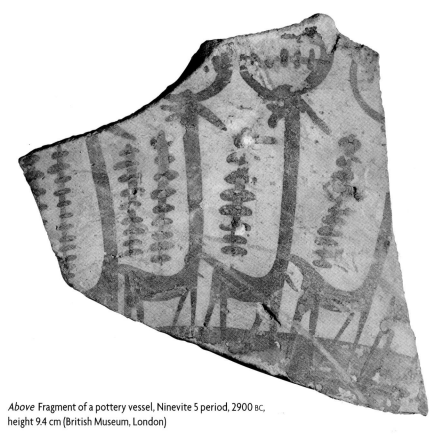

Above Fragment of a pottery vessel, Ninevite 5 period, 2900 BC, height 9.4 cm (British Museum, London)

Below Bevel-rimmed pottery bowl from Nineveh, Uruk period, 3300–3000 BC, diameter 16.2 cm
(British Museum, London)

Right Pottery bowl with foot,
Ninevite 5 period, 2800 BC
(Iraq Museum, Baghdad)

Below Pottery vessel with incised
and stamped ornamentation,
Ninevite 5 period, 2800 BC, height
11.3 cm (British Museum, London)

The deep sounding was dug down from the highest point in the very centre of Kuyunjik on 15 October 1931. Originally a square measuring 12 by 12 metres, the pit became smaller the further down it went. Steps were dug into the sides, with the workmen posted on them to pass the soil up out of the pit. Campbell Thompson's assumption that Nineveh had been built on natural rock was not confirmed. The pit went down and down. Several times Campbell Thompson contemplated calling a halt to the operation because of the threatening manner in which the steep walls of the shaft loomed over the heads of the men digging it. Mallowan, as an enthusiastic archaeologist, had to use all his powers of persuasion to keep him from doing so.[17] He even countered Campbell Thompson's argument that he would not find enough volunteers for work in the dangerous pit, since no special finds were to be expected and consequently no *bakshish* possible as the finder's reward, by secretly paying the men *bakshish* for almost every painted potsherd.[18] Work on the pit therefore went on until there was no more doubt that they had reached the virgin soil. They had been digging for eleven weeks, and the pit went 25 metres down. Contrary to expectations, three-quarters of the massive mound proved to be prehistoric.

The deep sounding at Nineveh was the first attempt to establish a chronological scheme for prehistoric Assyria.[19] Mallowan distinguished five levels, which he named Ninevite 1 to 5, from top to bottom. They covered three and a half millennia, from the middle of the sixth millennium to the middle of the third millennium BC. Max and Agatha found two levels particularly fascinating because of the unusually attractive pottery they contained. One was Ninevite 2 (or the Halaf period, *c.*5300–4500 BC), which was characterized by handmade but exquisite and beautifully painted pottery. For the first time the great age of this pottery, which was already known from the Syrian site of Tell Halaf, could be determined. The other level was Ninevite 5 (*c.*2900–2550 BC), for which vessels on a foot, bowls painted with animal and other patterns, or pottery made of fine grey ware adorned with incised and indented patterns were typical.[20] Both wares, Halaf and Ninevite 5 pottery, were to occupy the Mallowans for several years to come.

Agatha Christie greatly enjoyed her first experience of living on an archaeological dig. She liked Mosul, she had made friends with 'C.T.' and Barbara Campbell Thompson, 'she had completed the final demise of Lord Edgeware, and had tracked down his murder successfully' while she was at Nineveh.[21] Unexpectedly, the deep sounding had made her something of an expert on prehistoric ceramics. In *Death in the Clouds* she gives a sample of her knowledge: 'There is no doubt about it. They are *all* wrong – the Germans, the Americans, the English! They date the prehistoric pottery all wrong. Take the Samarra ware …', she makes her character the famous archaeologist Monsieur

Dupont say. But his son Jean contradicts him: 'You must take the evidences from all sources. There is Tell Halaf, and Sakje Geuze ...'.[22] The Duponts are discussing the age of Samarra and Halaf pottery, a problem that Max had solved through digging the deep sounding at Nineveh.[23] The attractions of Halaf pottery had a part to play outside Agatha Christie's novels, too; they also determined the Mallowans' choice of their next excavation site. This place was a little village 4 kilometres east of Nineveh called Arpachiyah.

NOTES

1   A. Christie, *An Autobiography*, London 1977, p. 422.
2   Jonah 3: 3 and 4: 11.
3   H.A. Layard, *Nineveh and its Remains*, London 1849; idem, *Discoveries in the Ruins of Nineveh and Babylon*, London 1853.
4   Christie, *Autobiography* (n. 1), p. 452.
5   Ibid. pp. 451f.; M. Mallowan, *Mallowan's Memoirs*, London 1977, pp. 69f.
6   Christie, *Autobiography* (n. 1), p.453.
7   Ibid.
8   Mallowan, *Memoirs* (n. 4), p. 69.
9   Christie, *Autobiography* (n. 1), p. 453; Mallowan, *Memoirs* (n. 4), pp. 69, 73.
10 Mallowan, *Memoirs* (n. 4), p. 69.
11 Christie, *Autobiography* (n. 1), pp. 454f.; Mallowan, *Memoirs* (n. 4), p. 74. According to Max Mallowan the table cost only three pounds.
12 A. Christie, *Lord Edgware Dies*, London 1933.
13 Christie, *Autobiography* (n. 1), p. 454; Mallowan, *Memoirs* (n. 4), pp. 72f.
14 Christie, *Autobiography* (n. 1), p. 454; Mallowan, *Memoirs* (n. 4), p. 70.
15 Christie, *Autobiography* (n. 1), p. 458; Mallowan, *Memoirs* (n. 4), pp. 69, 72, 77.
16 Christie, *Autobiography* (n. 1), pp. 455, 458f.; Mallowan, *Memoirs* (n. 4), p. 69.
17 Mallowan, *Memoirs* (n. 4), p. 79f.
18 Mallowan, *Memoirs* (n. 4), p. 84.
19 R. Campbell Thompson and M. Mallowan, 'The British Museum Excavations at Nineveh, 1931–32', *Annals of Archaeology and Anthropology* 20 (1933), pp. 71–186; R.V. Gut, 'Das prähistorische Ninive', *Baghdader Forschungen* 19, Mainz 1995.
20 Christie, *Autobiography* (n. 1), pp. 458f.; Mallowan, *Memoirs* (n. 4), pp. 81, 83f.
21 Christie, *Autobiography* (n. 1), p. 460; Christie, *Lord Edgware* (n. 11).
22 A. Christie, *Death in the Clouds*, London 1935.
23 Halaf pottery: Ninevite 2c; Samarra pottery: Ninevite 2b (c.5400 BC).

Arpachiyah

Stuart Campbell

When Mallowan's excavation at Arpachiyah began in 1933, very little was known of the prehistory of north Mesopotamia. Indeed, Arpachiyah was one of the first sites specifically chosen to address a prehistoric period. It had been selected largely on the basis of the pottery with elaborate, painted decoration that littered the surface of the tell. This was a type of pottery known as Halaf after Tell Halaf in north Syria where Baron von Oppenheim had first described it. Although it is now well known that this pottery characterizes a large area across north Mesopotamia and flourished between about 6000 and 5300 BC, it had only been observed in north Iraq in 1928 during the excavations at Nineveh. It was only in 1932, at the same site, that its stratigraphic position was established in the 90-foot (27.5-metre) deep sounding excavated by Mallowan under the direction of Campbell Thompson.

Almost everything Mallowan's first independent excavation uncovered was new and with few parallels. Many of his observations and conclusions have remained definitive until the last decade. The Halaf period is now known as one in which society was becoming steadily more complex. The economy was predominantly based on agriculture and herding of domestic animals. Settlements were generally of a small size, between 1 and 2 hectares, but in the last ten years archaeologists have started to discover much larger sites, up to 20 hectares in size, which must have formed larger population centres. The material culture was elaborate with extensive exchange systems between sites. Although recognizable urban states did not arise for more than 1,000 years after the end of the Halaf, it seems probable that some of the key changes in society were already taking place.

The site takes its name from the village of Arpachiyah, a few miles north-east of Nineveh, but the mound itself is called Tepe Reshwa. In 1933 it was surrounded by farmland, although today it is enclosed by a housing scheme and the village is being overtaken by the urban spread of Mosul. The mound is relatively small, perhaps 150 metres in diameter and standing 5.50

Left Fragment of a pottery vessel with snake decoration from Tell Arpachiyah (British Museum, London)

Above Fragment of a pottery vessel with a bull's head from Tell Arpachiyah, Halaf period 5000–4800 BC, height 16 cm (British Museum, London)

metres above the plain, although we now know that there is a further 2 metres below the level of the present plain. There is certainly a little fourth-millennium-BC occupation on the summit of the mound and some indications of much later remains as well, but the major occupation of the site was during the Halaf and Ubaid periods – perhaps between about 5800 and 4900 BC.

Mallowan knew of the site during his excavation of the deep sounding at Nineveh and in 1932 he selected it as the site of his proposed excavation, since it offered easy access to prehistoric levels. He was fortunate that, at the age of twenty-eight, he was able to obtain funding of £2,000 from several sources, including the British Museum and the British School of Archaeology in Iraq. His staff was small, consisting of himself as archaeologist, John Rose as architect and illustrator, and Agatha Christie, who seems to have worked mainly reconstructing pottery and printing the photographs. They were, however, able to carry out a vast quantity of recording, and most impressively the excavation report was completed only six months after the end of excavation and published in 1935. Although Mallowan wished to carry out a second season in 1934, he felt unable to do so because of a disagreement over the division of the finds between the excavation and the Iraq Museum, a disagreement sufficiently serious to involve correspondence with the League of Nations.

Mallowan employed a very large number of workmen on the site, up to

Aerial view of Tell Arpachiyah, 1933 (photo: Royal Air Force)

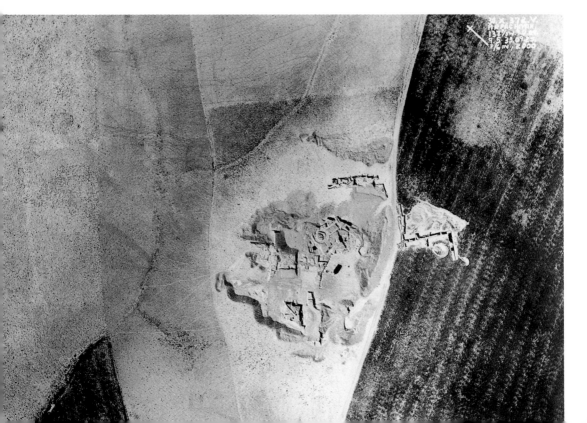

The 180-man Tell Arpachiyah excavation team, with Max Mallowan and Agatha Christie in the front

about 180 men, who were able to excavate a very significant portion of the site in only six weeks. Although he employed the foremen from Nineveh, the bulk of the men were untrained and, as he candidly states in the report in the journal *Iraq*, 'to enable the men … to obtain some initial training', excavation commenced on the lower portions of the mound. It is perhaps not surprising that rather little architecture was discovered in this initial phase of work. He was justified, however, in that his excavation of the centre of the mound was much better and produced a series of ten levels of architecture, labelled TT ('top of tepe') and numbered from the top down.

The site clearly has a very long history and for some time the sequence excavated by Mallowan provided the basic divisions of the Halaf, although we now know of earlier Halaf phases elsewhere. In fact, Mallowan did not excavate down to the natural soil underlying the tell. Very little is known of the early stages of the occupation, apart from the pottery. The earliest phase is characterized particularly by deep, straight-sided bowls, often decorated with cross-hatching or rows of large lozenges. Other shapes are known but they are limited and the decoration tends to be bold and relatively simple. A striking motif used in the early phase is the bull's head, or bukranion, that occurs repeatedly within the Halaf. Mallowan firmly interpreted it as representing a

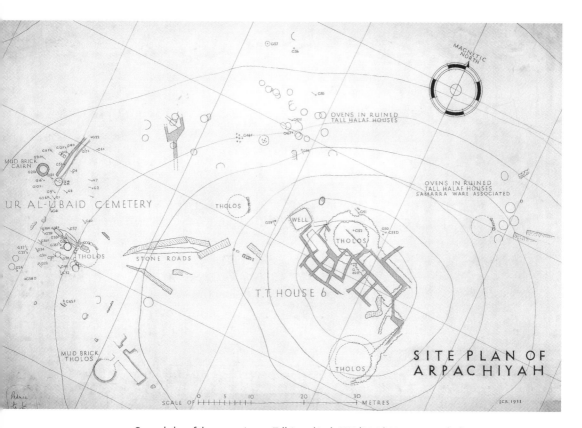

General plan of the excavations at Tell Arpachiyah, 1933 (British Museum, London)

male divinity and its prominence certainly argues for some specific symbolism.

We have more definite information on the archaelogy of Arpachiyah with the lowest level of the excavations at the centre of the site, TT10. In this level and the subsequent TT9 the stone foundations of circular buildings were excavated. Other tholoi from this broad phase were among the rare buildings rescued from the excavations in the outer area of the mound. Mallowan labelled these buildings tholoi, misleadingly pointing to architectural parallels with Mycenaean tombs in Greece. The name, however, has become accepted for these distinctive structures which are seen at many other Halaf sites across north Mesopotamia. Mallowan suggested they had a domed roof and there is evidence of this at a few sites; more often they seem to have had vertical walls and probably a flat roof. The TT9 and 10 examples are substantial, with diameters of between 5 and 7 metres, but the character of the centre of the site changes at this point and the tholoi of TT8 and TT7 are much larger. In these levels the tholoi have stone foundations approximately 1.5 metres wide constructed of river boulders and the circular rooms are around 10 metres in diameter. Furthermore they have rectangular rooms attached which themselves are an additional 10 metres long, giving a strikingly monumental character to the buildings at the centre of the site in the Late Halaf.

It is TT6, the last level of Halaf occupation at the site, that gives Arpachiyah its greatest claim to fame. A series of cobbled paths, which probably belong to this phase, lead towards the centre of the site. The architecture of the excavated structure is rectilinear rather than circular but the rectangular antechamber of one of the earlier massive TT7 tholoi remains in use or is rebuilt to provide architectural continuity with the preceding level at the centre of what seems a rather sprawling building. This building was either deliberately or accidentally burnt down, preserving an unparalleled wealth of objects that had been in the building in its final stage of use. A vast range of artefacts is preserved. Probably the most famous are the pottery plates decorated in up to three colours with densely packed geometric patterns of amazing complexity. The walls of these vessels are only a few millimetres thick and the finest examples stand comparison with the best pottery of any period. These are certainly likely to have been prestige items and there remain few or no parallels at other sites. Other pots, though, are much simpler and may represent the normal domestic assemblage of a Halaf house. Alongside the pottery are a number of stone vessels, usually rather rare in the Halaf and including one made from obsidian. Obsidian was also ground and polished into plaques which may have been sewn to clothing or strung as large beads, in one case in combination with cowrie shells. Other finds suggest more ritual activities: two figurines, one male and one female; a very stylized figurine made of pumice; human knuckle bones and carved stone representations of knuckle bones.

Interpretation of the TT6 'Burnt House' is uncertain. Mallowan suggested that it was a potter's workshop or a chief's residence. There are some clues to the activities carried out in the Burnt House from other finds. Stamp seals with incised geometrical patterns are found regularly but usually in very small numbers at Halaf sites. We know that they were pressed into wet clay to seal containers and to mark property. In the Burnt House at least ten seals were found together with twenty-six sealings. This is an unparalleled concentration of seals and suggests that the individual or institution within the Burnt House exercised significant control over the circulation of goods within society. Support for this comes from obsidian in particular. This volcanic glass was being imported from its sources in central and eastern Anatolia into north Mesopotamia in significant quantities during the Halaf and used to make sharp-edged chipped stone tools. It is probably no coincidence that thousands of waste chips of obsidian were found in the Burnt House. It is probable that,

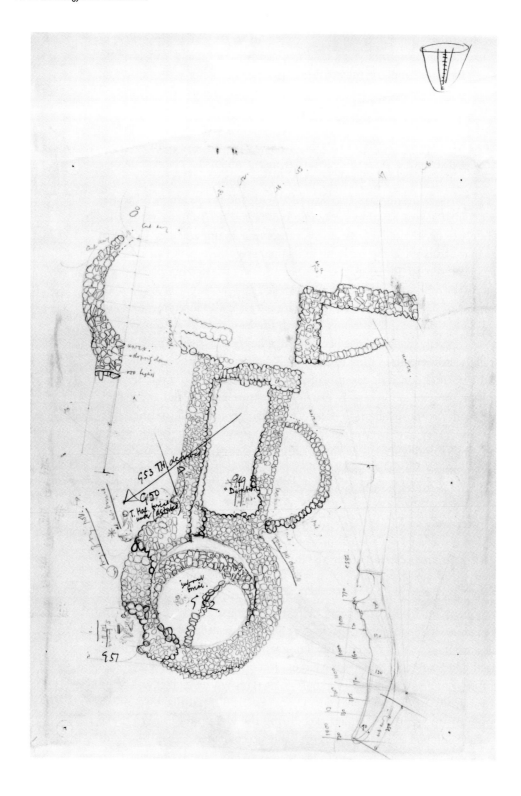

Above Stone foundations of a circular building with rectangular antechamber at Tell Arpachiyah, 1933

Left Drawing of the tholos from level TT7 of about 4500 BC at Tell Arpachiyah, 1933
(British Museum, London)

Above Workman next to a large storage jar at Tell Arpachiyah, 1933

Above right Painted pottery plate from the TT6 Burnt House at Tell Arpachiyah, about 4500 BC, diameter 10 cm (British Museum, London)

Right Painted pottery bowl from the TT6 Burnt House at Tell Arpachiyah, about 4500 BC, diameter 18 cm (British Museum, London)

Above Stamp seal from Tell Arpachiyah, steatite, diameter 2.5 cm
(British Museum, London)

Right Page from Max Mallowan's excavation diary at Tell Arpachiyah, 1933
(British Museum, London)

in part at least, the wealth of the occupants of the Burnt House was based on control of the obsidian trade.

We do not know why the TT6 building burnt down. Mallowan attributed it to Ubaid invaders who smashed pottery and burnt it in an orgy of destruction. It may have been accidental or it may even have been a deliberate ritual act, perhaps signifying the end of a whole series of significant building in TT8, TT7 and TT6.

The settlement of Arpachiyah was probably abandoned for a brief period after the destruction of the TT6 Burnt House. The latest well-documented occupation of the site was in the Ubaid period, *c.*5200 BC. Several poorly preserved building levels were discovered in TT1–5 and probably all belong in this phase. There was also an Ubaid cemetery on the western slope of the site. Around fifty graves were excavated, generally of individuals laid with the heads to the east or south-east and often accompanied by two or more pots. One interesting link between the people buried in this cemetery and the earlier Halaf occupants of the site is the practice of cranial deformation – by bandaging the heads of infants – which was used by both groups. Dental abnormalities may also suggest that the people buried in the Ubaid graves were related to some of the Halaf occupants.

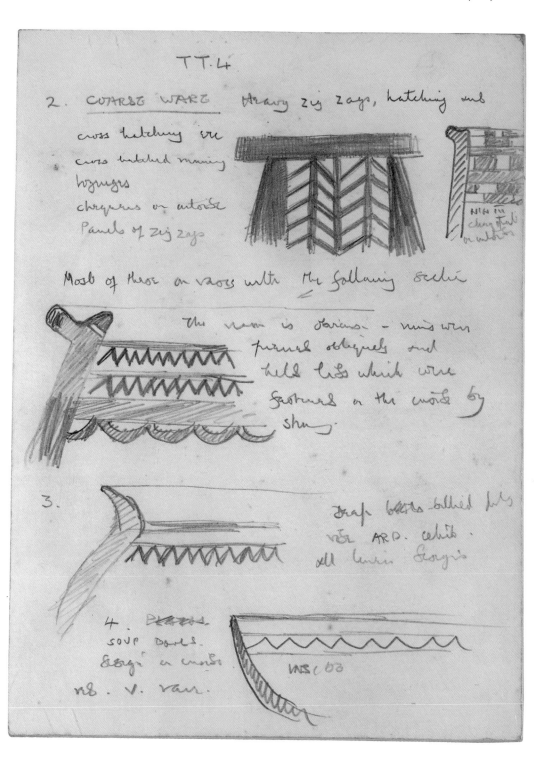

TT.4

2. COARSE WARE Heavy zig zags, hatching and

cross hatching are

cross hatched running

lozenges

chequers on autoise

Panels of zig zags

Most of these on vases with the following section

The rim is various — rims were

pierced obliquely and

held lids which were

fastened on the inside by

string.

3.

Drap blacks bellied lids

see ARD. white.

all burin Georgi's

4. SOUP BOWLS.

Georgi's on inside

nb . V. var.

Building at the top of the mound at Tell Arpachiyah, Ubaid period, about 4200 BC

Workmen on the west side of the mound at Tell Arpachiyah, 1933

Arpachiyah has remained the focus of work on the Halaf. Ismail Hijara carried out a further excavation of the site in 1976. He excavated a long narrow trench running from the summit of the mound – probably from the level of TT6 – down towards the west of the mound. This demonstrated that the outer areas of the mounds, in which Mallowan found almost no architecture, were in fact densely packed with structures. His excavations have also provided an important and carefully excavated pottery sequence starting on the natural floor under the site and running through to levels contemporary with TT6. A particularly notable find, demonstrating the wealth of the site that Mallowan left behind, is a bowl decorated with dramatic scenes of humans and animals. Tom Davidson carried out another important study, again in the mid-1970s, looking at the chemical composition of the clay used to make the pottery of Arpachiyah in comparison with the contemporary site of Tepe Gawra, some 25 kilometres to the north. His results suggest that Arpachiyah may have exported large quantities of pottery to neighbouring settlements and this could have formed another basis for the wealth and importance of Arpachiyah.

In many ways Mallowan's excavations at Arpachiyah still hold a key for our understanding of the later prehistory of north Mesopotamia.

Note: Dates are calibrated.

BIBLIOGRAPHY

C. Breniquet, 'A propos du vase halafien de la Tombe G2 de Tell Arpachiyah', *Iraq* 54 (1992), pp. 69–78.

S. Campbell, 'The Halaf Period in Iraq: Old sites and new', *Biblical Archaeologist* 55/4 (1992), pp. 182–7.

T.E. Davidson and H. McKerrell, 'The neutron activation analysis of Halaf and Ubaid pottery from Tell Arpachiyah and Tepe Gawra', *Iraq* 42 (1980), pp. 155–67.

I. Hijara, *The Halaf Period in Northern Mesopotamia*, London 1997.

I. Hijara *et al.*, 'Arpachiyah 1976', *Iraq* 42 (1980), pp. 13–54.

M.E.L. Mallowan and J.C. Rose, 'Excavations at Tall Arpachiyah, 1933', *Iraq* 2 (1935), pp. 1–178.

T. Molleson and S. Campbell, 'Deformed skulls at Tell Arpachiyah: the social context', in S. Campbell and A. Green (eds), *The Archaelogy of Death in the Ancient Near East*, Oxford 1995, pp. 45–55.

TROUSERED "MOTHER GODDESSES" DRESSED LIKE MODERN KURDS;

THE EARLIEST KNOWN CYLINDER SEAL; AND OTHER TREASURE FOUND WHILE DIGGING DOWN 60 FT. AT CHAGAR BAZAR.

FIG. 4. AKIN TO SARGONID PERIOD OBJECTS AT UR AND NINEVEH: A DAGGER, A PIN (WITH DOVES AT ONE END), AND A KNIFE, ALL OF COPPER, FROM A GRAVE IN THE ELEVENTH SETTLEMENT AT CHAGAR BAZAR, REPRESENTING A NEW AND METAL-USING POPULATION (c. 2700 B.C.).

FIG. 5. PROBABLY THE EARLIEST OF ITS KIND EVER FOUND? A PRIMITIVE CYLINDER SEAL, WITH ITS DESIGN—FOUR FIGURES, WITH BIRD-LIKE HEADS, DANCING.

FIG. 6. A BEAUTIFULLY CARVED ARCHAIC STONE AMULET SHOWING CONSIDERABLE SKILL IN ANIMAL MODELLING AND MINIATURE WORK.

FIG. 7. AT THE BOTTOM OF THE 60-FT. SHAFT SUNK AT CHAGAR BAZAR, WITH STAIRWAYS FOR WORKERS: EXCAVATIONS APPROACHING REMAINS OF THE FIRST OF FIFTEEN SUPERIMPOSED CITIES.

FIG. 8. THE LARGEST OF THE "MOTHER GODDESS" FIGURINES, THE FIRST OF THEIR KIND EVER FOUND WITH THE STOOLS THAT FORM THEIR SEATS: A TURBANED EXAMPLE.

FIG. 9. DEEP EXCAVATIONS AT CHAGAR BAZAR: WORK IN THE PREHISTORIC LEVELS, WITH NATIVE LABOURERS ASCENDING AND DESCENDING THE STAIRWAY CUT IN THE SIDE OF THE SHAFT.

FIG. 10. AN ARCHAIC TERRA-COTTA HEAD BELIEVED TO REPRESENT A BIRD, POSSIBLY A VULTURE: AN OBJECT FROM ONE OF THE LATER CITIES AT CHAGAR BAZAR, BUT PROBABLY MADE BEFORE 2000 B.C.

FIG. 11. WEARING THE SAME COSTUME AS MODERN KURDISH PEASANT WOMEN: PREHISTORIC TERRA-COTTA FIGURINES OF THE MOTHER GODDESS, PAINTED WITH DETAILS OF DRESS, INCLUDING STRIPED JACKET AND TROUSERS.

The above photographs illustrate Mr. Mallowan's article opposite, and, like those on the two succeeding pages, are numbered to correspond with his references to particular objects found during his excavations at Chagar Bazar, a mound in northern Syria containing successive levels of occupation representing fifteen separate settlements on the site. They range in date from before 4000 B.C. to about 1500 B.C., after which the place was unoccupied until Roman times. The word "tall" means "mound," and this explains the letter T before names on the map reproduced opposite. Regarding the above illustrations, one or two further details may be added. Thus, concerning Fig. 4, it is noted: "The dagger and the curved knife closely resemble objects found in the royal cemetery of Ur. The pin surmounted by a pair of doves is a very rare object." The bird-headed figures on the seal impression in Fig. 5 are described as engaged in a ritual dance. "Mother Goddess" figurines (Figs. 8 and 11) have never before been found with the stools that form their seats. Measurement rules shown in any photograph throughout the series are marked in centimetres.—[PHOTOGRAPHS BY COURTESY OF THE TRUSTEES OF THE BRITISH MUSEUM.] (SEE ARTICLE OPPOSITE.)

Chagar Bazar

Augusta McMahon

From 1935 to 1937 Max Mallowan excavated at the site of Chagar Bazar on the upper Khabur in north-east Syria.[1] Chagar Bazar was one of many sites the Mallowans identified in their 1934 survey of the region and was chosen for excavation first. The concurrent excavations at Chagar Bazar and Tell Brak were based at a house constructed just off the mound (eloquently described, with photographs, in Agatha Christie's *Come, Tell Me How You Live*), and she frequently expressed her preference for the village and ambience of Chagar Bazar. The site lies on the west bank of the Wadi Dara, which feeds the Wadi Khanzir, a tributary to the Khabur River; it is on the modern road between Hasseke and Amuda and was surely on a number of ancient routes which crossed this region.

The mound of Chagar Bazar is *c*.12 hectares at maximum, and its greatest height is 21 metres above the modern plain. It has a distinct high peak

Left Report of the excavation at Chagar Bazar in the *Illustrated London News*, 23 November 1935

Below Mid-1930s view of the River Khabur in Syria

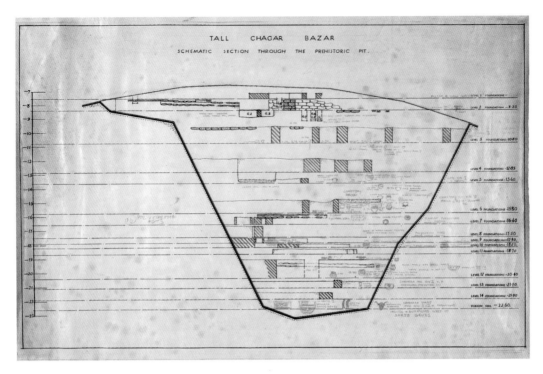

Stratified schematic section through the prehistoric pit at Chagar Bazar (British Museum, London)

at the south end and a lower and longer mound to the north; the two high areas are separated by an erosion gully. The sides of the mound are steeply eroded, particularly on the north and east, with a more gradual slope down to the south, where a modern village is located. Until 1934 very little archaeological work had been done in the Khabur area, and Chagar Bazar's relatively small size and the presence of a wide temporal range of deposits made it an ideal starting point for Mallowan's investigations.

The three seasons of excavation at Chagar Bazar revealed that the site was first occupied some time during the prehistoric Halaf period, the later sixth millennium BC, and was finally abandoned in the mid-second millennium BC in the Old Babylonian period. Fifteen occupation levels were identified, of Halaf, Ninevite 5, Early Dynastic to Akkadian, and Old Babylonian periods. There were gaps in occupation during the fourth millennium BC and the later third to early second millennia BC. The invaluable help of Agatha Christie Mallowan during the excavations was invariably acknowledged in the publications with such laconic notes as 'my wife was also present throughout, and assisted in the mending of the pottery and in the photography'.[2]

Prehistoric levels

Mallowan chose Chagar Bazar to excavate primarily because of the Halaf pottery on the surface. The 1934 survey identified a cluster of sites with this distinctive painted pottery in the area, especially just north of the site, and Mallowan proposed that Chagar Bazar was a provincial centre for production and diffusion of this ware. A deep (15 metres) stratigraphic sounding, Pit M, was located at the north-western end of the site in 1935 to investigate the pre-historic settlement. The Halaf period is represented within it by Levels 7–15, just under 7 metres of deposit. Although no complete building plans were uncovered in any level, there were substantial constructions with thick walls (*c.*1 metre wide) in Levels 10 and 11 and a possible mud-brick platform in Level 12. Otherwise the partially exposed structures were built of mud-brick or pisé and appear to have been simple private houses.

The pottery is mostly Late Halaf in date, and there is some possible

Drawings from Max Mallowan's excavation diary in Germayir, 1936 (British Museum, London)

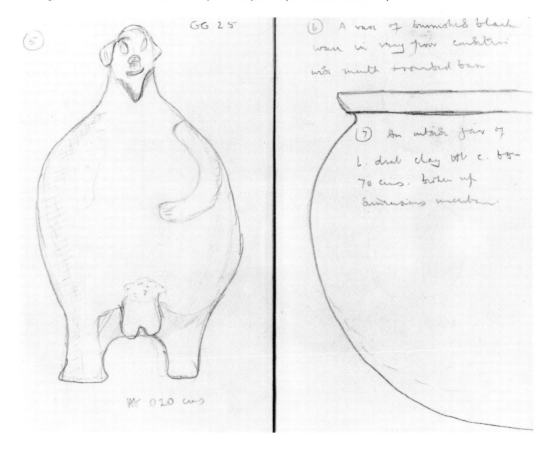

Transitional pottery from Level 7, bridging the gap between Halaf and Ubaid material, the latter being the next ceramic assemblage produced in the area. Level 12 already includes examples of polychrome painted pottery (red and black with white over-painting), which is associated with Late Halaf only, so all of Levels 12 through 7 can be ascribed to this period, *c.*4800–4500 BC. Chagar Bazar was temporarily abandoned at the point of the Halaf to Ubaid transition, the abandonment being marked by up to 2 metres depth of weathered deposit (Level 6). But the date the site was established remains uncertain. Halaf sherds together with Samarran pottery, a painted pottery tradition more at home in a separate zone on the mid-Tigris, are reported from the lowest levels (13–15), directly above virgin soil. Yet the date of that earliest pottery, within the *c.*700-year span allotted to production of Halaf material, remains uncertain.

Objects from Halaf levels include baked clay figurines, seated 'Mother Goddess' figures, which may have been associated with religious or magical ritual. There were also a handful of stone stamp seals with incised geometric patterns, a few pieces of ornamental obsidian and a single copper bead, indication that early experimentation with metallurgy was underway in the region if not actually at the site.

Mallowan proposed that Chagar Bazar was the hub of a network of corridors of communication running through the upper Khabur region, and that the site was a regional centre for prehistoric sites on the Wadi Khanzir and Wadi Dara. His reconstruction was based on a large estimated site size (possibly 12 hectares, relatively large for that time) and on the substantial walls and platform in the Late Halaf levels. He also proposed that the site's

Sandstone moulds for casting weapons from Chagar Bazar, 2400–1900 BC, length 40 cm (British Museum, London)

main focus of attention was to the east, to the Mosul triangle, and that it owed its cultural traditions, especially the painted pottery, to influence from that direction. This proposal has been partially validated by Neutron Activation Analysis, which indicates the close relationship of pottery from other Wadi Dara sites with a clay source near Chagar Bazar;[3] yet that study indicated that the situation was quite complicated, with at least one vessel from Chagar Bazar possibly coming from Tell Halaf, further west in the upper Khabur. Despite the limited evidence, Chagar Bazar can be identified as an important site in the Late Halaf period, with both local and mid-range contacts in the region.

Vessel with incised decoration from Chagar Bazar, Ninevite 5 period, about 3000 BC, height 13.1 cm (British Museum, London)

Historic levels

Although the Halaf occupation was the primary reason for Mallowan's choice of Chagar Bazar, he also hoped to excavate a 'cross-section of the main periods of occupation of the Khabur region from prehistoric times down to the historical period,'[4] to explore the region's settlement history. Third-millennium-BC levels were uncovered in the deep sounding of 1935, and an excavation across the ridge of the main mound in 1936 concentrated on the second-millennium-BC occupation but reached down into third-millennium levels also. A few additional weeks' work in 1937 expanded that area and produced an archive of Old Babylonian cuneiform tablets.

Third millennium BC

After the post-Halaf abandonment Chagar Bazar was reoccupied in the mid- to late third millennium BC. At this time, there was a regional transition from a network of independent city-states with local artifactual traditions to grad-

Left Grave 151 at Chagar Bazar, showing a skeleton in flexed position with pottery vessels, about 1400 BC

Below Workers on the dig at Chagar Bazar

ually increasing cultural influence from southern Mesopotamia; this was followed by a partial political takeover by the southern 'Akkadian empire' from c.2250 BC.

At the north-western end of the site the deep sounding exposed graves of Ninevite 5 date (cut into Level 6), followed by a substantial Ninevite 5 settlement (Levels 4 and 5), in turn covered by Early Dynastic and Akkadian levels (Levels 2 and 3). Both Levels 4 and 3 were composed of private houses, with the irregular plans, shared walls and narrow streets typical of naturally developing sites in this region. Contemporary levels were also excavated at the centre of the site, where substantial walls (some 2.5 metres wide) belonging to Levels 3 to 5 were exposed below the second-millennium-BC houses in Area BD. Mallowan proposed that these were public buildings, but the area exposed was limited and this remained speculation.

More recent surveys in the upper Khabur region have revealed microregional differences in proportions of and presence of painted versus incised Ninevite 5 pottery. The Ninevite 5 pottery at Chagar Bazar includes painted, incised and excised examples. The presence of the painted portion of the assemblage links Chagar Bazar to the east half of the upper Khabur (since painted Ninevite 5 ware may be less frequently represented in the west). But there seems to be a greater popularity of incised ware in both levels. And temporal variations within the Ninevite 5 ceramic sequence have been identified in excavations at Tell Muhammad Arab and Tell Leilan, which indicate that greater popularity of incised ware, where both types of decoration are present, may point to a date later in the Ninevite 5 period. The question of the site's regional association versus date within the Ninevite 5 period still remains unanswered.

For Levels 2 and 3, Early Dynastic and Akkadian seal impressions, an Early Dynastic cylinder seal and two inscribed clay 'ration dockets' allow dating with reasonable accuracy, and a rich array of metal objects testifies to the wealth present at the site during this time. Black burnished pottery (an imitation of 'stoneware') was typical of the ceramic assemblage. Tell Brak has more extensive deposits of this time range, yet Tell Brak is a very different site from many contemporary settlements in the area, since Brak is an Akkadian outpost under the fourth king of that dynasty, Naram-Sin (and possibly earlier). Chagar Bazar offers parallels to this time range and, as a less strategic site, reveals more of the unalloyed local material.

Left Decorated copper pin for fastening robes, from Chagar Bazar, 1900–1400 BC, length 14 cm (British Museum, London)

Right Stone horse's head amulet from Amuda, length 2.5 cm (British Museum, London)

Second millennium BC

The largest horizontal area of excavation (Areas BD, TD and AB) was devoted to exposure of the second millennium BC. The material of this date was called Level I, further divided into four sub-phases and in places 3.5 metres deep. A date for the beginning of Level I is offered by tablets datable to *c.*1778 BC found on the lowest floors, while a sherd of 'Nuzi' ware in the final sub-phase indicates that Level I runs to approximately 1500 BC. This sequence conveniently links with the final occupation of Tell Brak. During this time there was a remarkable geopolitical evolution in northern Mesopotamia, from a kingdom under Shamshi-Adad to the coalescence of the Mitanni regional state.

Area BD, near the centre of the site, exposed a group of houses. The stratigraphy was very complex, with many rebuildings and structural adaptations. The earliest sub-phase had been badly destroyed by later construction, while the final one was greatly eroded, so the houses, as identified, belong mostly to the middle two phases. The structures are so tightly clustered that it is sometimes difficult to distinguish individual buildings, but where identifiable, the plan usually included a courtyard with three or four rooms attached to one end and graves below the floors. The walls were mudbrick, and there were occasional limestone pavings and some evidence for vaulted brick roofs. The dense occupation is a configuration more usually associated with urban spaces than with town or village sites, a category that the size of Chagar Bazar (*c.*8–10 hectares at this date) would seem to indicate. The arrangement may have been the result of a gradual infilling of the area (in response to changes in political or economic conditions) or perhaps the

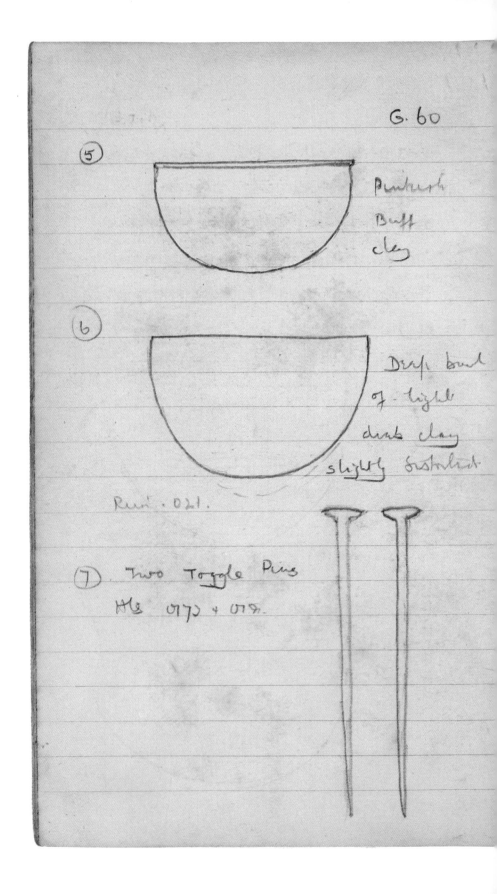

G. 60

⑤   Pinkish
                            Buff
                            clay

⑥   Deep bowl
                            of light
                            drab clay
                            slightly friable?

Rim . 021.

⑦   Two Toggle Pins
    Mé   0172 & 0173.

G. 60

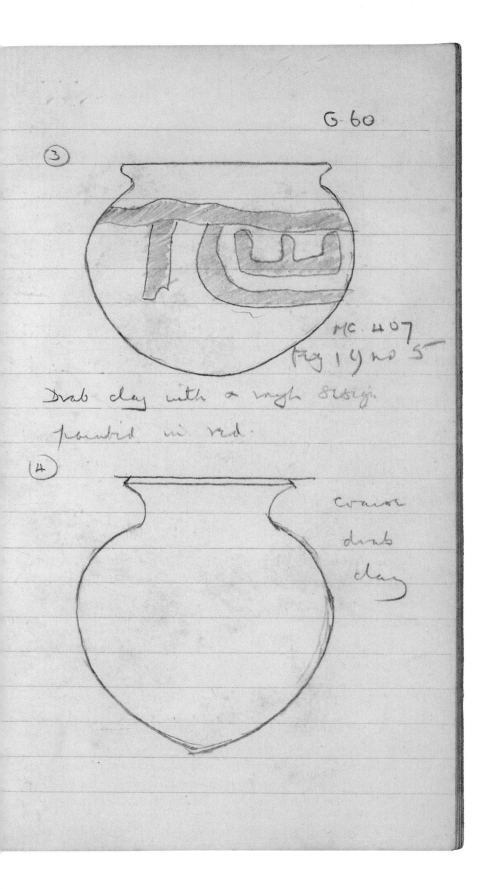

③

④

MC. 407

Fig 1 9 no 5

Drab clay with a rough design
painted in red.

coarse
drab
clay

Above Copper battle-axe from Chagar Bazar, grave 131, 1800–1700 BC, length 27 cm
(British Museum, London)

Previous double page Drawings of finds from Chagar Bazar in the excavation diary of 1935
(British Museum, London)

Below Drawing of the battle-axe

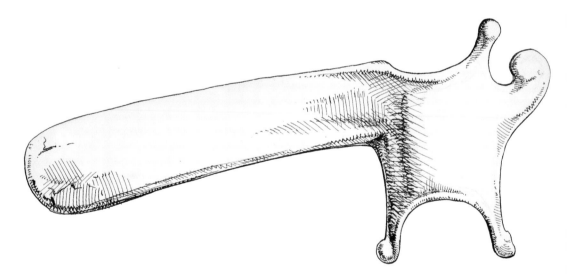

resumed occupation of the site in the second millennium BC began with such a closely spaced plan.

The graves below the house floors were of adults and children, each placed separately in a pit or built tomb and usually accompanied by burial offerings. These range from a pottery jar or two through richer arrays of

Painted pottery vessel from Chagar Bazar, Khabur Ware, early second millennium BC, height 23.5 cm
(British Museum, London)

bronze weapons and pins, with rarer inclusions of silver jewellery. The occupational layers within the houses included baked clay animal figurines, chariots and toy wheels. There was a single cylinder seal from Room 42 in the southern house area, with a finely carved scene in 'Syro-Hittite' style consisting of a heraldically posed kneeling human figure and two winged griffins, flanked by additional human figures. An additional cylinder seal from a grave of Level I, carnelian with gold caps, has an unfinished scene of a human figure and a deity in Old Babylonian style.

The rooms in the northern portion of Area BD were interpreted as part of a 'temple-palace', supported by references in the cuneiform tablets to the king and to a temple institution. But burials under the floors of those rooms indicate a residential, rather than religious, purpose for the building. However, the physical separation of this structure from the houses to the south by an open area, plus the thicker walls and greater care in their construction, do suggest a different status. The burials are marked by a greater richness of offerings, including gold jewellery, necklaces of semi-precious stone beads (carnelian, agate and quartz) and bronze vessels or utensils; there is also a greater frequency of vaulted tombs, when compared to the southern sector burials. Altogether these factors may mean that the structure was the residence of a high-status family. The slightly earlier building partially cleared in the western end of Area TD, south of BD, may have had a purely public function, given its regular layout with ranges of small rooms, the tablets in one room and the lack of graves. The presence of these three distinct functional areas, low-status and high-status residences and a public building is unusual in a site of relatively small size and allowed reconstruction of the internal landscape of the settlement to a degree not often possible.

The excavation at Chagar Bazar allowed the date for a distinctive pottery with geometric painted decoration (Khabur Ware) to be pinned down to the first half of the second millennium BC. This pottery had been encountered on the surface of many sites in the upper Khabur region and on the upper Tigris around Mosul, but its date remained uncertain until it was found *in situ* exclusively in Level I at Chagar Bazar. Since 1937 there has been excavation of contemporary Old Babylonian material at Tell al-Rimah, Mari and Tell Leilan, which have provided an expanded corpus of pottery and objects for the Old Babylonian period, but Chagar Bazar remains a key site.

Agatha Christie on site at Chagar Bazar with her shooting-stick

Pottery cuneiform tablet from Chagar Bazar, height 2.8 cm (British Museum, London)

Textual material

Cuneiform tablets were found in the second-millennium-BC levels in Areas BD and TD. The tablets are mostly economic – lists of agricultural products, animals and rations for workers – providing valuable information about the economic and political history of the region. Many texts indicate that Chagar Bazar was linked with the state administration of the kingdom of Shamshi-Adad, which stretched from Mari on the mid-Euphrates across the upper Khabur. There is reference made to 'contributions' from Iasmah-Adad (second son of Shamshi-Adad and ruler at Mari), consisting of grain, beer, flour and similar commodities. These contributions were originally inter-preted as indications that Chagar Bazar was under the control of Iasmah-Adad.[5] A few tablets, however, had seals of 'servants' of Shamshi-Adad; and given the proximity of Chagar Bazar to Tell Leilan (identified as Shubat-Enlil, the capital of Shamshi-Adad, only in 1985), it is possible that Chagar Bazar was under the control of the father, rather than the son. Gadd's interpretation of the situation was formed before Shubat-Enlil had been physically located, and the functional placement of Chagar Bazar within the upper Khabur regional state can now be reassessed.

However, some tablets do refer to shipments of grain intended for feeding draught animals belonging to Iasmah-Adad. This suggests that

Iasmah-Adad possibly owned land in the region. In addition, there are references to 'the palace' and the 'house of Shubat-Enlil', and it is unclear whether the same establishment is meant and whether it was located at Shubat-Enlil, at Mari or at Chagar Bazar itself. And there are records of deliveries of animals and dispatches of employees attached to Ekallatum. This was the third city of Shamshi-Adad's kingdom, located on the upper Tigris and ruled by his eldest son, Ishme-Dagan. Despite the unanswered question of who controlled the site, what is clear is that there was royal interest specifically in the place and generally in the surrounding region. The lists of rations supplied to an array of workers (grain grinders, bakers, cleaners, gardeners, animal herders and weavers) suggest that there were a royal estate and royal workshops on the site or in the vicinity. An additional intriguing set of texts records that the site was briefly used as a regional centre for a census of nomadic tribes in the area, which involved a visit by the king and his retinue.

Ancient name of the site
The tablets refer several times to a NU/ BE-Sha-an-nim (KI), which may be read Nushannum, Beshannum or Til-Sha-annim. It is not conclusively proven that this is the ancient name of Chagar Bazar, but it is likely. Other options are Ashnakkum and Hassum-of-Membida, which appear in contemporary texts from Mari and are located somewhere on the upper Khabur.[6]

NOTES

1   Archaeological reports: M.E.L. Mallowan, 'Excavations at Chagar Bazar and an Archaeological Survey of the Habur Region of North Syria, 1934–5', *Iraq* 3 (1936), pp. 1–86 (1934 survey and 1935 excavation); M.E.L. Mallowan, 'Excavations at Tall Chagar Bazar and an Archaeological Survey of the Habur Region, Second Campaign, 1936', *Iraq* 4 (1937), pp. 91–177 (1936 excavation); M.E.L. Mallowan, 'Excavations at Brak and Chagar Bazar', *Iraq* 9 (1947), pp. 1–259 (final report, incorporating the brief 1937 season). Additional summary: J. Curtis, 'Chagar Bazar', in J. Curtis (ed.), *Fifty Years of Mesopotamian Discovery: The Work of the British School of Archaeology in Iraq, 1932–1982*, London 1982, pp. 79–85.
Texts: C.J. Gadd, 'Tablets from Chagar Bazar, 1936', *Iraq* 4 (1937), pp. 178–85; C.J. Gadd, 'Tablets from Chagar Bazar and Tall Brak', *Iraq* 7 (1940), pp. 22–66; P. Talon and H. Hamadi, *Old Babylonian Texts from Chagar Bazar*, Akkadica Supplementum X, Brussels 1997.
2   Mallowan, 'Excavations at Chagar Bazar' (n. 1), p. 1.
3   T. Davidson and H. McKerrell, 'Pottery Analysis and Halaf Period Trade in the Khabur Headwaters Region', *Iraq* 38 (1976), pp. 45–56.
4   Mallowan, 'Excavations at Chagar Bazar' (n. 1), p. 5.
5   Gadd, 'Tablets from Chagar Bazar and Tall Brak' (n. 1).
6   Talon and Hamadi, *Old Babylonian Texts* (n. 1), pp. 4–7.

Tell Brak

David and Joan Oates

T ell Brak is one of the most impressive archaeological sites in the Near East. It rises to a height of over 40 metres and occupies an area of some 60 hectares, dominating the landscape of the lower Wadi Jaghjagh in north-eastern Syria. The site lies on a major ancient road from the Tigris Valley in modern Iraq via Chagar Bazar to Mardin and the metal resources of Anatolia, or westwards to the Euphrates and the distant Mediterranean. From the top of the tell on a clear day one can see both the great mountain of Jebel Sinjar, some 45 kilometres to the south in Iraq, and Mardin and the mountains of the Tur Abdin, the same distance to the north in south-eastern Turkey. This itself explains to some extent the importance of the site.

Max and Agatha Mallowan first saw Brak in November 1934 on his survey of the northern basin of the River Khabur in north-eastern Syria. It was clear to Mallowan that Brak was a site of major importance, 'a magnificent site' to use his words, but at that time virtually no archaeological work had been carried out in this part of Syria, then under French mandate. Mallowan sensibly chose to look first for a smaller site 'before attempting to come to grips with so formidable a mound'. Thus work began first at Chagar Bazar, some 65 kilometres NNW of Brak, where excavation was carried out in the spring of 1935 and 1936. In the spring of 1937, his third season at Chagar Bazar during which an important collection of cuneiform tablets was recovered, he at last felt confident to take on the greater challenge of Brak, returning there also in the spring and autumn of 1938. During these seasons Mallowan was fortunate to have working with him various members of the family of Hamoudi, son of Sheikh Ibrahim of Jerablus, who had worked with Woolley and Hogarth at Carchemish and later with Woolley at Ur. The excavation of Tell Brak was a bold decision, and it is an illustration of Mallowan's extraordinary flair and good fortune as an excavator that in such a vast area he happened upon its most important building, the Naram-Sin Palace.

Above General view of the excavation area of Tell Brak, 1938 (photo: Agatha Christie)

Previous double page Aerial view of Tell Brak (photo: Georg Gerster)

Agatha was with her husband throughout these campaigns, and in the spring of 1938 they were joined by her daughter Rosalind who was responsible for the drawings of Nuzi pottery and the very fine restored Nuzi beakers published in *Iraq* in 1947.[1] Agatha did all the photography, even developing the photographs herself, and helped with the cleaning and recording. They had built a charming and spacious dig house at Chagar Bazar, noted for its beehive domes, but for the excavations at Brak they rented a large, derelict house in an Armenian village on the Jaghjagh, which still survives a few kilometres from the mound. Perhaps fittingly, mud-bricks from this house, which afterwards became a police post but later totally derelict, were used in the construction of the storehouse of the current Brak excavations. Agatha much preferred Chagar Bazar to Brak, not only because of the comforts of the dig house, but also because of the flowers, Chagar Bazar receiving marginally more spring rain than Brak. One has the impression, in fact, that a stint at Brak was viewed as more punishment than pleasure. We must remember, however, that at that time the countryside immediately around Brak was much more desolate than it is today, with no settled inhabitants apart from the Armenian community on the Wadi Jaghjagh. An aerial photograph taken at the time of the excavations by the Aviation Française en Syrie shows a solitary group of Bedouin tents around a well on the north side of the mound, a seasonal encampment of nomadic tribesmen who came north from the Euphrates valley in spring in search of grazing for their flocks. The green plain on which we look down from the tell sixty years later is the product of deliberate settlement and, particularly in the last generation, the mechanization of agriculture and the proliferation of irrigation pumps. But it is still covered with a profusion of wild flowers, certainly less plentiful than those that Agatha admired in the 1930s but still beautiful and still with the same bee-eaters and rollers flying overhead.

Mallowan's work at Brak and Chagar Bazar is significant first and foremost for the archaeological framework it provided in a then unknown yet extremely important area of northern Mesopotamia. The extensive nature of his excavations also added historical and cultural dimensions to the very basic chronology established earlier in the famous deep sounding at Nineveh. Mallowan never discovered the ancient name of Brak, which we now believe to be Nagar, a city mentioned in the texts from Ebla as one of the most important in the third-millennium Near Eastern world, noted also for its unusually strong mules and its acrobatic dancers! The two most important buildings excavated by Mallowan were the so-called Eye Temple of the fourth millennium BC and the 'Naram-Sin Palace', actually a vast and heavily fortified storehouse built c.2250 BC by one of Mesopotamia's most renowned monarchs, at a time when Brak-Nagar had become an administrative centre of the Akkadian empire.

The Naram-Sin Palace was a massive structure, over 100 metres long, with outer walls about 9 metres thick. The plan consisted of large courtyards surrounded by some forty long storage magazines. The attribution to the

Watercolour by Guilford Bell of the Armenian village of Tell Brak

SUBARTU POTTE

SUBARTU POTTERY

PAINTED HABUR WA

CLAY VASES

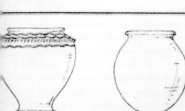

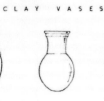

C L

BLACK BURNISHED WARE   CLAY VASES AND COPPER IMPLEMENTS

LAY VASES

ROSETTE
DECORA

STAMP SEALS AND AMULETS

AL UBAID WARE

T HA

HALAF WARE

BRAK SHOWING OBJECTS

SUBARTU WHITE PAINTED
POTTERY AS AT BILLA NUZI
ASHUR NINEVEH ATSHANA HA

CYLINDER SEALS WITH SACR
TREE DESIGN

S I G N S

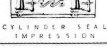

C Y L I N D E R   S E A L
I M P R E S S I O N

C . 1350 - 1550   B C

HURRIAN LEVEL

ᴇ L Y   R E P R E S E N T E D   A T   B R A K

PAINTED POTTERY IRANIAN
DESIGNS AS AT GIYAN

PERIOD OF HAMMURABI OF BABYL
AND SHAMSHI ADAD I OF ASSYRIA

C . 1550–1800 B.C.

RECONSTRUCTED
POST AKKADIAN
PALACE

THIRD DYNASTY OF
UR LEVEL

MESOPOTAMIAN INFLUENCE

RECONSTRUCTION OF THE
DESTROYED AKKADIAN PAL

POTS AS AT UR GAWRA ASHU

ꜱE C H A R I O T   A N D   F I G U R I N E

C . 2000–2100 B.C.

SARGONID LEVEL

G R E E N   S T O N E
A M U L E T

PALACE BUILT BY NARAM SIN (
AGADE AND HABUR UNDER
AKKADIAN CONTROL

OBJECTS AS AT UR KHAFAJA
AND MARI

SILVER BEAD AS AT TROY AND
ALACA HUYUK

C Y L I N D E R   S E A L
I M P R E S S I O N

E N G R A V E D   B O N E
I N L A Y S

NARAM SIN
I N S C R I P T I O N
ON MUD BRICK

C . 2300 – 2200 B.C.

EARLY DYNASTIC
JAMDAT NASR AND
URUK LEVEL

E Y E   I D O L S

SECTION
THROUGH
A SHAFT

LATE JAMDAT NASR PLATF
BUILT OF SUN-DRIED BRIC
SURMOUNTED BY TEMPLE
STONE BUTTRESSED WALLS

STAMP SEALS AS AT URUK

ALABASTER IDOLS

THOUSANDS OF VOTIVE BEA

C . 3100 B C

AL UBAID & T HA
LEVEL

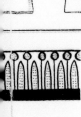

ᴺNTED POTTRY DESIGNS MOST'LY POLYCHROME

CHALCOLITHIC LEVEL — EARL

ARPACHIYAH T HALAF
AND AL UBAID WARE

BEGINNINGS OF STOCK BREE
AND FARMING ON THE HABUR

4TH MILLENIUM B C

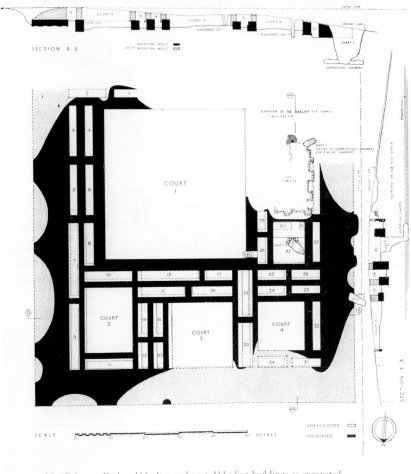

The Palace at Brak. Akkadian and post-Akkadian buildings as excavated.

Above Ground plan of the Naram-Sin and later palaces ('Excavations at Brak and Chagar Bazar', *Iraq* 9, 1947)

Previous double page Schematic plan showing the classification of objects at Tell Brak ('Excavations at Brak and Chagar Bazar', *Iraq* 9, 1947)

famous south Mesopotamian king Naram-Sin is based on the presence of mud-bricks stamped with his name in the foundations of the building. Mallowan's discovery of these bricks provided the first, and still the most precise, chronological link between the history of northern Mesopotamia in the third millennium BC and that of the better-documented south. Cuneiform tablets and seal impressions found in the building, and also during the current series of excavations directed by David Oates, further attest Akkadian control of the site. Found in contemporary houses nearby (Areas CH and ER) were treasure hoards of silver and other precious materials and a vast range of pottery, metal tools and other material objects that now provide an important and well-dated archaeological corpus.

The Naram-Sin Palace was rebuilt by the successors to the Akkadians at Brak, erroneously identified by Mallowan as southern kings of Ur in 'the reign of Ur-Nammu'. More recent information suggests that the successor to the Akkadian was a Hurrian-speaking kingdom, attested by a seal impression with a cuneiform inscription found by Mallowan but only recently translated.[2] Hurrian kingdoms are known at this time also at nearby Tell Mozan, ancient Urkesh, a site tested by Mallowan during his Khabur survey, and at Nineveh.

The Eye Temple was one of Mallowan's most important discoveries, so named because of the thousands of 'Eye Idols', small alabaster figures with very large eyes, found in the foundations of the temple platform, together with a fragment of copper panelling stamped with an eye design recovered from the sanctuary itself. An altar stood at one end of the sanctuary, its sides decorated with an elaborate frieze composed of decorative bands of blue limestone, white marble and green shale and encased in a gold surround that had been fastened to a wooden backing with gold-headed silver nails. One section can now

Pottery vessel with gold jewellery from Tell Brak before restoration (photo: Agatha Christie)

be seen in the Aleppo Museum; the other is in the British Museum. The blue limestone ornament consisted of panels of cone-like objects, a favourite medium of decoration in the fourth-millennium Uruk period. Indeed the walls of the temple were decorated with a mosaic of coloured clay and limestone cones, while large eight-petalled stone rosettes ornamented the outer face of the north wall of the shrine.

The Eye Temple itself rested on a platform 6 metres deep, which incorporated the remains of at least three earlier buildings. The latest, below the surviving temple, was the so-called White Eye Temple, defined by a white gypsum plaster floor. The walls and packing were said to be of red mud-bricks. The foundations of the Grey Eye Temple, so named after the grey bricks of the walls and the packing of this phase, contained rich deposits of amulets, Eye Idols and hundreds of thousands of beads. As Mallowan wrote, 'it is no exaggeration to say that the foundations of the earlier Eye Temple had literally been sown with beads and even the mud-bricks themselves contained beads within them'.[3] This level had been heavily plundered late in the third millennium BC, and Mallowan came across many of the earlier plunderers' tunnels, where he himself recovered the large quantity of objects that had been left

Cylinder seal impression with sacrifice scene from Tell Brak, 2300–2100 BC, height 2.5 cm (British Museum, London)

behind. One can only imagine the wealth that may have been removed by the earlier plunderers. In the current excavations we have recovered Eye Idols in the context of house deposits of the middle of the fourth millennium, that is, earlier than Mallowan had suspected. This dates the Grey Eye Temple to approximately the same time, and the earlier Red Eye Temple to some time in

Alabaster Eye Idols, from the foundations of the Grey Eye Temple at Tell Brak, 3500–3300 BC, height 3.5 cm (British Museum, London)

the first half of the fourth millennium. This redating makes the fine alabaster head recovered by Mallowan in one of the plunderers' tunnels in the grey-brick stratum one of the earliest pieces of human sculpture ever found.[4] Mallowan's Eye Temple plan shows stone revetments along the mud-brick walls, but these can now be dated to the middle of the third millennium, demonstrating that the Eye Temple itself continued in use for some considerable time after the Uruk period. The foundation trenches of Naram-Sin's Palace are dug into it, so it cannot have survived later than the end of the Early Dynastic period.

Mallowan dug a number of house structures at Brak, providing for the first time a range of north Mesopotamian pottery types that could be dated to the third millennium. The houses themselves had interesting features, including what he identified as a small chapel with associated child burials. On the basis of a small hole penetrating the altar and opening out in the adjacent room, Mallowan suggests the possibility that this hole served as a speaking-tube for an oracle-like association with the chapel. The houses from Area ER produced a small number of cuneiform tablets of the Akkadian period, including a well-known list of workmen from cities or small settlements in the neighbourhood of Brak (including Urkesh = Tell Mozan, and Šehna = Tell Leilan).

Above Stone rosette and drawing from the Eye Temple at Tell Brak, 3300–3000 BC, diameter 17.5 cm (British Museum, London)

Right Pearls attached to a necklace of steatite, carnelian and rock crystal, from Tell Brak, 3200–3000 BC

Below Altar frieze from the Eye Temple at Tell Brak, 3300–3000 BC, length 113 cm (British Museum, London)

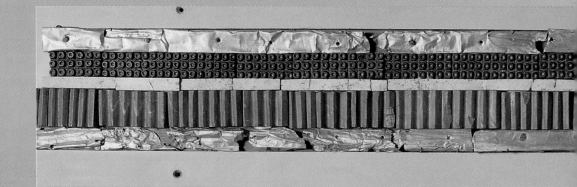

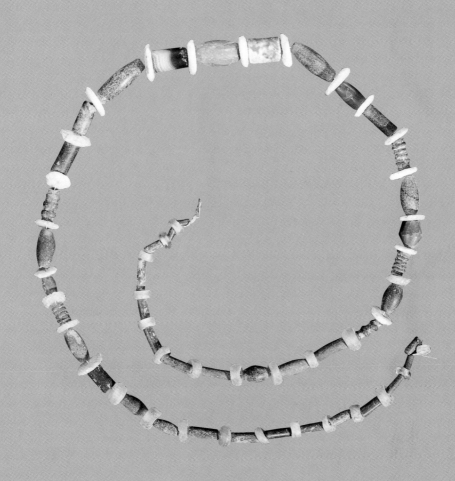

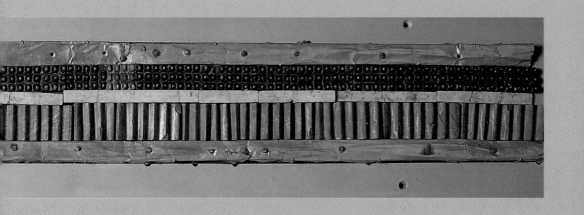

Above Raising baskets with a cable winch from the underground rooms of the Eye Temple at Tell Brak (photo: Agatha Christie)

Right Report of the excavations at Tell Brak in the *Illustrated London News* of 20 May 1939

On the high north ridge of Brak Mallowan also excavated a number of houses of the second millennium BC, finding here both material of Mitanni date and, below that in a deep sounding, the same early second-millennium painted Khabur ware that he had previously identified at Chagar Bazar. This material greatly expanded our knowledge of the second millennium and provided unusual discoveries such as the famous painted 'face-vase', now in Aleppo.[5] To the east of this group of houses he came upon what he describes as a 'heavy terrace which flanked the steep northern slopes of the mound'. Renewed excavations, begun with his enthusiastic encouragement in 1976, revealed after many seasons that this 'heavy terrace' was the outer wall of a temple and palace of the fourteenth and early thirteenth centuries BC.

THE EARLIEST KNOWN CARVED HEADS IN SYRIA, FOUND AT BRAK.

11. A LANDMARK IN THE HISTORY OF SCULPTURE : A BOLD AND FORCEFUL CARVING OF A HUMAN HEAD FOUND AT BRAK—THE EARLIEST PIECE OF SYRIAN STONE CARVING OF THE KIND, SEEN FROM THE FRONT AND THE SIDE. (ACTUAL SIZE.)

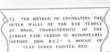

13. THE METHOD OF DECORATING THE OUTER WALLS OF THE EYE TEMPLE AT BRAK, CHARACTERISTIC OF THE JAMDAT NASR PERIOD IN MESOPOTAMIA (BEFORE 3000 B.C.) : A MOSAIC OF CLAY CONES PAINTED RED.

15. ANOTHER CARVED HEAD FROM BRAK WITH PART OF ITS CONICAL HAT MISSING, AND BROKEN IN TWO BY PLUNDERERS WHO WERE LOOTING THE TREASURE HOARD UNDER THE TEMPLE. (7 CM. HIGH.)

14. ANOTHER OF THE STONE HEADS FROM BRAK—THE EARLIEST IN SYRIA ; WITH A CONICAL HAT SIMILAR TO THAT OF MODERN SYRIAN MOUNTAIN TRIBES. (9.2 CM. HIGH.)

12. TWO LIMESTONE MACE HEADS—SYMBOLS OF ROYAL AUTHORITY FOUND AGAINST THE OUTER WALL OF THE TEMPLE. (LOWER HEAD 7.2 CM. HIGH.)

The most remarkable thing among the carvings brought to light at Brak is the head illustrated in Fig. 11. The face is vigorously modelled, the much simplified ears betray it as the work of a very early sculptor who was still in the experimental stage of carving the human head. The recessed forehead suggests that it may have been intended to mount an inlay of gold foil in the manner of much later Syrian carving. Almost the only feature which betrays it as being Mesopotamian is the peculiar method of joining the prominent nose and eyebrows. It may perhaps represent the sculptor's conception of the Northern Syrian, Subaraean type. Like the other heads illustrated here it was probably once attached to a wooden body.

Stone frog from the Grey Eye Temple at Tell Brak, 3500–3300 BC, length 6.7 cm (British Museum, London)

Unfortunately the war put an end to Mallowan's work at Brak, and when it was over he divided his time between the Professorship of Western Asiatic Archaeology at the Institute of Archaeology, University of London, and the excavations at Nimrud of the British School of Archaeology in Iraq, of which he was the first Director. Had he returned to Brak, he would no doubt have anticipated the recent excavations in uncovering not only the Mitanni Palace, but also the great Akkadian temple of the sun god Shamash and the temple, probably dedicated to the god of donkeys and other steppe animals, with its own caravanserai overlooking the Anatolian trade route. There are the marks of his trenches above or nearby all these buildings but the work remained unfinished.

NOTES

1 *Iraq* 9 (1947), pls 86–7.
2 Ibid., pl. 24.1.
3 Ibid., p. 33.
4 Ibid., pl. 1.
5 Ibid., pl. 40.

Nimrud

John Curtis

The great Assyrian city of Nimrud is represented nowadays by a string of
mounds stretching along the east bank of the River Tigris in northern
Iraq. The site was occupied from prehistoric times onwards and was an
important Assyrian centre from at least the thirteenth century BC. It achieved
real prominence, though, only in the reign of King Ashurnasirpal II (883–859
BC), who made Nimrud the capital of an empire which was soon to stretch
from Western Iran to the Mediterranean Sea. Thereafter, although Nimrud
was not always the capital of Assyria – an honour shared with Nineveh and
Khorsabad – it remained one of the chief cities of Assyria until it was destroyed
by the combined forces of the Medes and the Babylonians in 614–612 BC. In
Late Assyrian times the walls of Nimrud enclosed an area of about 360
hectares. Within this enclosure the most prominent feature was the citadel
mound or acropolis in the south-west corner covering 20 hectares. Here stood

The ziggurat at Nimrud (photo: Joan Oates)

the most important palaces, public buildings and temples. In the south-east corner of the city was a large building founded by the King Shalmaneser III (858–824 BC), which was a 'review palace' or arsenal and is known today as Fort Shalmaneser after the founder. The city was known to the Assyrians themselves as Kalḫu, and it is referred to in the Bible as Calah.

The first proper excavations at Nimrud were made by the great nineteenth-century archaeologist and traveller Sir Henry Layard, who worked there between 1845 and 1851. He found gigantic stone figures of winged bulls and lions, stone wall slabs decorated with scenes of warfare and hunting, stone obelisks, carved ivories, bronze bowls and a host of small antiquities. His discoveries created a sensation in an era when people were familiar with the Bible and its references to the Assyrians, and both Layard and Nimrud (which he mistakenly identified as Nineveh) became household names. After Layard a number of other archaeologists worked at Nimrud, including Hormuzd Rassam, W.K. Loftus and George Smith, but from 1879 onwards the site was effectively abandoned. In truth, however, the vast mounds had scarcely been touched, and they still had huge potential. It is much to Sir Max Mallowan's credit that he recognized this, and the promise of further interesting discoveries must have been uppermost in his mind when he decided in 1949 to apply for permission to re-open the excavations. In addition, both he and his wife were enchanted by the site of Nimrud and its environs, and this must have been a further incentive. On her first visit to Nimrud, when Max was working with Campbell Thompson at Nineveh, Agatha Christie had found it

> a beautiful spot ... The Tigris was just a mile away, and on the great mound of the Acropolis, big stone Assyrian heads poked out of the soil. In one place there was the enormous wing of a great genie. It was a spectacular stretch of country – peaceful, romantic, and impregnated with the past.[1]

Working at Nimrud was a big commitment, however, and the decision was not to be taken lightly. But Mallowan was not the sort of person to be intimidated by the size of the task, and he describes his visit to the Director of Antiquities of Iraq as follows: 'Suddenly any thought of caution which I may have had, left me, and I was moved to ask if we might return to Nimrud, where a hundred years back the first British expedition had made some startling discoveries.'[2] At

Previous double page Aerial view of Nimrud with the River Tigris in the background (photo: Georg Gerster)

Left Relief with bird-headed genie by the tree of life, 875–860 BC, height 141 cm (British Museum, London)

View of the excavation at Nimrud from the ziggurat (photo: Donald Wiseman)

this time Mallowan was Director of the British School of Archaeology in Iraq as well as Professor of Western Asiatic Archaeology in the London University Institute of Archaeology.

Permission to excavate at Nimrud was duly given by the Iraqi authorities, and the work on behalf of the British School of Archaeology in Iraq started on 17 March 1949. Altogether there were to be thirteen seasons of excavation, each lasting about two months, which took place almost every year in the late spring until the project was brought to a halt in 1963. Usually there was a work-force of about 200, which included up to twenty skilled workmen known as Sherqatis, who came from the villages on the Tigris opposite the ancient city of Ashur. Mallowan directed the excavations in person until 1957. For the 1958 season David Oates assumed the mantle of field director, but Max Mallowan remained as director of the project and even in the 1958 season the Mallowans joined the expedition for the last fortnight. After the revolution of 14 July 1958, when the Hashemite monarchy was overthrown by Abdul Karim Kassem, Mallowan found it difficult to come to terms with the new political situation, and although he and Agatha visited Iraq in 1959 they were not present for the campaigns between 1960 and 1963 which were directed from 1960 until 1962 by David Oates and in 1963 by Jeffrey Orchard.

Max Mallowan, Barbara Campbell Thompson and Agatha Christie visiting Nimrud during the excavation at Nineveh in 1931–2 (photo: Reginald Campbell Thompson)

For the first eight seasons of the British School excavations at Nimrud when Mallowan was field director, the work was concentrated on the citadel mound.[3] To begin with, the centre of attention was the North-West Palace, founded by Ashurnasirpal II and partly restored by several later kings. This is the largest building on the citadel, measuring about 200 metres north–south. In the centre of the palace were the state apartments that had been partially cleared out by Layard a century before. Most of these chambers were elaborately decorated with sculptured stone slabs as well as painted plaster and glazed bricks. In some of the more important gateways were the massive stone guardian figures that are such a familiar feature of Assyrian art. For his part, Mallowan focused on the northern or administrative wing of the palace, where there were offices and storerooms, and on the domestic quarters and private apartments on the south side of the palace. In the course of this work he made many outstanding discoveries.

One of the most informative findings relates to the building of the palace itself. This was a yellow sandstone stela found outside one of the main doors to the Throne Room. In a small frame at the top is a representation of King Ashurnasirpal accompanied by the symbols of various gods. Most of the surface of the stela, though, is covered with a long cuneiform inscription detailing

Workers on the dig at Nimrud, 1949 (photo: Agatha Christie)

his titles and military achievements, the building of his palace at Kalhu and the works he did in and around the city. It ends with the description of a great banquet that was organized to celebrate these achievements, and lists vast quantities of food and wine that were provided for the 70,000 guests. Also containing important historical information were clay tablets inscribed in cuneiform found in a cluster of rooms in the administrative wing.[4] These were part of the royal archive of the eighth century BC and included administrative and legal documents as well as letters to various kings with official reports from around the empire. Other rooms in the administrative wing yielded large amounts of pottery, and seals and sealings, including one showing a king stabbing a lion that is thought to be the royal seal. An amphora with a pseudo-hieroglyphic inscription probably made in Phoenicia is just one of the many valuable items found in this part of the palace.

The majority of the objects were found in the earth and debris covering the floors of the palace, but some others were recovered from graves. One particularly rich burial, under the floor of Room DD, was that of a woman who had been placed in a baked clay coffin. She wore a necklace of semi-precious stones and a bronze brooch or fibula from which was suspended a gold chain and a pendant in a magnificent gold setting that has come to be known as the

'Nimrud Jewel'. It is a large chalcedony stamp seal engraved with a design showing two musicians. This grave obviously belonged to a rich and important woman. It now seems possible that this part of the southern wing of the palace may have been the harem, as between 1988 and 1990 Mr Muzahim Mahmud of the Iraq Department of Antiquities found in this vicinity four subterranean tombs with barrel-vaulted roofs. Three of them contained extraordinary amounts of gold jewellery and are among the wealthiest graves ever found in the ancient Near East. Inscriptions show that in these tombs were buried 'queens' or 'palace women' of four different Assyrian kings including Ashurnasirpal II, Tiglath-pileser III (744–727 BC) and Sargon (721–705 BC). Ironically one of the tombs was under the floor of Room MM that was cleared out by Mallowan, but its existence was not suspected at that time.

Some of Mallowan's best discoveries in the North-West Palace were made in wells that were cleared out with the help of equipment borrowed from the Iraq Petroleum Company. The first well, in Room NN, was found to be 25.4 metres deep and lined with 331 courses of baked bricks, many of them inscribed with the name of Ashurnasirpal. The bottom of the well was filled to a depth of 10 metres with wet sludge, and it was in this deposit that a series of

Plan of the North-West Palace of Ashurnasirpal II, Nimrud, 1949–53 (British Museum, London)

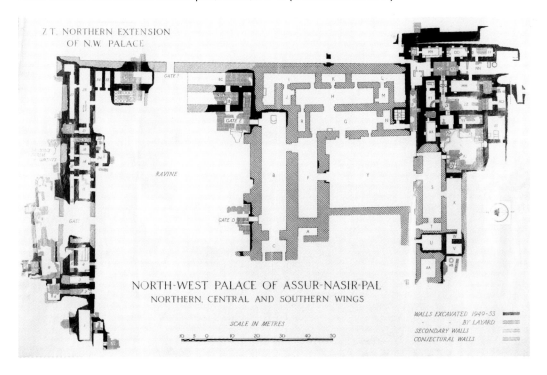

Z.T. NORTHERN EXTENSION OF N.W. PALACE

RAVINE

NORTH-WEST PALACE OF ASSUR-NASIR-PAL
NORTHERN, CENTRAL AND SOUTHERN WINGS

SCALE IN METRES

WALLS EXCAVATED 1949–53
" " BY LAYARD
SECONDARY WALLS
CONJECTURAL WALLS

rich finds was made. Firstly, there were about seventy pottery jars which had been used to draw water from the well and had fallen back into it when the rope broke. Then, there were various items of horse harness, including a pair of ivory blinkers decorated with winged sphinxes, a bronze cheekpiece from the end of a bit in the form of a galloping horse, and shell ornaments which had decorated a bridle. The ivories recovered from the well included four outstanding examples. The face of a woman carved from a section of ivory tusk is especially well known and is often referred to as the 'Mona Lisa' or the 'Lady of the Well'. She has an alluring smile and a plump face framed by long tresses of black-coloured hair. Another ivory face of a woman is in a very different style. It is less naturalistic and less appealing and was nicknamed by the excavators the 'Ugly Sister'. Two splendid ivory plaques each show a lioness mauling an African against a background of lotus and papyrus plants. These plaques were originally overlaid with gold leaf and were inlaid with carnelian and lapis lazuli. The curly hair of the African is represented by gold-topped ivory pegs. Lastly, miscellaneous finds in this well included a small collection of bronze dogs.

Another well, in the north-west corner of Courtyard AJ, was found to be unstable and clearing it out would have been too dangerous. It was left to the

Left Relief with a winged genie in front of the tree of life uncovered in the North-West Palace of Ashurnasirpal II, Nimrud, 1950 (photo: Agatha Christie)

Below Excavations in the North-West Palace of Ashurnasirpal II, Nimrud (photo: Agatha Christie)

Department of Antiquities of Iraq to find important ivories here at a later date. The third well had been previously discovered by Layard in the so-called 'Room of the Bronzes' (AB), where he had found a large collection of bronze bowls, cauldrons, furniture and horse harness. He had cleared out the well to a depth of *c.*18.25 metres before hitting water. In the sludge below this level Mallowan found sixteen ivory writing-boards and others of wood. They were made so that they could be fixed together with hinges and were all coated with a thin layer of wax in which traces of cuneiform writing were sometimes preserved. Excavation in this well was brought to a sudden halt when the bottom caved in with a great roar, showing just how dangerous this sort of undertaking was. Fortunately, the man who was clearing out the well had been hauled to the surface a few moments before. It remains a mystery why so many valuable objects came to be at the bottom of wells, but the most likely explanation is they were thrown down at a time of civil unrest or when Nimrud was sacked

Right Ivory relief panel showing a bearded man, from Fort Shalmaneser at Nimrud, 9th–8th century BC, height 26.6 cm (British Museum, London)

Below Inscribed brick of Ashur-etel-ilani, 630–627 BC, height 30 cm (British Museum, London)

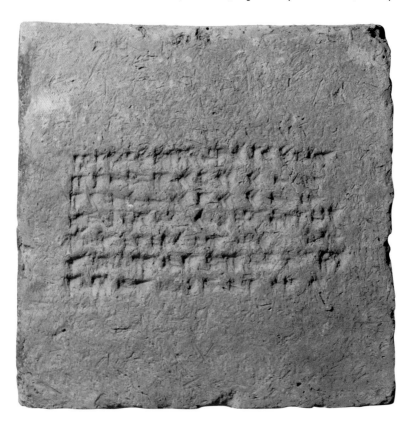

THE ILLUSTRATED LONDON NEWS

The World Copyright of all the Editorial Matter, both Illustrations and Letterpress, is Strictly Reserved in Great Britain, the British Dominions and Colonies, Europe, and the United States of America.

SATURDAY, AUGUST 16, 1952.

FIG. I. "A MONA LISA OF 2600 YEARS AGO", THE LARGEST AND FINEST CARVED IVORY HEAD EVER FOUND IN THE ANCIENT NEAR EAST—AN ASSYRIAN POLYCHROME IVORY HEAD FOUND IN A WELL AT NIMRUD. (NATURAL SIZE.)

On pages 255-256 Professor Mallowan describes some of the outstanding discoveries made in the fourth season's excavations at Assyrian Calah, Nimrud, in Iraq. The most remarkable of these is the ivory head we show here, of which the Professor writes: " It was indeed a thrilling moment when we saw this lady emerge from the deep waters of the well where she had lain immersed in mud for more than 2600 years. Carefully we wiped away the dirt from her face, her hair and her crown. What we beheld was a thing of beauty still radiant with life. The warm brown tones of the natural ivory set against the dark black tresses of hair that framed the head combined with the soft, rounded curves of the face to give an extraordinary impression of life. The slightly parted lips appeared to have a light reddish tint ; the black pupils of the eyes were encased in dark lids ; the crown, fillets and stand were of a rather darker brown than the face. Originally crown and base must have been decorated with ivory studs, of which only one remained. Full use was made of the graining of the ivory, which showed to advantage on the crown, while the cheeks were cleverly contrived to display a concentric graining where they were fullest. Large lumps of sludge which had turned to the consistency of a cement had imprisoned the head from the back and at the sides, and thus prevented a number of vertical cracks from causing the face to disintegrate. It was, in fact, this fortunate circumstance which had saved for us what may be deemed to be at once the largest and the finest carved ivory head that has ever been found in the ancient Near East. We cannot be certain of the exact time at which this head was made, but for various reasons a date of about 720 B.C. is probably not far off the mark."

Above Ivory woman's head from the well in the North-West Palace at Nimrud, the so-called 'Mona Lisa', (*Illustrated London News*, 16 August 1952)

Left Ivory woman's head from the well in the North-West Palace at Nimrud, the so-called 'Ugly Sister', 9th–8th century BC, height 13.7 cm (Metropolitan Museum of Art, Rogers Fund, 1954)

around 612 BC.

Apart from the fine ivories in the wells, many others were discovered by Mallowan both in the North-West Palace and in other buildings at Nimrud. In fact, one of the first discoveries made by the Mallowan expedition at Nimrud was a beautiful modelled ivory cow with head turned back to lick a now miss-ing suckling calf. Ivories are so common at Nimrud they might almost be said to be a hallmark of the site. They came in a variety of shapes and sizes, includ-ing carved and incised plaques, openwork compositions and figures in the round, and show a wide range of decorative scenes. But comparatively few of them were actually made in Assyria. The majority were produced in the areas of Syria and Phoenicia to the west and are decorated in styles that are charac-teristic of those regions. For example, the plaques with the lioness and African show evidence of Egyptian influence and probably come from Phoenicia where that influence was strong. Most of these ivories were originally made to decorate furniture, boxes, horse harness, chariots and so on, all of which were brought to Nimrud from different parts of the Near East by the victorious Assyrian kings who had received them as tribute or plunder.

The many ivories that were discovered all had to be carefully conserved.[5] Here, Agatha came into her own. Max records:

> For the preservation of the objects and their treatment in the field, Agatha's controlled imagination came to our aid. She instantly realized that objects which had lived under water for over 2000 years had to be nursed back into a new and relatively arid climate. The 'Lady at [sic] the Well' was therefore kept under damp towels for several weeks and we reduced the humidity day by day until she was accustomed to a drier atmosphere.[6]

About cleaning the ivories, Agatha Christie herself says:

> I had my part in cleaning many of them. I had my own favourite tools, just as any professional would: an orange stick, possibly a very fine knit-ting needle – one season a dentist's tool which he lent, or rather gave me – and a jar of cosmetic face-cream, which I found more useful than any-thing else for gently coaxing the dirt out of the crevices without harm-ing the friable ivory. In fact there was such a run on my face cream that there was nothing left for my poor old face after a couple of weeks![7]

This was work that Agatha found both exciting and rewarding – in her own words: 'How thrilling it was; the patience, the care that was needed; the delicacy of touch.'[8] A particularly memorable moment – 'one of the most

Right Ivory lion's head from Fort Shalmaneser at Nimrud, 9th–8th century BC, height 5.5 cm (British Museum, London)

Below Openwork ivory panel with lion from Fort Shalmaneser at Nimrud, 9th–8th century BC, height 14 cm (British Museum, London)

exciting days of my life'[9] – was when the sludge was washed off the 'Lady of the Well', which had been entrusted to her for cleaning. In later seasons at Nimrud so many ivories were found that professional conservators had to be enlisted to help with their cleaning, but the efforts of Agatha and others in the early seasons are still respected and admired.

Elsewhere on the citadel, the British School expedition worked in a number of different places. Further investigation of the Ninurta Temple located between the North-West Palace and the ziggurat, previously excavated by Layard, yielded a cache of cylinder seals and beads. A statue of Shalmaneser III found in fragments in the outer town and reassembled by the Mallowan expedition is thought to have been set up originally in this temple. Examination of the Nabu Temple in the south-east part of the citadel, previously excavated mainly by Hormuzd Rassam, showed that there were twin shrines to Nabu the god of writing and his consort Tashmetum. The cuneiform tablets found in this temple included literary and administrative texts as well as the so-called Vassal Treaties of Esarhaddon. These are treaties between King Esarhaddon (680–669 BC) and the Medes of Western Iran whereby the Medes agree to recognize and support the Assyrian crown prince Ashurbanipal as the legitimate successor to the Assyrian throne. Also from the Nabu Temple was a rich collection of ivories, many of them in the incised style that is thought to be characteristic of Assyrian workmanship. In the adjacent Burnt Place a large collection of ivories had been found by W.K. Loftus. Further excavations here produced more ivories, a chariot linch-pin in bronze with the figure of a kneeling man at the top, and a series of clay figurines that were buried in foundation boxes. They included spear-bearers and winged genies.

In the nearby Governor's Palace Mallowan found an important archive of

Ivory relief panel with winged sun disk from Fort Shalmaneser at Nimrud, 9th–8th century BC, length 55.7 cm (British Museum, London; purchased with assistance from the NACF)

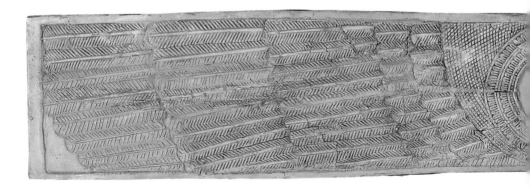

administrative tablets showing that this building had been the residence of the governor of Nimrud in the eighth century BC. There were also painted plaster decoration and in one of the rooms a collection of about 100 pottery vessels, including a large number of beakers in the thin high-quality pottery known as Assyrian Palace Ware. It is thought that in the seventh century BC the governor's residence might have shifted further south to what is known as the 1950 Building. Mallowan excavated just one corner of this evidently large structure. Particularly valuable from an archaeological viewpoint was Mallowan's work on a complex of private houses abutting the town wall in the north-eastern part of the citadel, as this produced an archaeological sequence going back to the Middle Assyrian period, *c*.1200 BC. In a grave under one of these houses was found a pottery drinking cup in the shape of a beautifully modelled ram's head. In addition to all this, the Mallowan expedition cleared a stretch of stone wall on the west side of the citadel overlooking the old bed of the River Tigris. The river has now shifted several kilometres to the west. Lastly, in the south-east part of the citadel, partly on the site of the Nabu Temple, Assyrian remains were found to be covered by a succession of later settlements. In particular, the careful excavation of a series of villages dating from the Hellenistic period (*c*.240–140 BC) produced an abundance of pottery wine-jars and bowls, clay figurines and coins, and shed much light on the material culture of this period. By this time Nimrud had shrunk from the vast city of Late Assyrian times to a modest village in a corner of the citadel, but nevertheless the villagers lived in some comfort.

Beyond the confines of the citadel Mallowan dug a series of trenches between the ziggurat and the north-west corner of the outer town wall. In one of these (PD5) he found part of a palace evidently founded by Adad-nirari III

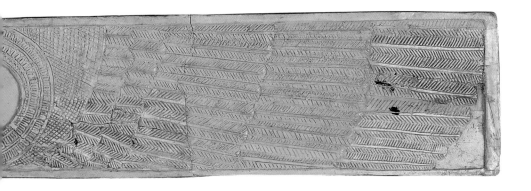

Storage vessels as found at Nimrud (photo: Agatha Christie)

(810–783 BC). There were well-preserved painted designs on the wall plaster. Traces of another palace, known as the 'Town Wall Palace', were found on the south side of the outer town. The most important building in the outer town, though, is undoubtedly Fort Shalmaneser. The discoveries here were made mainly in the years 1958–63, when the field directorship had been handed over to David Oates, but the decision to investigate this building had already been taken in 1957. During five years of excavation the ground plan of this vast building was established, and many of the rooms were cleared out, producing a carved stone throne base, a large decorative panel of glazed bricks, extensive and varied collections of carved ivories, and interesting collections of metalwork. But the earlier excavations on the acropolis of which Mallowan had been in direct charge were no less fruitful, producing inscribed clay tablets, metalwork, glass, pottery, cylinder seals, stamp seals, foundation figures, decorated shell and so on.

Throughout his time at Nimrud Mallowan was accompanied by Agatha Christie, whom he described as 'a wonderful helpmate, an ever-smiling hostess, a brave and happy companion … and in addition was photographer and helped with the cleaning and registration of the small finds'.[10] She also helped Max to pay the workmen.[11] In the first season the small team of four people lived in a mud-brick house belonging to the local sheikh.[12] After that a dig-house was built on the eastern edge of the acropolis mound with a fine view both of the plain below and in the far distance the Zagros Mountains. The staff slept in tents. The dig-house still stands, now used by the Iraq Department of Antiquities. It originally had four rooms, one of which was a small dark-room.[13] When in due course the dig-house was extended, Mallowan tells us that a room was added for Agatha 'where for a part of the morning she sat and wrote her novels quickly and straight on to the typewriter. More than half a dozen of them were written in this way, season after season.' [14] Agatha herself says about the dig-house:

> Finally, a year or two later still, I petitioned to be allowed to have a small room added on of my own. This I would pay for myself. So, for £50, I built on a small square, mud-brick room … It had a window, a table, an upright chair, and the collapsed remnant of a former 'Minty' chair, so

Preparations for transporting sculpture from Nimrud, 1950s (photo: Agatha Christie)

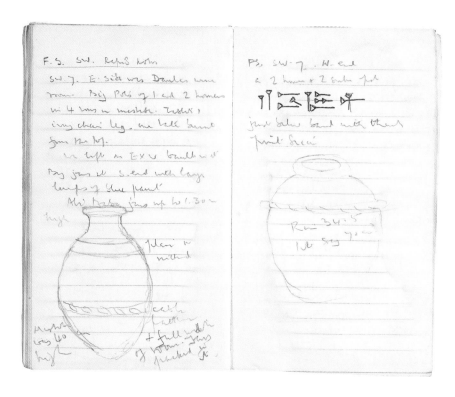

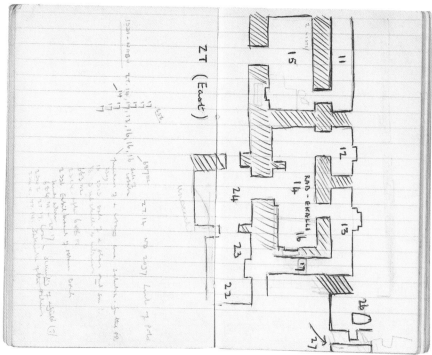

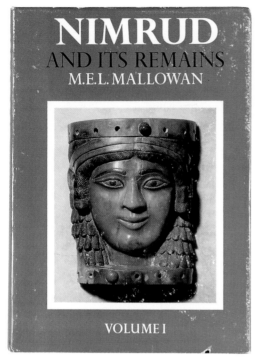

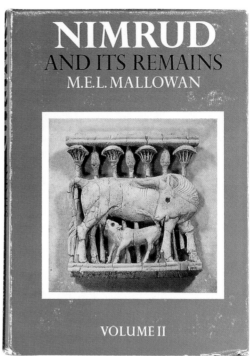

Above Jackets of the two volumes of Mallowan's *Nimrud and its Remains* (Collins 1966)

Above left Max Mallowan's Nimrud diary of 1957 (British Museum, London)

Left Max Mallowan's Nimrud diary of 1952 (British Museum, London)

decrepit it was difficult to sit on, but still quite comfortable. On the wall I hung two pictures by young Iraqi artists ... On the door, Donald Wiseman, one of our epigraphists, fixed the placard in cuneiform, which announces that this is the Beit Agatha – Agatha's House, and in Agatha's house I went every day to do a little of my own work.[15]

We are further told that the room 'measures about three metres square. It has a plastered floor with rush mats and a couple of gay coarse rugs ... There is a window looking out east towards the snow-topped mountains of Kurdistan.'[16]

The significance of Mallowan's excavations at Nimrud is undisputed. A great deal was learned about the topography of Nimrud, and great contributions were made to our understanding of the history, art and archaeology of Assyria. With hindsight we can say that Mallowan's decision to excavate at Nimrud was fully justified, and our only regret should be that the British School did not continue the excavations for longer. He also took advantage of

'Beit Agatha', Agatha's house at Nimrud, where she began her autobiography (photo: Donald Wiseman)

his presence at Nimrud to dig at the nearby site of Balawat where in 1878 Hormuzd Rassam had found a pair of embossed bronze gates dating from the reign of Shalmaneser III. In two brief campaigns in 1956–7 Mallowan found another pair of bronze gates but in this case dating from the reign of Ashurnasirpal II showing the king hunting wild animals and leading his army into battle.[17] These were set up in a temple dedicated to Mamu, the god of dreams.

As a measure of the extent to which Mallowan's excavations have contributed to our knowledge about Nimrud, we may compare Layard's plan of the Acropolis, published in 1849,[18] with Mallowan's plan.[19] We find that the plan of the North-West Palace is greatly extended, and quite absent from Layard's map are plans of the temples between the ziggurat and the North-West Palace: the Governor's Palace, the Nabu Temple, the Burnt Palace, the 1950 Building and the TW53 houses. And all this is without taking Fort Shal-

The dig-house and the sleeping tents at Nimrud, 1952 (photo: Joan Oates)

maneser into account. Similarly the many finds made by the British School
expedition, but particularly the carved ivories and the cuneiform tablets, have
contributed immeasurably to our understanding of Assyrian history and
Assyrian arts and crafts. Mallowan was right to take great pride in this achievement, and who can blame him for bracketing himself with the great Victorian
archaeologist Sir Henry Layard by calling his sumptuous two-volume work
Nimrud and its Remains, reflecting the title Layard had chosen for his 1849
account of *Nineveh and its Remains*. And it is surely not inappropriate that Mallowan's report should have been dedicated to his beloved wife: 'I dedicate this
book to my wife, Agatha Christie Mallowan, who shared with me in the joys
and trials of excavating Nimrud and lightened our labours through her imagination, her skill, and her kindness.'

NOTES

1   A. Christie, *An Autobiography*, London 1977, p. 456.
2   M.E.L. Mallowan, *Nimrud and its Remains*, London 1966, vol. 1, p. 29.
3   For accounts of the British School of Archaeology in Iraq excavations at Nimrud, see
    preliminary reports in *Iraq*; Mallowan, *Nimrud* (n. 2); J.N. Postgate and J.E. Reade, 'Kalḫu',
    Reallexikon der Assyriologie 5 (1980), pp. 303–23; J.E. Reade, 'Nimrud', in J.E. Curtis (ed.),
    Fifty Years of Mesopotamian Discovery, London 1982, pp. 99–112.
4   For publications of the cuneiform tablets found at Nimrud, see *Cuneiform Texts from
    Nimrud*, vols I/2–V, London 1972–96.
5   For publications of the ivories found at Nimrud, see *Ivories from Nimrud*, fascicules 1/2–V,
    London 1967–92.
6   M. Mallowan, *Mallowan's Memoirs*, London 1977, p. 262.
7   Christie, *Autobiography* (n. 1), pp. 456–7.
8   Ibid., p. 457.
9   Ibid.
10 Mallowan, *Memoirs* (n. 6), p. 245.
11 Ibid., p. 290.
12 Ibid., pp. 246–7.
13 Mallowan, *Nimrud* (n. 2), p. 52.
14 Mallowan, *Memoirs* (n. 6), p. 290.
15 Christie, *Autobiography* (n. 1), p. 525.
16 Ibid., p. 11.
17 For accounts of Mallowan's excavations at Balawat, see D. Oates, 'Balawat (Imgur Enlil):
    the site and its buildings', *Iraq* 36 (1974), pp. 173–8; J.E. Curtis, 'Balawat', in *Fifty Years of
    Mesopotamian Discovery* (n. 3), pp. 113–19.
18 A.H. Layard, *Nineveh and its Remains*, London 1849, vol. I, plan opp. p. 332.
19 Mallowan, *Nimrud* (n. 2), plan I.

Life on Site

'*Le camping* begins': Life on an Archaeological Site in the 1930s

Charlotte Trümpler

When, in 1930, Agatha Christie met Max Mallowan in Ur while he was working on the archaeological excavations and married him in September of the same year, she cannot have known what life with an archaeologist would really entail. She described the impressions she had gained in Ur as a tourist thus: 'The lure of the past came up to grab me. To see a dagger slowly appearing, with its gold glint, through the sand was romantic. The carefulness of lifting pots and objects from the soil filled me with a longing to be an archaeologist myself.'[1] On her first journey with Max from Ur to Nippur in the spring of 1930, however, she seems to have taken less interest in the places they visited. She said later that without her companion's explanations of these sites, which often consisted solely of walls, she would not have found them very exciting. However, she could not maintain this attitude after her marriage, for even on honeymoon she had to acknowledge her husband's passion for his career. Agatha sat enjoying the sun on a fine day in the theatre of Epidaurus, while Max spent hours deciphering an inscription in the gloom of the museum. She had tried for some time in vain to lure him outside, but he finally left the building happy, 'having deciphered one particularly obscure Greek phrase which, as far as he was concerned, had made his day'.[2] She used this little incident in her short story 'The Oracle at Delphi',[3] in which a pale, thin, bespectacled young man spends hours on his knees in the ruins of Delphi deciphering Greek inscriptions which appear to his mother tedious beyond belief.

Greek inscription at Delphi (photo: Max Mallowan)

Above Excavation at Ur, 1920s (photo: Max Mallowan)

Below Cook with Christmas cake at Ur, 1926 (photo: Max Mallowan)

ARPACHIYA LAND LEASE ?

سند ايجار واستيجار

المأجور وحدوده ونوعه وموقعه نمرة ✳ عدد ✳

ارض زراعيه واقعه في قريه بموجب السند الخاقاني نمرة ٤٤ وتاريخ ذي القعده ١٣٥٩
و ١٧ تشرين اول ١٤٤٣

اسم المؤجر وشهرته ومحل اقامته نائله بنت رشيد سلطان قريه اربجيه

اسم المستأجر وشهرته ومحل اقامته ام ال ل لميلس بلداه مدير حفريات بريتش موزيم في الاربجيه

مقدار الاجرة اى بدل الايجار وكيفية تأديته سبعه وعشرين دينارا عراقيه بالسنه تدفع نقدا اول شباط من كل سنه

مدة الايجار ثلاث سنه

مبدأ الايجار وانتهاؤه ٧ شباط ١٩٣٣ الى ٧ شباط ١٩٣٦

تاريخ عقد الايجار ٧ شباط ١٩٣٣

ماهي مقادير حصص الشركاء في المأجور المشترك

هيئة المأجور حين العقد ارض زراعيه مقدارها مايه وخمسه وثلاثون دونم

لاي شيئ يستعمل المأجور لاجراء الحفريات فيه والحصول على الاثار القديمه

بيان الاشياء والادوات التي سلمت الى المستأجر حين الايجار

الشرائط العمومية

المادة الاولى – المستأجر مجبور على رد وتسليم مفتاح الماجور عند انقضاء مدة الايجار . فان لم يفعل ذلك فانه يضمن ايفاء كلما سيحصل من الضرر والخسار للمتصرف بالاجرة المضاعفة للموجر عن كل يوم يمضي بعد انقضاء عمدة الايجار روبية

المادة الثانية – اذا ظهر عارض بصورة تمنع امكان استعمال الماجور حينئذ تكون التعميرات الاساسية من قبل المتصرف غير ان ما يتعلق بمصارفات الانشاء والتعمير والزبينات والترتيبات والغريثات فيصرف ويمضى ذلك من قبل المستاجر وعند مشاهدة اللوازم لا يكون المستاجر مانعا لاجراء التعميرات الاساسية مهما اتسع مقدارها خلال مدة الايجار وليس للمستاجر ان يغير او يبدل تقسيمات المأجور باي وجه كان ما يأذن له الموجر بذلك

Contract for hire of the land at Tell Arpachiyah, 1933 (British Museum, London)

17

INCORPORATING :-
STEPHEN LYNCH & C?
LYNCH BROTHERS, LT?
GRAY, MACKENZIE & C?
AND GRAY, PAUL & C?

Telegraphic Address:-
MESPERS

CODES
A.B.C. 5TH Edition.
BENTLEYS

THE MESOPOTAMIA PERSIA CORPORATION,
LIMITED.

Mesopotamia

№ FOR/M/1/138

Baghdad, 4th February 19 33

M.E.L. Mallowan Esqr,
~~Maude Hotel~~ C/o Railway Rest House
~~Baghdad~~ Mosul

Dear Sir,

"ADDRESS" 2 Cases Expedition Equipment and Household
material ex s/s "Shahristan" Voy.30 and
"Shamal" V.94

"ADDRESS" 2 Cases comprising one-4 Burner valor
Cooking Stove, forwarded to Railway Rest
House, MOSUL

We beg to hand you herewith our debit note No.LD/33/21

amounting to I.Dinars 18/155, being charges incurred by us on the

above packages.

We further enclose the invoices in respect of the

former two packages, as they are no longer required by us.

Yours faithfully,
for the Mesopotamia Persia Corporation Ltd.

THE UNDERMENTIONED EQUIPMENT IS ALL USED AND IS ALL EXPEDITION MATERIAL.

4 table napkin cases

4 finger bowls

5 meat dishes

65 plates

4 bowls

11 tea cups

40 saucers

I cream jug

2 milk jugs

6 soup bowls with lids

I2 coffee saucers

IO coffee cups

I mustard pot

2 pepper pots

2 salt cellars

3 vegetable dishes with lids

I sauce boat

I colander

4 frying pans

I frying basket

I steamer with lid

5 saucepans

2 pie dishes

2 strainers

I egg-beater

I fish slice

I mixing bowl

5 table cloths

I9 table napkins

Left and above Correspondence and list of household utensils for the dig at Tell Arpachiyah, 1933
(British Museum, London)

Workmen on the dig at Tell Arpachiyah before the start of a race, 1933

Since Katharine Woolley, the wife of the excavator of Ur, did not tolerate the company of another woman for any length of time, Max, who wanted to have Agatha with him while he was on a dig, decided to look for a different site. He received an offer from Reginald Campbell Thompson to direct the excavation of a deep pit on Campbell Thompson's site at Nineveh. Agatha spent a month as a guest on this expedition. She and Barbara Campbell Thompson visited the dig every day, although she was not yet involved with the excavations herself, and was working on her crime writing at the time. None the less, this visit was an experience of crucial importance to her, as she comments in looking back on it: 'I enjoyed my first experience of living on a dig enormously.'[4]

'Glorious dishes, vases, cups and plates'

When Campbell Thompson had completed his last season in Nineveh, Max decided to carry out an excavation by himself. He had already made it his business while working at Nineveh to study prehistoric material, especially in the field of early pottery. A small *tell*, or settlement mound, Tell Arpachiyah, only 6 kilometres east of Nineveh, seemed ideal. The expedition was financed by the Trustees of the British Museum, the British School of Archaeology in Iraq and an anonymous sponsor – in fact Agatha Christie herself.

In February 1933 Max and Agatha travelled to Mosul in Iraq with the

The workmen after the race with their prizes

architect John Rose. They first had to clear up the complicated question of landownership of the site in a series of difficult negotiations. It transpired that fourteen different people all claimed to own the land on which the mound stood. They were taken to a bank in two horse-drawn carts to put their thumb-marks on the contract, which provided in detail for all eventualities and stipulated that the agreement must be upheld and the team of excavators must not be impeded in any way, on pain of a fine of £2,000.[5]

Max was under great pressure during his first independent dig, for only if it was successful would it further his career. But after some rather disappointing initial finds, the rest of the excavation turned out extremely well. A potter's kiln was discovered, with many pottery vessels.

> It was ... a crowning piece of luck. The potter's shop was all there, under the soil. It had been abandoned when burnt, and the burning had preserved it. There were glorious dishes, vases, cups and plates, polychrome pottery, all shining in the sun – scarlet and black and orange – a magnificent sight ... I was bursting with happiness.[6]

Agatha had taken art lessons the previous autumn, hoping to learn to draw to scale. Her teacher did not find it easy to overcome her ignorance and indeed her lack of skill. But she worked hard and willingly to help John Rose draw

1. Cow + Calf
2 Sheep
3 Ram
4. 3 Chicken
5 2 Chicken X
6 1 Chicken
7. 1 other Rice
8. 50 Eggs
9. 25 Eggs
10. 10. Eggs

Dates + Ahlawa 1/4 Rice

the pottery found on the dig in Arpachiyah, although despite her lessons she was never very good at it, and she did not repeat the attempt on later excavations. As well as acting as photographic technician, Agatha discovered an enthusiasm for restoring pottery, a task she carried out with much love, skill and patience. It suited her passion for jigsaw puzzles, and she was to be a great help to the team in this way on many other digs.

The accommodation in Tell Arpachiyah consisted of a small rented house with a number of storerooms and a wonderful view of both the river Tigris and the mound of Kuyunjik in Nineveh. As with all the other expedition houses used by Max and Agatha, several dogs from the neighbourhood lived there, and the Mallowans looked after them with affection.

The domestic staff consisted of a cook, a house-boy and an amusing Irishman who acted as driver. No further details are recorded of the housekeeping arrangements from this period spent by the Mallowans at Tell Arpachiyah, but lists preserved in the archives of the British Museum offer a fascinating insight into the expedition's equipment.[7] They cover ten pages and enumerate every item transported to Mosul in four crates by the Mesopotamia Persia Corporation Ltd. The equipment itself consisted of used expeditionary material in the form of household utensils, together with some new purchases from the Army & Navy Stores and Woolworth's. These interesting lists clearly show the influence of Agatha Christie, who thought it important for the food to be good on a dig, and made sure there was European kitchen equipment available. Second-hand utensils included four cake tins, a colander, four finger bowls, a frying basket and four frying pans, two baking tins, 65 plates, a mustard pot, four napkin rings, six tablecloths – and also, newly purchased from Woolworth's, four dessert bowls, a large dessert dish, two nutcrackers, two steak platters and two crystal water-bowls.

Other lists feature drawing implements, large quantities of different kinds of paper, restoration materials and books. Among the books, Turkish, Arabic and Sumerian grammars, an Arabic and an English dictionary, and the Bible are especially noteworthy. These carefully compiled records clearly illustrate the meticulous exactitude, forethought and experience that had to go into the preparations for even a relatively small dig.

Numerous medicaments indicate the provision made against possible illness. One could not simply call in a doctor if someone fell sick in the desert. The knowledge Agatha Christie had acquired as assistant in a pharmacy gained her something of a reputation as a 'medicine woman' among the local population. The large quantities of medicines the expedition took with it,

Sketch of the race-track and list of prizes, from Max Mallowan's notebook (British Museum, London)

Manuscript notes for *Come, Tell Me How You Live*

Come
Tell Me How
You Live

AGATHA
CHRISTIE
MALLOWAN

Cover of the first edition of *Come, Tell Me How You Live*, Collins 1946

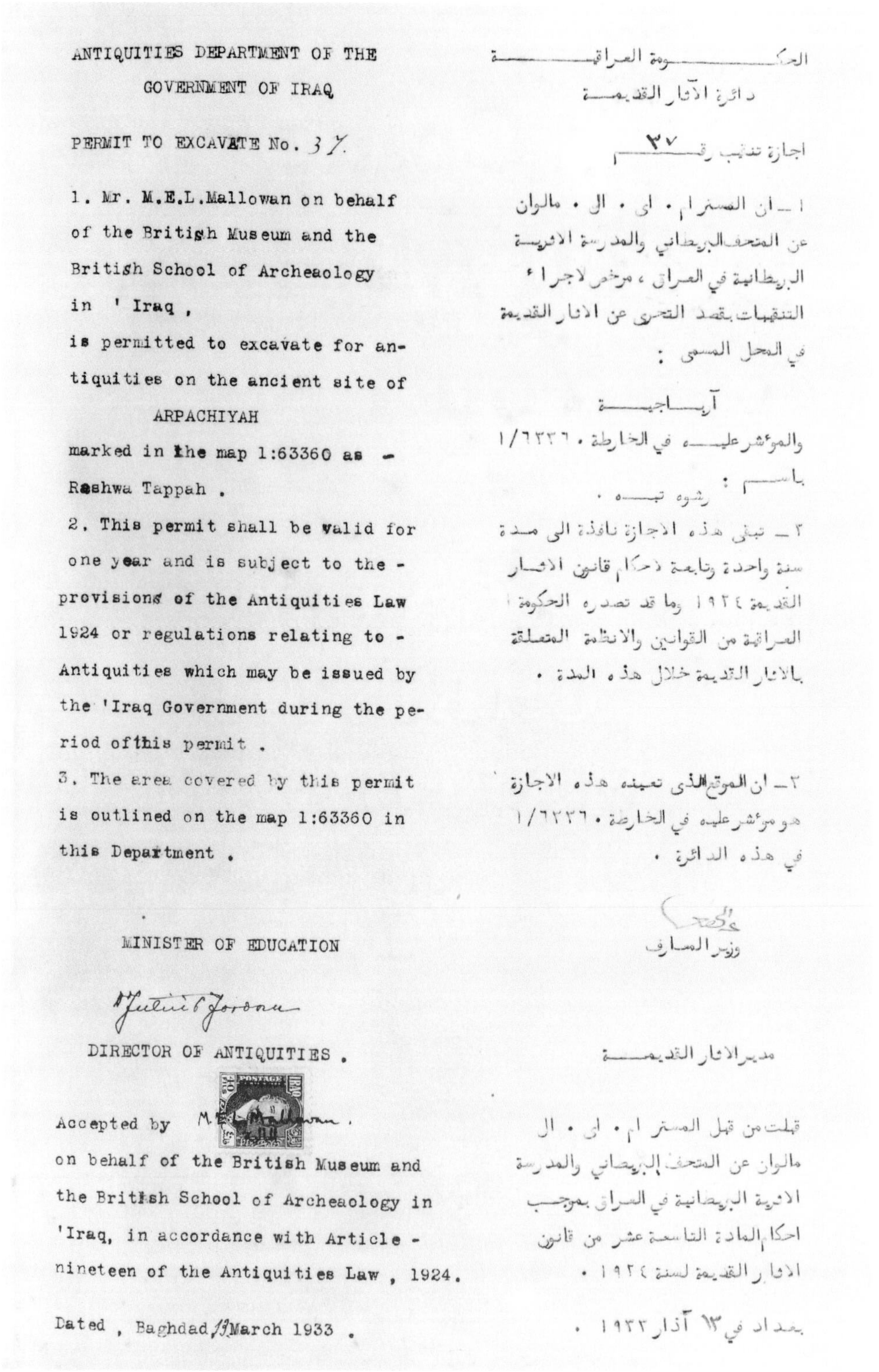

ANTIQUITIES DEPARTMENT OF THE
GOVERNMENT OF IRAQ

PERMIT TO EXCAVATE No. 37.

1. Mr. M.E.L.Mallowan on behalf of the British Museum and the British School of Archeaology in 'Iraq, is permitted to excavate for antiquities on the ancient site of

ARPACHIYAH

marked in the map 1:63360 as - Rashwa Tappah.

2. This permit shall be valid for one year and is subject to the provisions of the Antiquities Law 1924 or regulations relating to Antiquities which may be issued by the 'Iraq Government during the period of this permit.

3. The area covered by this permit is outlined on the map 1:63360 in this Department.

MINISTER OF EDUCATION

Julius Jordan

DIRECTOR OF ANTIQUITIES.

Accepted by M.E.L. Mallowan

on behalf of the British Museum and the British School of Archeaology in 'Iraq, in accordance with Article nineteen of the Antiquities Law, 1924.

Dated, Baghdad 13 March 1933.

الحكومة العراقية
دائرة الآثار القديمة

اجازة تنقيب رقم ٣٧

١ ـ ان المستر ام . اي . ال . مالوان
عن المتحف البريطاني والمدرسة الاثرية
البريطانية في العراق ، مرخص لاجراء
التنقيبات بقصد التحري عن الاثار القديمة
في المحل المسمى :

آرپاجية

والمؤشر عليه في الخارطة ١/٦٣٣٦٠
باسم :
رشوه تبه .

٢ ـ تبقى هذه الاجازة نافذة الى مدة
سنة واحدة وتابعة لاحكام قانون الاثار
القديمة ١٩٢٤ وما قد تصدره الحكومة
العراقية من القوانين والانظمة المتعلقة
بالاثار القديمة خلال هذه المدة .

٣ ـ ان الموقع الذي تعينه هذه الاجازة
هو مؤشر عليه في الخارطة ١/٦٣٣٦٠
في هذه الدائرة .

وزير المعارف

مدير الاثار القديمة

قبلت من قبل المستر ام . اي . ال
مالوان عن المتحف البريطاني والمدرسة
الاثرية البريطانية في العراق بموجب
احكام المادة التاسعة عشر من قانون
الاثار القديمة لسنة ١٩٢٤ .

بغداد في ١٣ آذار ١٩٣٣ .

Excavation permit granted by Julius Jordan for Tell Arpachiyah on 13 March 1933 (British Museum, London)

especially the many bottles of aspirin and quinine, six bottles of castor oil and herbal laxatives, show that Agatha's account of the workmen's illnesses presents an accurate picture. Since their diet was low in fibre, many of the local people suffered from constipation, which could be relieved only by taking huge quantities of laxatives.

Full of ideas to make their dig as lively as possible and motivate their workmen, the Mallowans decided to organize a race for them at the end of the season. Some of the older men were afraid that their dignity might suffer if they ran in the race against younger men, but after long negotiations all of them eventually agreed to take part. Max sketched the racetrack of the 'A.A.A.A.' – Arpachiyah Amateur Athletic Association – in his journal of the dig and listed the prizes:[8]

1.   *Cow and Calf*
2.   *Sheep*
3.   *Ram*
4.   *3 Chickens*
5.   *2 Chickens*
6.   *1 Chicken*
7.   *1 Bag Rice*
8.   *50 Eggs*
9.   *25 Eggs*
10. *10 Eggs*

The other competitors each received as many dates and as much halva (a sweetmeat made of honey and sesame) as they could hold in their two hands. Two photographs show the men waiting expectantly at the start, and with their prizes at the end of the race. The surprise winner was a very poor workman who owned almost nothing.

After the end of the season the archaeological finds were to be divided up by Dr Julius Jordan, the German Director of Antiquities in Baghdad. According to local law, half the finds must stay in Iraq while the rest went to the country from which the archaeologist came, in this case England. Unfortunately nationalist feeling was emerging in Iraq during these years, and Max had difficulty in getting his finds to London. Dr Jordan did not play a very laudable part in this situation. He was a National Socialist who did not want to foster the interests of the English; indeed, he was the first Nazi Agatha Christie had ever met. It was a considerable shock to her to realize that this educated, musical man could express such hatred for Jews. Next year Iraq passed a stricter law, severely restricting the export of archaeological finds, and foreign archaeologists transferred their activities to Syria and the neighbouring countries.

Max Mallowan in the car 'Queen Mary' in the yard of the expedition house, Tell Brak, 1938 (photo: Agatha Christie)

'The landscape is full of tells and brown Bedouin tents'

In 1934 Max decided to study several tells in the Khabur valley, in the relatively unexplored north-east part of Syria, to establish a chronology of the prehistoric pottery of the area. The aim of this survey conducted in November and December 1934 was to investigate as many tells as possible and find the most suitable for excavations to take place over a period of several years. It was a good season to carry out such a survey, since surface finds were particularly easy to spot when the vegetation had died down. On the other hand the weather could be very changeable, and heavy rainfall could make driving impossible.

We are well informed about the Mallowans' excavations in Syria at this time from a short but very entertaining autobiographical work by Agatha Christie entitled *Come, Tell Me How You Live*. It makes a good complement to the memoirs of Max Mallowan, who of course concentrated chiefly on the archaeological perspective.[9] Agatha Christie's book describes in detail their experiences on their digs, and reflects her attitude to the local people and the other members of their expeditions.

Agatha's journeys to Syria always began with the purchase of suitable clothing, which could present problems in England in the middle of winter. In happy anticipation of her coming travels she would try department stores for everyday washable cotton dresses to fit her full figure, and hats that would stay on in the strong desert winds. She describes herself being sent on from the ordinary clothing department with its fur-trimmed suits to the sailing department, which was full of tight-fitting shorts for slender young girls, and so to the tropical department, where in desperation she buys a shantung silk dress 'suitable for the wives of Empire Builders',[10] which turns her into a

Map showing the tells investigated by Max Mallowan in 1934 on the Khabur survey (British Museum, London)

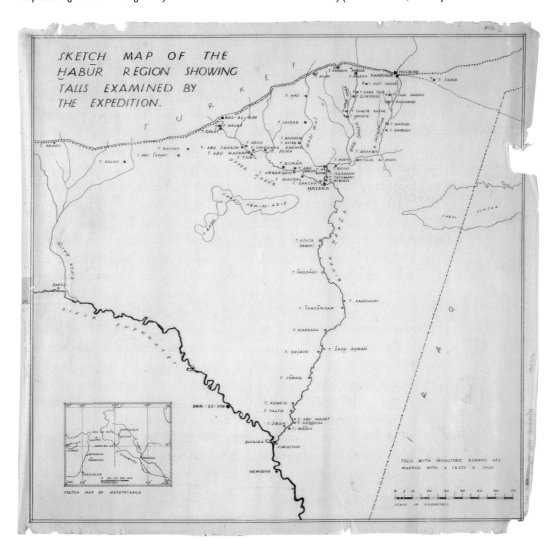

memsahib. Later, on the dig, it failed to win the approval of Max, who thought it unsuitable for an archaeological expedition.

Before the war visitors to the Orient travelled either by train or ship, and on reaching the Middle East continued by bus or rail. Although these journeys were often very arduous, they gave Agatha great pleasure, since she loved travelling by train. In her view flying to Iraq, as she did after the Second World War, was not just expensive but boring, and it also did away with the pleasure she took in approaching her journey's end by slow stages.

Preparations for the Khabur survey and the later excavations were made in Beirut, where the headquarters of the Syrian Antiquities service – Direction du Service des Antiquités – was located during the French mandate in Syria. The director of the time, a Frenchman called Henri Seyrig, was extremely civil and helpful to the Mallowans. He dealt quickly and smoothly with such formalities as getting the necessary permit to dig, and at the end of the expedition he divided the finds equitably. He and his wife became close friends of the Mallowans and often visited them in England.

It was important to find a suitable motor vehicle to stand up to months of wear and tear in the desert. The expedition bought a four-cylinder Ford with a high-built chassis to overcome the problem of potholes; its majestic appearance earned it the name of Queen Mary. This faithful and extremely practical vehicle was lightweight (a matter of some significance if it got stuck) and could hold four tents: two for the European members of the expedition, one for the kitchen and the servants, and one for toilet facilities.

'Here, some five thousand years ago, was *the* busy part of the world'
The account of the investigation of the tells is one of the most delightful episodes in Agatha's Syrian memoir, and shows her casting an amused eye on what she saw as the odd business of going round countless mounds to look for archaeological remains. According to the archaeological records, Max Mallowan studied sixty tells.[11] It was necessary to walk round the mounds several times to find enough material, and on one occasion Agatha suddenly found herself swaying as she walked. At first she put this feeling down to a disturbed sense of balance, but it turned out that the outer sole of her left shoe and the inner sole of her right shoe were worn right down, as a result of walking round and round in the same direction all the time.

This intense concentration on the ground caused her to remark, pithily: 'I begin to understand why archaeologists have a habit of walking with eyes downcast to the ground. Soon, I feel, I myself shall forget to look around me,

The architect Robin Macartney and the archaeologist Richard Barnett at Chagar Bazar, 1935

Sheikh Hamoudi and Leonard Woolley, 1930s

or out to the horizon. I shall walk looking down at my feet as though there only any interest lies.'[12] However, it gave her great pleasure to search for fragments and reflect on what she had found: 'Here were the beginnings of civilisation, and here, picked up by me, this broken fragment of a clay pot, hand- made, with a design of dots and cross-hatching in black paint, is the forerunner of the Woolworth cup out of which this very morning I have drunk my tea.'[13]

The choice of future sites for excavation depended on three factors: first, there must be a village somewhere near from which workmen could be recruited; second, there must be a source of water – a river or a well – as close as possible; and the third and most important criterion was that the tell must be archaeologically productive. In this particular case it was important to Max that the mound should have prehistoric pottery even on its upper level, because of the expense of digging. To Agatha's regret, several of the mounds that were particularly attractive as part of the landscape and aesthetically appealing contained only Roman pottery near the top. 'Min Ziman er Rum' ('it's Roman' in Arabic) was Max's dismissive verdict on identifying a tell as a Roman settlement.

The accounts of this first visit to Syria look almost entirely on the bright side of the experience, although it cannot always have been easy for Agatha. Thanks to her fertile imagination, she could withdraw into a world of her own when she was unable to join the conversation of other members of the team for one reason or another, either her inadequate command of the local language or her lack of archaeological knowledge.

Besides the Mallowans, the team on the Khabur survey consisted of only five members and the Arab foreman Sheikh Hamoudi, whom Max had met at Ur when he was working for Leonard Woolley. Hamoudi had previously worked on the site at Carchemish with Woolley and T.E. Lawrence (Lawrence of Arabia). Two of his sons, Alawi and Yahya, accompanied him on the later excavations at Chagar Bazar and Tell Brak. The Hamoudi family came from Jerablus where they still live today, proudly venerating the long-dead Sheikh Hamoudi. A rather bad cook called Isa, who had in fact never

Sheikh Hamoudi and his sons outside their house in Jerablus, 1939 (photo: Agatha Christie)

cooked at all before joining the Mallowans, a fact evident from the dishes he served, was supposed to look after the physical well-being of the members of the expedition. Queen Mary and a taxi were driven by two chauffeurs, each with his different idiosyncrasies.

The scientific team consisted of Max and a very shy and silent architect, Robin Macartney, whom Max had recruited on the recommendation of his colleague Aurel Stein.[14] Macartney had a rather pessimistic nature, and his

Beehive Houses near Ras-el-Ain. North Syria

Houses near Ras el-Ain, by Robin Macartney, 1935

shyness could make him seem supercilious and arrogant, so that he made Agatha feel insecure at first. After living with the others under extreme conditions in the desert, however, Macartney ceased to be cool and unapproachable, and became more adept at showing his feelings. His great passions were for horses and painting. When Agatha had recognized his real gifts she asked him to design several jackets for her crime stories. He painted some extremely artistic and original pictures, some of which have recently been reproduced by HarperCollins as jackets for the novels. A picture of the Syrian village of Ras el-Ain by Macartney hung in the Mallowans' bedroom in Devon all their lives, and can still be seen there today.

Agatha discovered how hard camping could be when she fell ill with stomach trouble. Since the temperature in the tents rose to over 55° in the

Sheikh Ahmad Kaderi, still from the film made by Agatha Christie at Tell Brak in 1938

daytime, and Max could not leave her alone in the desert, she had to endure the bumpy ride to the tells suffering from nausea and a high temperature. On reaching the tell to be investigated she lay down in the shade of Queen Mary and tried to rest, although she was tormented by the pestering of great swarms of flies. At such moments she felt sorry she had ever joined the expedition at all.

After intensive study the choice for the future excavation site fell on the mound of Chagar Bazar, where attractive and promising Tell Halaf pottery of the fifth century BC had come to light. It was a suitable place, since there was quite a large village called Kamichlie only 40 kilometres to the north, with a shop, a post office and a bank. The landowner, Sheikh Ahmad, was a friendly but grasping character with a long red beard. It was with him that the expedition had to negotiate over terms for the use of the excavation site.

'Mice in your hair – mice! Mice! MICE!'

The following year, on 10 March 1935, Max Mallowan and the Haut Commissariat de la République Française en Syrie et Liban – Direction du Service des Antiquités – signed the agreement for the dig at Chagar Bazar.[15] The Mallowans spent 1935 to 1937 carrying out excavations on this mound. A letter

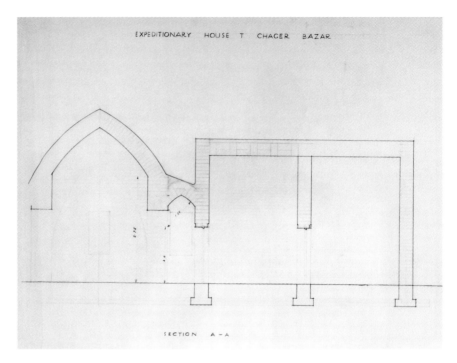

EXPEDITIONARY HOUSE T CHAGER BAZAR

SECTION A - A

Plan of the expedition house at Chagar Bazar (British Museum, London; drawing by Robin Macartney)

from Henri Seyrig to various authorities shows that the archaeological and household equipment was the same as Mallowan had used at Arpachiyah. It had obviously been stored in Mosul in the meantime.[16]

During the first season's digging the team rented a large mud-brick building in Amuda which Agatha disliked from the first, since it was infested by great numbers of mice. This plague of mice assumed such gigantic proportions on the first night that for the first and only time in all her years on digs Agatha became hysterical. But the intruders were driven out when the team borrowed a 'highly professional cat', a talented hunter who otherwise showed no feelings of any kind and would not tolerate such human activities as conversation while it was at work.

The expedition intended to build a house of its own at Chagar Bazar as soon as possible. Robin Macartney designed a very individual plan, based on the buildings with pointed arches common in northern Syria. The high dome over the central area, however, presented practical problems. Over 10,000 mud bricks were used, and when finished the house consisted of two bedrooms, a drawing-office, a storeroom for antiquities, a living-room, a kitchen and a dark-room. The interior was cool and very comfortable. Agatha

The expedition house at Chagar Bazar, 1935 (photo: Agatha Christie)

compared the entire building to a church consecrated to a 'venerable saint'. To Max's displeasure, Sheikh Ahmad sprinkled all four corners with blood from a freshly slaughtered sheep, which was a magic spell supposed to bring luck, but it spoilt the attractive appearance of the newly erected brick building.

When the excavations at Chagar Bazar were over in 1937, the house passed into the hands of the avaricious sheikh, who had raised money on his future ownership of it years in advance. Even during the dig he had made the most of the high credit he might be expected to enjoy: in addition to his existing four Kurdish wives he acquired a fifth, a pretty Yezidi girl. To the last he kept trying to get as much money and as many presents as he could out of Max. Every time the Mallowans set out for England he asked them to procure expensive gifts, in double quantities if possible, for instance two gold watches: 'One can then lend one to a friend.' When the house became his he was still trying to negotiate for compensation 'for spoiling of the garden'.[17] The French officer presiding over the transactions queried this point. 'Asked to produce any trace of ever having had a garden, or indeed knowing what a garden *is*, the Sheikh [climbed] down.' A contract still in the British Museum archives established that with the transfer of the house and a horse to the

Kaméchlié, le 9 Mai 1938.

En considération des services rendus à monsieur Mallowan par Cheikh Ahmad de Tchagher-Bazar au cours des fouilles
faites à Tell-Tchagher-Bazar de 1934 à 1937, il sera versé
150 L.S. à Cheikh Ahmad.

La maison voutée construite par monsieur Mallowan à
Tchagher-Bazar devient immédiatement la propriété de Cheikh
Ahmad.

Le contrat dressé le 15 mai 1935 entre Monsieur Mallowan et Cheikh Ahmad est résilié et annulé.

En acceptant cette somme de 150 L.S., Cheikh Ahmad
ainsi payé de ses services passés ne pourra, à ce sujet, plus
rien réclamer à monsieur Mallowan.

A la signature du présent quittus Cheikh Ahmad rece-
vra en Bakchiche un cheval de monsieur Mallowan.

Monsieur Mallowan et Cheikh Ahmad soussignés décla-
rent ainsi réglées toutes questions d'intérêt entre eux.

Monsieur Mallowan.   Cheikh Ahmad Kaderi.

M.E.L.Mallowan

                    Le Capitaine AZZIS
            Officier des S.S.Chef du Poste de Kaméchlié.

sheikh any claims to further compensation would be invalid. The document of agreement between Sheikh Ahmad Kaderi and Monsieur Mallowan was drawn up by the French officer in Kamichlie on 9 May 1938.[18]

In 1935 Mallowan's colleagues were Robin Macartney and the archaeologist Richard Barnett from the British Museum, and in 1936 and 1937 they were joined by Colonel Burn, a retired army officer who spoke fluent Arabic, and the architect Louis Osman. Richard Barnett was a good counterweight to Macartney, being very sociable and talkative. Unlike Macartney, too, Barnett had a good knowledge of Arabic and could talk easily to the workmen. Macartney refused to the end to learn Arabic, and communicated with the workmen through various kinds of whistles and gesticulations.

When visitors came – and they were something of a nuisance on a dig – Barnett would show them round enthusiastically, lifting the burden from other members of the team, including Agatha, whose natural shyness always made her awkward with strangers.

Left Agreement between Sheikh Ahmad Kaderi and Max Mallowan, dated 9 May 1938 (British Museum, London)

Below Cheerful workmen at the end of a day's work (*fidos*), 1935 (photo: Richard Barnett)

'A confusion of tongues'

The workmen on the dig – some 140 of them in all, were a mixture of Arabs, Kurds, Yezidis ('so-called devil-worshippers',[19] according to Agatha) and Christians. The best workers were Turks who had smuggled themselves over the border wearing Arab headdresses, and put their Turkish caps back on as soon as they were in Syria. Although it was not easy to control so many different nationalities, speaking several different languages, Max succeeded in organizing the dig without any major incidents. His diplomacy was required, for instance, to settle the delicate matter of the day of rest. The Muslims, who outnumbered the Christians, wanted it to be Friday. The Armenians, on the other hand, refused to work on a Sunday. Finally Max decided to make Tuesday the day of rest, since no practising religion has its feast-day on a Tuesday.

To encourage the workmen to keep a sharp eye open and dig with great care, Max paid *bakshish* for every good find. They were intrigued by the

Max Mallowan assessing the finds and recording the *bakshish* payable, Chagar Bazar, 1936
(photo: Agatha Christie)

difficulty of predicting how he would assess an object. The little boys whose job it was to look through the contents of the baskets of soil a second time in search of finds could earn as much money in this way as a grown spademan or pickman. Every afternoon, just before work ended, the workmen lined up to show Max any special finds. If these items found favour with him, he would write down the sum earned beside each name in a book, and when pay-day came the *bakshish* was paid out along with the regular working wage. Every worker remembered exactly what he was owed and would put the record straight if he was paid too little or even too much.

Pay-day was a great occasion. A photograph shows Max sitting in the car Queen Mary and paying the workmen – as Agatha said, 'looking rather like a booking-clerk at a railway station'.[20] In the first years of excavation the workmen refused to accept pay in French francs, the official currency of the country, demanding Turkish mejidis instead. The banks, on the other hand, would accept only French francs. Consequently the chauffeur Michel had to exchange the official currency for mejidis in the bazaar. As the mejidi was a huge and heavy coin that was also dirty and stank of garlic, transporting and paying out the money was an extremely unpleasant activity. Mejidis were finally withdrawn during 1937 and 1938.

Agatha, who thanks to her gift for observation could describe human beings very accurately, enjoyed analysing the different ethnic groups. In many brief anecdotes she pinpointed the fundamental differences between Arab and Kurdish women, who – although their life-styles and religion were the same – were very different in nature. Reserve, shyness and modesty were characteristic of the Arab women, who avoided looking Agatha straight in the eye, while the confident Kurdish women would strike up a conversation themselves. Among the Kurds the women and not the men dominated family life, which she demonstrated by citing the example of a Kurdish woman who stormed into the crowd of workmen on pay-day and immediately took her husband's money from him, to the horror of the Arab men present. No Arab woman would ever have addressed a man directly, while the Kurdish women cheerfully exchanged banter with any man. These different attitudes were also expressed in their clothing: the Kurdish women wore bright, colourful clothes, while the Arab women usually chose black or other dark colours.

'Some of the lazier ... when taking their baskets to the dump, do not return at once'

At Chagar Bazar Agatha's archaeological involvement became more intensive, professional and demanding. She had developed into an indispensable member of the team, leaving her own career as a writer in abeyance. She usually went to the tell every day and examined the latest finds from the

XIV

Amount   Baksh.   Total

- J. OSMAN MEDEI   19 days = 855 - 25 = 830 + 98 = 928   928
- K. HAJI HASSAN   15 1/2 — = 697 1/2 - 50 = 647 1/2 + 33 1/2 = 680   680
- A. MAHALI HUSSEIN   13 — = 585   +9 = 594   594
- J. JASIM MOHD   13 — = 585 - 162 1/2 = 422 1/2 + 13 = 435 1/2   435 1/2
- J. JUMA' MOHD.   13 — = 585 - 137 1/2 = 447 1/2 + 25 = 472 1/2   472 1/2
- Do. MOHD MUSA.   6 — = 270   +5 = 275   275

XV

- H. MAHMOUD SHIBLI   12 — = 540 - 60 = 480 + 14 = 494   494
- H. JASIM MOHD.   12 — = 540 - 210 = 330 + 14 = 344   344
- H   MOHD HADI   12 — = 540   +8 = 548   548
- H. GHARAF HAMD   12 — = 540 - 20 = 520 + 19 = 539   539
- H. ALI MUSTAFA.   12 — = 540 - 50 = 490 + 12 = 502   502
- J. MOHD HUSSEIN AHMADH   — = 495 - 62 1/2 = 432 1/2 + 8 = 440 1/2   440 1/2
- K. ISA IBRAHIM   5 — = 225 - 25 = 200 + 1 = 201   201
- H. ABO EL GEDRUS   3 1/2 — = 157 1/2   +3 = 160 1/2   160 1/2
-     ABO 'ISA   4 1/2 — = 202 1/2 - 10 = 192 1/2 + 5 = 197 1/2   197 1/2

XVI

- J. JASIM MOHD   19 — = 855 - 50 = 805 + 108 = 913 + 135 for 3 days Ham = 1048 =
- J. JASIM ALI   14 — = 630 - 138 = 492 + 14 = 506   506
- J. MAHMUD HASSAN MOHD'   — = 495 - 162 1/2 = 332 1/2 + 12 = 344 1/2   344 1/2
- A. JEDA HALIL   11 — = 495   +22 = 517   492
- K. HALAF DAWAN   11 — = 495 - 25 = 470 + 28 = 498   498
- A. OBEID 'ISA.   11 — = 495 - 105 = 390 + 6 = 396   396
- J. ISMAIL HUSSEIN.   11 — = 495 - 62 1/2 = 432 1/2 + 8 = 440 1/2   440 1/2

XVII

- J. MOHD KHARAJI   14 — = 630 - 98 = 532 + 123 = 655   655
- K. HUSSEIN HAMOUD.   11 — = 495 - 25 = 470 + 10 = 480   480
- K. MUSTAPHA ALI   11 — = 495 -)5 = 420 + 15 = 435   435
- K. SUMER SHAHR   11 — = 495 - 150 = 345 + 8 = 353   353
-     YAPRAIM HAWADIS   4 — = 180   +3 = 183   183
- K. AWAD JASIM   10 — = 450 - 50 = 400 + 5 = 405   405
- J. HAMAD HALAF   11 — = 495 - 212 1/2 = 282 1/2 + 9 = 291 1/2   291 1/2   16
- K. HAMUD GASUB   8 — = 360 - 125 = 235 + 7 = 242   242 -   12
- A. IBRAHIM AWWADIS

XVIII		Advance	Back'd	Total

ALI KERKES 14 days = 630 - 88 = 542 + 12 = 554 | 554

KAISAR EL 'ISA 11 — = 495 +29 = 524 | 524

RAMADHAN HALAF 11 — = 495 - 75 = 420 + 6 = 426 | 426

HAMED UWAIYIS 11 — = 495 +8 = 503 | 503

ISA BERHO 11 — = 495 - 50 = 445 + 5 = 450 | 450

HASSAN MAHMUD 9 — = 405 - 25 = 380 + 4 = 384 | 384

MUSTAPHA JUMA HAMAD 11 — = 495 - 62½ = 432½ + 25 = 457½ | 457½

GARABET CIRCISSIAN 6 — = 270 + 1 = 271 | 271

MOHD HINDI 4 — = 180 + 4 = 184 | 184

XIX

IBRAHIM MOHD. 14 — = 630 - 138 = 492 + 27 = 519 | 519

ALI JURI 11 — = 495 + 17 = 512 | 512

OTHMAN MOHD 11 — = 495 - 75 = 420 + 5 = 425 | 425   450

ARAB IBRAHIM 11 — = 495 - 50 = 445 + 7 = 452 | 452   495 122½

MOHD ALI 11 — = 495 + 10 = 505 | 505   372½

SATUF EYOUB 11 — = 495 - 62½ = 432½ + 9 = 440½ | 440½   495 167½

ALI MUSTO   327 7/16

MUSTAPHA 'ISA 9 — = 405 - 50 = 355 + 7 = 362 | 362   337½

MUSTAPHA ALI 3 — = 135 + 1 = 136 | 136

XX

ALI HUSSEIN 10 — = 450 - 122½ = 327½ + 9 = 336½ + 45 = 381½   381½

HALOUF JUMA 10 — = 450 - 167½ = 282½ + 10 = 292½ + 45 = 337½   381½

HAJI HASSAN 10 — = 450 - 62½ = 387½ + 11 = 398½ + 45 = 443½   292½ 45

FARAJ SULEIMAN 10 — = 450 + 8 = 458 | 458   337½

ABD ER RAHMAN 10 — = 450 + 8 = 458 | 458   495

EYOUB HAMAIDI 10 — = 450 - 30 = 420 + 5 = 425 | 425

KRIKOR WARTAN 3 — = 135 = 135 | 135

HORUNT AWADIS 4 — = 180 - 25 = 155 + 1 = 156 | 156

HASSAN SALEH . 2 — = 90 + 1 = 91 | 91

9992½

Above Pay-day at Chagar Bazar, with Max Mallowan in Queen Mary, 1935
(photo: Richard Barnett)

Previous double page Max Mallowan's pay-book for Tell Brak (British Museum, London)

excavations, a habit that she continued year by year until her last participation
in a dig, at Nimrud, when she was sixty-eight years old.

One of her tasks now was to keep an eye on the basket-boys, some of
whom did not empty their baskets quickly enough on the dump but lounged
around wasting time, sometimes even curling up for a nap. At the end of the
week, in what she described as her role as master spy, she would report to
Max. More important, however, was her work restoring and labelling pottery.
She continued with the restoration work she had begun at Tell Arpachiyah,
and developed great skill in it. In 1936 the director of the hospital in Aleppo
and his wife, Ernest and Dora Altounyan, visited the Mallowans. They stayed
at Chagar Bazar for some days, treating the sick workmen, and Dora painted
a picture in oils of Agatha sitting in the dining-room restoring pottery. Max
was very fond of this picture because Agatha looked so happy in it.

However, Agatha's main occupation was taking and developing photographs of the dig. This activity was of such central importance that a whole
chapter is devoted to it (cf. my essay 'A dark-room has been allotted to me').
Another of her responsibilities was to organize and supervise the household
staff. Besides the Armenian chauffeur Michel, who in principle would have
liked to remove all Muslims from the face of the earth and several times tried
to do so when driving the car, they comprised the cook Dimitri and the
house-boys Ali, Ferhid, Mansur and Subri.

Over a period of months Agatha Christie tried to teach the conspicu-
ously clumsy Mansur how to set the table properly. Their mutual lack of
understanding made the relationship between him and Agatha difficult. He
would regularly use a teacloth to clean a dirty headlight on the car, because it
removed smears so well, but dried the dishes with a dirty sheet. There were

Agatha Christie supervising the workmen at Chagar Bazar

no limits to his ingenuity in laying the table: he might put forks on top of a cup and saucer, knives on the left of the plates, or two forks to the right of a plate. Mansur faced equally insoluble problems in cleaning the rooms and making beds. After scouring the enamel basins on the washstands, he would first sweep the dust vigorously up from the floor and then make the beds, which he did in one of two ways: either there would be no bedclothes covering the sleeper's feet or the sheet was half tucked under the mattress, so that it covered only part of the bed.

As the senior house-boy, Mansur was responsible for the Mallowans' personal comfort, much to Agatha's regret, for she preferred the much more intelligent and skilful Subri, who cheerfully looked after Colonel Burn and Louis Osman. His 'general appearance of ferocity' and the fact that he kept a sharpened knife under his pillow were no particular drawback, nor was the fact that he spent his holidays visiting relatives in prison, where many of them were serving sentences for murder. He was a Christian and came from Turkey, having been expelled from that country by Mustafa Kemal.

For all her understanding and tolerance, Agatha Christie's accounts of the way the house-boys did their work are written from the viewpoint of an Englishwoman who would have liked her household to be run just as it was at home.

75 ALEP - Hopital Civil

Above Postcard showing the hospital in Aleppo, Syria, 1930s (Fouad Debbas collection, Beirut)

Right Agatha Christie restoring pottery at Chagar Bazar, oil painting by Dora Altounyan, 1936

'Lemon curd is a great success'

Sometimes Agatha taught the expedition's amiable cook Dimitri how to make a new European dish. Dimitri came from Antioch, and every year he turned up punctually at the beginning of the dig, even though no one had told him the exact date. He looked forward to being with the Mallowans and to the wage he would earn, since his brother had died leaving twelve children, and Dimitri had to provide for the family. He was the only one of the household servants to carry no weapon. He was a gentle kindly man and lavished care on the many puppies of the various dogs that lived at Chagar Bazar.

In time Agatha learned which were the best dishes to try. Anything that had to be served as soon as it was ready, for instance omelettes or chips, was unsuitable, since all meals were made at least an hour in advance and kept waiting in the oven. Dimitri cooked an excellent stuffed lamb, however, and it was always served on special occasions. Agatha developed culinary ambitions of her own in the expedition's kitchen, and on one occasion tried her hand at a vanilla soufflé, which turned out remarkably well. But teaching a Syrian cook to prepare something as difficult as a soufflé demanded considerable optimism and willingness to experiment.

Left Dimitri the cook in
the expedition house kitchen
at Tell Brak, 1938
(photo: Agatha Christie)

Right Agatha Christie at home
in Winterbrook House,
Wallingford, 1950

Going shopping in Kamichlie was like an excursion back to civilization. The party would first go to 'Harrods', as they called the shop kept by a man called Yannakos, where they bought canned food, bread and wine. Meat was purchased in the form of live sheep, which grazed the land around the expeditionary house until they were slaughtered – as far from the house as possible, on Agatha's orders. Chickens were bought either ready slaughtered or still alive, in a miserable state and tied in bundles together.

The chauffeur Michel had a tendency towards thrift, *economia*, which could not be overcome. It was expressed in ridiculous purchases, for instance of 200 oranges, which were very cheap in such quantities. The fact that half the oranges were already mouldy, and in any case there were far too many for six people, did not stop him 'saving' in this way. He had a mania for driving until the petrol tank was nearly empty, even at the risk of being stranded in the middle of the desert, and he refused on principle – again for reasons of economy – to take any spare cans of petrol.

A special occasion was a visit to the post office, where the postmaster, in dirty pyjamas and unshaven, would appear only after long and intensive efforts to find him. To spare himself other visits from customers, or perhaps merely in order to appear particularly generous, he would always press on the Mallowans several other letters addressed to total strangers.

In the spring of 1937 the Mallowans began working on another dig near Chagar Bazar, at Tell Brak, and continued their work there in the spring and autumn of 1938. Tell Brak was the most imposing and important tell at the far end of Khabur. Max had already decided to investigate it when he first visited the area in 1934, but he had wished to begin with a more easily surveyed site. In the spring of 1937 both sets of excavations were conducted in parallel, an arduous task, since the archaeological teams had to change sites every other day. Agatha and Max made up one team, Colonel Burn and Louis Osman the other.

They rented a former caravanserai, which with ten rooms and a kitchen, as well as a large courtyard, made an ideal expedition house. The courtyard in particular was a great gain: the cars could be unloaded and the men paid there, and it provided space for pottery to be laid out and restored. It was adorned with ancient ceramic vessels in which Agatha sometimes put flowers, for in spring the desert became a huge sea of blooms, covering the hills with colours of every shade.

After the day's work the archaeological team often went on excursions all over northern Syria. Once, setting out from Chagar Bazar, the Mallowans, Macartney and Barnett visited Tell Halaf, the famous prehistoric pottery site at the name of which Max would always respectfully lower his voice. As Agatha said, the journey 'had something of the reverence of a pilgrimage to a shrine'. It was at Tell Halaf, a town of the sixth and fifth centuries BC, that the finest pottery of that early period had been found. For an archaeologist concerned with the prehistoric ceramics of this culture, Tell Halaf is a Mecca. It reminded Agatha of a journey to Berlin where they had met the excavator of Tell Halaf, Baron Max von Oppenheim. Poor Agatha had to spend hours in the museum listening to him and Max Mallowan arguing about dates and examining large quantities of ugly reproductions of early Tell Halaf statues, although she wanted nothing more than a chair to sit down on. At moments such as these it cannot have been easy to be an archaeologist's wife.

In the spring of 1938 Rosalind Christie, Agatha's daughter, visited the dig. She enjoyed her stay there very much, and even took an active part in the work. Unlike her mother, she was a gifted artist, and the fine drawings of Nuzi pottery she made were published in the record of the excavations.[21] With the

Agatha Christie and Max Mallowan in a field of flowers in Syria, 1938

Above Colonel Burn with house-boys packing crates in the yard of the expedition house at Tell Brak, 1938 (photo: Agatha Christie)

Right Agatha Christie and Max Mallowan on a visit to Tell Halaf, 1935 (photo: Richard Barnett)

Below The expedition house at Tell Brak, 1938 (photo: Agatha Christie)

Drawing of a forged animal figure, 1935 (British Museum, London)

architect Guilford Bell, who came out to rejoin the party in 1938 and worked on both digs, she went out riding on horseback, to the great surprise of the workmen.

The dig in Tell Brak was extremely successful, producing a quantity of objects of very high quality. In the last season of digging, during the autumn of 1938, however, there was a serious incident that clearly illustrates the potential dangers of such excavations and at the same time gives a glimpse of the mentality of the local people.

Many finds of beautiful animal amulets in stone or ivory had earned the workers plenty of *bakshish*. Since *bakshish* represented good additional earnings, the idea of the money undoubtedly induced some of the men to try their hand at forgery now and then. On the dig in Tell Brak, however, the animal amulets led to something much worse. They were found at a certain depth in a shaft that was supposed to be cut straight down from the top. However, to get at the area containing amulets as quickly as possible the men began undercutting at the bottom of the shaft, without permission and indeed against Max's express orders. During a midday break some of them crept into the shaft from the far side of the mound and went on with the undercutting, planning to say that the figures were finds from their own part of the site and earn *bakshish* for them. But the overhang broke away, burying five men, and only one of them was brought out alive. After the matter had been settled with the sheikh and the French security officer, Max posted a guard at the scene of the accident, fearing further illicit digging. He himself waited out of sight during the next day's midday break, and caught three more workmen in the act of coming to dig at the same spot. The rest of the men showed little respect for the dead, making fun of them in song and gestures. The members of the archaeological team had already noted on other occasions that death counted for very little in these countries.

'Various obscure and ambiguous [amulets] are labelled discreetly by the convenient name of "cult object" …'

At the end of the dig the director of the Service des Antiquités, Henry Seyrig, or his deputy would carry out the division of finds. In Syria, in contrast to Iraq, the excavator himself had to divide all the finds into two halves, as equal as possible in value. The director of the Service des Antiquités then came to the dig to decide which half was to remain in the museum in Aleppo. Long lists of finds in the journals of the excavations have a red S for Syria against them, as a record of their ultimate location. The process of pre-selection was agony for Max, since he had to spend days examining all the archaeological objects and was in constant fear, as he divided them up, that the best pieces might remain in Syria. To make the division as equitable as possible the objects had to be sorted by genre, and then each piece was assessed for its value and aesthetic appearance. Finally, it was up to the other members of Max's team to say which half they would choose. If the majority picked a certain half, Max, fearing it was too strong, tried to achieve a better balance by moving some of the more valuable finds to the other. After a while this game became a manic activity that concluded only with the arrival of the Frenchman appointed to make the choice. The finds were then packed in large crates and loaded on a lorry to take the Syrian half to Aleppo and the other half to be put on a ship for England. The house was boarded up and all the furniture placed in two rooms.

After their last dig in Syria in 1938 the Mallowans visited their friends Claude and Odile Schaeffer, the excavator of Ras Shamra and his wife, on the west coast of Syria, where they all spent Christmas together.[22] Like many other archaeologists, the Schaeffers remained good friends of the Mallowans. The last trip abroad that Agatha Christie ever took with her husband, in 1972, was to the Côte d'Azur, where they went – in flight from photographers – to stay with the Schaeffers.

In the autumn of 1938 the catastrophe about to overwhelm Europe was already casting its shadow before it. None of the excavators could be sure of being able to continue their activities in future. Their farewell to Syria was a particularly melancholy one that year. The war interrupted archaeological activities in the Orient for a decade. Not until 1949 did the Mallowans return, but this time to Nimrud in the north of Iraq.

Agatha wrote her account of her visit to Syria during the difficult days of the Second World War, when she and Max were apart, in order to bring those happy times back to her mind and in fear that they might be forgotten. She closes her book with the following remarks:

> I love that gentle fertile country and its simple people, who know how to laugh and how to enjoy life; who are idle and gay, and who have dignity, good manners, and a great sense of humour, and to whom death is not terrible.
>
> *Inshallah*, I shall go there again, and the things that I love shall not have perished from this earth ... Spring, 1944.[23]

NOTES

1   A. Christie, *An Autobiography*, London 1981, p. 389.
2   Ibid., p. 440.
3   In A. Christie, *Parker Pyne Investigates*, London 1934.
4   A. Christie, *Autobiography* (n. 1) p. 476.
5   British Museum, Archive ANE 196.2, p. 39.
6   Christie, *Autobiography* (n. 1), p. 479.
7   The British Museum, Archive ANE 196.2, pp. 17–27.
8   The British Museum, Archive ANE 193.3.
9   A. Christie Mallowan, *Come, Tell Me How You Live*, London 1999; M. Mallowan, *Mallowan's Memoirs*, London 1977.
10   Christie, *Come, Tell* (n. 7), p. 20.
11   The British Museum, Archive ANE 197.1, pp. 1–36.
12   Christie, *Come, Tell* (n. 7), p. 48.
13   Ibid., p. 55.
14   The British Museum, Archive ANE 196.2, p. 334.
15   The British Museum, Archive ANE 196.2, p.175.
16   The British Museum, Archive ANE 196.2, p.177.
17   Christie, *Come, Tell* (n. 7), p. 185.
18   The British Museum, Archive ANE 196.2, p. 215.
19   Christie, *Come, Tell* (n. 7), p. 85.
20   Ibid., pp. 155–6.
21   M.E.L. Mallowan, 'Excavations at Brak and Chagar Bazar', *Iraq* 9 (1947), pls 76–8.
22   Christie, *Come, Tell* (n. 7), pp. 202–3; O. Schaeffer, *Petits Souvenirs de Grandes Expeditions*, 1993, pp. 27f. (unpublished).
23   Christie, *Come, Tell* (n. 7), p. 205.

Agatha Christie, Nimrud and Baghdad

Joan Oates

In the 1930s Agatha Christie accompanied her husband Max Mallowan on his excavations at Nineveh and Arpachiyah in Iraq and on the pioneering survey and excavation he carried out in north-eastern Syria in the years just before the Second World War. Her account of these years in *Come, Tell Me How You Live* remains one of the more readable tales of life on a Middle Eastern dig.

After the war Max returned to Iraq with the intention of excavating at Nimrud, one of the capital cities of ancient Assyria where in the nineteenth century Layard had discovered royal palaces ornamented with the famous stone reliefs that now adorn the walls of the British Museum among others. Max and Agatha had visited Nimrud in the autumn of 1931, while they were working at Nineveh, and Max had decided then that Nimrud was where he would dig if he could ever afford to do so. Thus in 1949, by then holder of a new Professorship of Western Asiatic Archaeology at the Institute of Archaeology in London, he applied for and received permission from the Directorate-General of Antiquities in Baghdad to reopen British work at the site. As she had on previous digs, Agatha accompanied him to Nimrud, where for the first season they lived in somewhat primitive conditions in the sheikh's house in a nearby village, and Agatha acted as photographer as she had in the Khabur. She also helped with the cleaning and recording of antiquities, activities she continued to undertake throughout her time at Nimrud.

Nimrud was an extraordinarily beautiful place, in spring covered with wild flowers and the lush green that followed the winter rains but soon vanished with the onset of the arid summer heat. On a clear spring day one could see on the horizon the high, snow-covered mountains of Kurdistan, and herds of gazelle still roamed the fields below the tell – truly a landscape of great interest and beauty. It was at Nimrud in the early 1950s that I first came to know Max and Agatha. I was at that time a research student at the University of Cambridge and I had been encouraged by Max, then professor in London, to travel to Baghdad in order to study materials in the Iraq Museum relevant to

The ziggurat at Nimrud, with Agatha Christie to the left, 1950s (photo: Joan Oates)

the subject of my thesis. I found myself staying in the house that was then both the hostel of the British School of Archaeology in Iraq (BSAI) and the Mallowan's residence when they were in Baghdad. It was a lovely old courtyard house on the River Tigris in Karradet Mariam, with semi-underground *sirdabs* on the ground floor (rooms cooled by means of air shafts from the roof) and a balcony overlooking the Tigris where Agatha breakfasted. Another of her special culinary privileges was a large, late morning glass of pomegranate juice, carefully and lovingly pressed for her by our cook and houseboy, Ibrahim.

Max and Agatha always spent a month in Baghdad before the dig. Agatha loved the old house and delighted in buying for it local rugs, copper and other antique objects from the *suq*. Shopping in the *suq* was one of her favourite pastimes and I often accompanied her to her favourite shop, owned by Hassan Halabi, which was still in the same place and still functioning, now owned by his son, when I recently visited Baghdad (1998). She found many items irresistible and I remember, years ago, seeing large numbers of printed Persian bedspreads stored in the house in Devon. Furniture and other items inlaid with mother-of-pearl were a particular favourite, and the house in

Baghdad boasted an attractive collection of antique copper finger bowls bought by Agatha over the years. One of her greatest bargains was an out-sized Senna kilim bought in Mosul from the shop known as that of the 'Robber Baron' for eight Iraqi dinars (then £8). He had been unable to sell it owing to its unusual size, and this very beautiful trophy adorned the sitting-room of the Baghdad house for many years thereafter.

Undoubtedly her most perceptive purchases were in contemporary Iraqi art and I was often privileged to accompany her to the openings of exhibitions in Baghdad in the 1950s. This was in the days of the distinguished Iraqi painters Jawad Salim, Faiq Hasan and Akram Shukri, the latter a member of the Antiquities Department. Among her purchases were two paintings by our Antiquities Department representative in those early Nimrud days, Tariq al-Madhloum, who later wrote a Ph.D. dissertation on Neo-Assyrian art under Max in London, and who is himself now a most distinguished painter and sculptor, still working and teaching in Baghdad.

In 1956 the BSAI moved to a larger house in Karradet Mariam, where my husband David and I were to live for a number of happy years in the 1960s. Both the earlier school residence and this house were situated on the west bank of the Tigris, across the river from the main shopping area, and both adjoined steps down to the river's edge from which the local boatman would row us across to the other side and the joys of shopping in Rashid Street or in the *suq*. The new house was much larger and had two balconies overlooking the Tigris, ornate ceilings decorated with coloured glass inlay, and a courtyard with four orange trees. The main living-rooms were on the upper floor and circulation was by means of an internal balcony surrounding the courtyard. The house was ideal for archaeologists, with plenty of room on the ground floor for the storage of tents and equipment; it also served well for entertaining with its large rooms and balconies over the Tigris. The furniture and curtains, brought from the old house, still featured many items acquired in the late 1940s from a still surviving courtyard house across the river, lived in during the war by the archaeologist and then Adviser to the Antiquities Department, Seton Lloyd. We all loved the new house, which was bright and sunny in the winter, while the open-air plan and *sirdabs* made it tolerably cool even in the summer, when in the evening there was always a breeze off the river. There was also an incomparable view of the old city.

Both David and I spent many seasons with the Mallowans at Nimrud, travelling from Baghdad up to Mosul on the night train with our bedrolls wrapped in colourful *jajims*, woven in southern Iraq and purchased by Agatha on her many trips to the *suq*. Agatha liked Nimrud and in many small ways added greatly to the comfort of the younger dig staff. First and foremost was the food which she herself much enjoyed and to which she personally

Above The first house of the British School of Archaeology in Iraq, Baghdad, 1955
(photo: Agatha Christie)

Left Agatha Christie on the balcony of the first house of the British School of Archaeology in
Iraq, Baghdad

Previous double page The light railway at Nimrud, 1950s (photo: Agatha Christie)

contributed the luxury elements – including the lashings of rich water buffalo
cream on the hot chocolate soufflés miraculously baked by our Indian cook in
a kerosene-heated box oven. She paid for the taxi that carried her, and fortunate younger dig staff, on our Friday trips to see archaeological sites and the
countryside. The rest travelled in the old Dodge bought by Robert Hamilton
in 1948. She also hired and paid for the cook, though this was never without its
difficulties. There were many excellent Indian cooks in Baghdad, most of
whom had arrived as young boys with the Indian Army in 1917. Indeed, one of
our ancient servants, Sandu, proudly claimed to have saved the army when it
ran out of flour at the siege of Kut, by instructing them in the preparation of
the local unleavened bread. There was a cooks' coffee-house in Baghdad by the
river in Abu Nawas, to which Ibrahim would be dispatched each year to find a
suitable cook for the dig. Ibrahim himself was a first-class cook but he did not
enjoy the discomforts of the countryside and much preferred to stay in Baghdad as protector and defender of the household (as he once literally was, in July
1958, with the assistance of a gun which had once belonged to Seton Lloyd).
The problem in finding a cook lay not only in the fact that he would have to
survive in the wilds of the north and a somewhat inadequate kitchen but that
any wholly reliable and first-class Baghdad cook was always in full-time

Courtyard of the first house of the British School of Archaeology in Iraq, Baghdad, 1954
(photo: Agatha Christie)

employment. Those who frequented the coffee-house were more than likely
to be either overly fond of the bottle or mentally less than stable – sometimes
both. We always managed very well, nonetheless, with delicious and often
lavish meals. In addition to the soufflés and buffalo cream, I remember especially pilaus covered with crisp fried onions, almonds and raisins, and the
inevitable but delicious turkey dinners, the sources of which wandered about
the dig house courtyard. Often, however, the driver Petros, a man of considerable physical stature, was called upon to ration the cook's arak, at least until
dinner was successfully served; even an episode of madness, when the then
cook became persuaded that Max was indeed the Almighty, was turned to
good effect by 'the Almighty' decreeing that dinner should be prepared daily.
Agatha was also well-versed in medicine, having worked as a dispenser during
the First World War, and had her own favourite remedies, including the very
effective combination of kaolin (china clay) and brandy, which she dispensed
freely to the younger members of the dig staff on the rare occasions when they
were struck down with diarrhoea.

The Nimrud camp consisted of a mud-brick dig house and a row of
tents in which we slept, pitched at a right angle to the south end of the house.
Max and Agatha headed the queue of tents, next to the house, followed in the

Balcony above the courtyard of the second house of the British School of Archaeology in Iraq, Baghdad (photo: Joan Oates)

early years by Barbara Parker and myself. The water for the house and the workmen came from the Tigris, some 4 kilometres away, carried in metal water cans by two donkeys who were paid a workman's wage for plodding back and forth all day long. The water for the house was filtered through a large pottery vessel, from which it emerged crystal clear but hardly safe to drink. In theory it was then boiled in the kitchen, but one year the water seemed unusually delicious and we were somewhat startled to discover, as we were packing at the end of the season, that it had never been boiled at all. Baths were a once-a-week luxury, the water heated on a primus stove and poured into a large Victorian hip bath, which had been installed in a purpose-built, mud-brick bathhouse. Unfortunately, and occasionally rather startlingly, the cold water which was added to the hot still contained the odd frog or fish, and I remember one lady visitor who was more than a little startled to find a brightly striped lizard occupying the bath before her. A jug of hot water was supplied to everyone's tent both in the early morning and before dinner, the early morning ritual accompanied by a very welcome cup of tea. Max and Agatha always dressed for dinner, and the rest of us turned up at least cleaner than before. Work often continued after dinner, especially in the periods of large finds of ivory objects, with electricity supplied by a generator borrowed, along with much other equipment, from the Iraq Petroleum Company, whose Kirkuk establishment Max 'raided' at the beginning of each season.

The dig house had a kitchen, the domain of the cook and house boy (whose evening conversations, driver included, often focused on the various Christian heresies about which they were remarkably well informed); a large living- and dining-room; an office, where Max paid the workmen and which he shared with the epigraphist; and two large workrooms, the first serving also as the drawing office. The rooms were surrounded by mud-brick benches, which served for seating covered with the ever-present and colourful *jajims*, and could literally be cut down to insert drawing boards or other equipment, as mud-brick is such a wonderfully versatile construction medium. In the far corner of the end room was a dark-room where Agatha sometimes helped with the developing. She continued to assist in the cleaning of objects when

Second house of the British School of Archaeology in Iraq, Baghdad (photo: Joan Oates)

the dig staff were overworked, making a major contribution to conservation in suggesting that the final cleaning of the ivories should be done with hand lotion to prevent unnecessary drying of the surface. Undoubtedly her greatest contribution to archaeology, however, and a tribute to her great patience and perseverance, was her almost single-handed reconstruction of over thirty wood and ivory writing boards recovered from a well in 1953, in hundreds of small and very similar fragments – just the sort of jigsaw puzzle she loved. At the end of the house was a separate small room, built at her own expense, where Agatha kept her clothes (including the fur jacket she wore to dinner on cool evenings) and her typewriter, and where she worked on her books and attempted to conceal her presence from the many visitors whose major interest, regrettably, was more in her presence than in the archaeology. The writing of her autobiography was in fact begun in this small room.

Quweir ferry in Baghdad, 1950s (photo: Agatha Christie)

Top Covering up inscriptions at Nimrud, 1950s (photo: Agatha Christie)

Above Agatha Christie, Max Mallowan and Barbara Parker investigating ceramics
(photo: Donald Wiseman)

Previous double page Workman and excavation baskets at Nimrud, 1950s (photo: Agatha Christie)

Top Washing pottery in front of the dig-house at Nimrud, 1950s (photo: Agatha Christie)

Above Working on the dig-house at Nimrud, 1950s (photo: Agatha Christie)

Following double page Expedition tents at Nimrud, 1950s (photo: Agatha Christie)

THE ILLUSTRATED LONDON NEWS

©1957. THE ILLUSTRATED LONDON NEWS & SKETCH LTD. *The World Copyright of all the Editorial Matter, both Illustrations and Letterpress, is Strictly Reserved.*

SATURDAY, NOVEMBER 23, 1957.

A GOD OR PRINCE PLUCKING THE FLOWERING LOTUS : ONE OF A SERIES OF SUPERB IVORIES FOUND IN A HITHERTO UNTOUCHED ASSYRIAN PALACE AT NIMRUD.

This magnificent ivory is one of a remarkable group, perhaps the finest yet known and some of them unique, which will be illustrated in full in the second of a series of articles (beginning in this issue) by Professor M. E. L. Mallowan. The articles, which will be continued in our next two issues, concern the exceptionally rich harvest of the 1957 excavations at Nimrud by the British School of Archæology in Iraq, conducted by Professor Mallowan. A new site has been discovered, named by the excavators "Fort Shalmaneser," which seems to have remained undisturbed since its destruction in 612 B.C.; and it is believed that even more of these magnificent works await the spade. This particular example measures about 10 ins. by 4½ ins. (25.2 by 11.5 cm.), and it is shown after its cleaning by Sayid Akram Shukri in the Iraq Museum laboratories. It is now in the Iraq Museum. [*Photograph by Antran.*]

Postage—*Inland*, 4d. ; *Canada*, 1½d. ; *Elsewhere Abroad*, 5½d. (These rates apply as The Illustrated London News *is registered at the G.P.O. as a newspaper.*)

Ivory relief from Nimrud with bearded man and tree of life (*Illustrated London News*, 23 November, 1957)

Writing-boards from the North-West Palace at Nimrud, ivory and wax, 720–710 BC, height 34 cm
(British Museum, London)

Envelope addressed to Mrs Mallowan (Agatha Christie), 25 March 1952 (John Mallowan, London)

Arbil, Iraq, 1950s (photo: Agatha Christie)

Visit to Telul-eth-Thalathat, a Japanese excavation in Iraq, 1956, with Agatha Christie on the left and Max Mallowan in the middle

Aqrah, Iraq, 1953 (photo: Agatha Christie)

Spring at Nimrud, 1953 (photo: Agatha Christie)

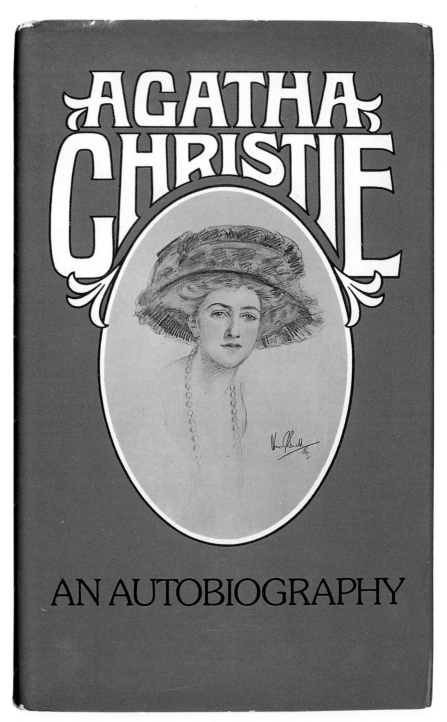

Above Jacket of the first edition of Agatha Christie's autobiography (HarperCollins 1977)

Right The Nabu Temple at Nimrud, Agatha Christie lying in the background, 1956 (photo: Joan Oates)

Agatha loved the wild flowers in the spring and often wandered into the nearby fields to pick them for the dig house. Wild tulips, irises, anemones and poppies were among the most spectacular. The birds too attracted her attention, especially the very colourful bee-eaters and rollers. She also enjoyed walking about the dig, at her own pace, often photographing its most interesting aspects – and especially the workmen, the flowers and the dogs. On Fridays Max organized day-trips, when we travelled all over north-eastern Iraq, pursuing both archaeological and scenic interests. Agatha was always willing to walk anywhere, however far, though she and her ever-present shooting-stick often lagged far behind. But she never gave up.

Evenings on the dig were enlivened by mathematical games, in which few of us were able to keep pace with her. There was also a most respectable library, enlarged each year by the books sent out for the dig by her publisher. Serious archaeological reading was served by the library of the School in Baghdad, much of which was transported to Nimrud each season. Never averse to betting, Agatha turned her attention from her own books once a season to run a sweepstake on the Grand National, the results of course arriving some days late in *The Times*, to which she regularly subscribed, even in Baghdad. The fine quality paper of the airmail edition was especially welcome when it came to packing the antiquities at the end of the season. Among the yearly entertainments were the annual poems, presented always on the morning of Easter Sunday. These were composed and typed by Agatha in the privacy of her own room, and concerned incidents on the dig or the foibles of the dig staff. There was always one for each member of the staff, including Max. Occasionally there were longer poems, often in the style of Lewis Carroll or in biblical cadence. One of my favourites was the Psalm to Toto in Calah, Calah being the biblical name of Nimrud (Assyrian Kalhu), while Toto was a local sheepdog adopted by Agatha and devoted to her. Unfortunately he cared rather less for the rest of us, including Max, often fiercely barring our way at night to the 'battlements', the primitive but not inadequate amenities on the city wall, not far from the tents. Agatha could never understand that some members of the dig staff were less devoted to Toto than she was. When I was last at Nineveh, Toto's offspring were still guarding the Nineveh dig house, and their presence, as descendants of Agatha's 'English' dog, was as important a local feature as the excavations.

Nimrud would not have been the same without Agatha. Certainly those of us who were there remember her with great affection.

'A dark-room has been allotted to me ...': Photography and Filming by Agatha Christie on the Excavation Sites

Charlotte Trümpler

We are relatively well informed about Agatha Christie's life in the Orient, and in particular about the digs, from her two autobiographical works and Max Mallowan's memoirs. These books, and the reports on his excavations in which Max gives a detailed account of who was responsible for which tasks, convey an excellent idea of Agatha's own activities.

Almost unknown until now, however, are certain other sources that form a very useful complement to the written material. They consist of a wealth of photographs, some of them extremely good: black and white prints and colour transparencies taken by Agatha Christie in the 1930s in Syria, and in Iraq after the war between 1948 and 1958. Even more sensational was the discovery of two 16-mm films, each running for forty-five minutes, which she shot on the excavation sites before and after the war. Both are of outstanding quality and in many respects are rarities. First, it is an unusual stroke of luck for a writer to have left not only her written memoirs but also filmed documentation to illustrate them. Second, the films represent a valuable record of a time now gone, and the first in particular, dating from the 1930s, shows a world in which it was still possible for different ethnic and religious groups to co-exist in close proximity. The really interesting feature is that these films do not simply record the excavations, showing the finds made and the levels uncovered, but also provide a unique and humorous account of everyday life on a dig. These fascinating pictorial documents were made only because Agatha was not an archaeologist herself, yet she had helped with the work on the site. In this way she maintained a certain distance from the archaeology but could still follow the course of the excavations from the viewpoint of an insider.

Although Agatha paid her own travel costs and her living expenses on the digs, she worked hard with the other members of the team when required.[1] Besides restoring pottery, her main occupation was taking and developing photographs of the excavations. The first mention of this activity of hers is in Max's foreword to his account of the excavations at Tell Arpachiyah in 1933, where he wrote that Agatha was responsible for developing and enlarging the photographs.[2] Agatha's own account of this dig says nothing about her photography; instead, she dwells exclusively on her restoration and drawing of pottery, the former an occupation she greatly enjoyed. It seems almost certain, then, that in this first season she was not yet taking photographs on the dig herself, and was involved in laboratory work only to a limited extent.

Since the beginnings of photography in the middle of the nineteenth century, photographs have been of incalculable value for archaeology.[3] This is partly because archaeological monuments were and are extremely attractive in themselves, and have therefore always provided desirable subjects for photographers.[4] Another reason is that photographs are indispensable for the scientific documentation of a dig, recording conditions that will be irrecoverably lost during the excavation process. Every dig destroys a cultural legacy. This loss can be compensated for only if as accurate and precise a record as possible is made of the state of the site as it was at the time of excavation. To this day, however, widely differing views are held about the importance of photography to archaeological digs. While some excavations are photographed with every technical method available, and an expert photographer is part of the team, other expeditions still economize in this area and take 'snapshots' without professional assistance.

In Max Mallowan's small-scale excavations he obviously set store by accurate documentation, but the financial means at his disposal did not allow an expensive photographic operation. In general, all important finds were photographed, but only from one angle – as was usual at the time – and in restoration work only one process was generally recorded. For pragmatic reasons, again, only a single photograph was usually taken of the state of any given site at the time of excavation. It was different after the war, and Max valued the medium of photography more highly in the major excavations at Nimrud.

Laboratory work was thus of great importance, for directly after photographs had been taken it was possible to check whether the pictures, for instance of a particular level, had been taken correctly before digging

Workmen at Chagar Bazar

28

IN ACCOUNT WITH THE TRUSTEES OF THE PERCY SLADEN MEMORIAL FUND.

ARPACHIYAH EXPEDITION EXPENDITURE. 1933.

1. Expenditure on journeys between London and Mosul by M.E.L. Mallowan

and J.Cruikshank Rose, architect to the Expedition.   £.   S.   D.

Jan. 16. Two through tickets from London to Baghdad.   88.   2.   9.

18. Hotel bill at Trieste.   2.

20. Tips on boat.   1.

Deck chairs.   4.

21. Car from Jaffa to Damascus.   4.

Meals on trains, tips, porters.   4.

22. Nairn desert transport. Excess baggage.   1. 13.   4.

Hotel bill in Damascus.   1.   5.

16. Baggage insurance to Mosul.   1.   4.

26.-Feb 1. Hotel bill in Baghdad: 10Dinars,800f.   10. 16.

Feb. 2-10. Hotel bill in Mosul. 9D. 873f.   18. 17.   5.

1. Fares from Baghdad to Mosul. 2D. 70f.   2.   9.   5.

Bedding, excess baggage, car from Baiji to Mosul. 1. 10.   10.

Porterage and taxis. 500fils.   10.   0.

May. 19. Mosul. Hotel bill for one day. 1D. 172f.   1.   3.   5.

23. Car from Mosul to Baghdad and expeditions to

neighbouring archaeological sites. 12D. 888f.   12. 17.   10.

24. Rose: Hotel bill in Baghdad 4 days.7D. 201f.   7.   4.   0.

Thos Cook. 2 tickets Baghdad-London.94D. 860f.   94. 17.   2.

25. Nairn desert transport. Excess baggage.   1.   5.   8.

26. Hotel bill in Beirut. 1322 Piasters.   1. 14.   0.

Tips on boat, landing Marseilles, excess luggage 4.

Meals in train through France & porterage.   2. 15.

2 Taxis on arrival in London (1 to Muswell Hill 1.   0.

£265 - 9s - 10

Expense account for the dig at Tell Arpachiyah, 1933 (British Museum, London)

continued. In addition, it was necessary to ensure that the finds were properly documented, since half of them would be staying in the country where they had been excavated.

In the introduction to his account of the survey of the Khabur region in 1934 and the first dig at Chagar Bazar in 1935, Max acknowledged the contribution made by his wife, who had been present throughout and helped both with the restoration of pottery and with photography.[5] Agatha, who certainly also took photographs of her own at Chagar Bazar, wrote in *Come, Tell Me How You Live* about her laboratory work in the expedition house in Amuda:

> I am now quite busy. In addition to repairing pottery, there is the photography – a 'dark-room' has been allotted to me. It somewhat resembles the 'Little Ease' of medieval times. In it, one can neither sit nor stand! Crawling in on all fours, I develop plates, kneeling with bent head. I come out practically asphyxiated with heat and unable to stand upright.[6]

She added a mild complaint to the effect that no one paid much attention to her sufferings, since Max was much more interested in the results than in the trouble she had taken with her work.

The first definite mention of Agatha's taking photographs on the dig herself occurs in Max's report on the 1936 season at Chagar Bazar, where he says that his wife was largely responsible for the restoration of pottery and the photographs taken on the site.[7] Her own comments on this second campaign at Chagar Bazar are confined to the remark that the dark-room in the newly built expeditionary house was more comfortable than the facilities in Amuda, since it had a chair and a table and she could stand upright in it.[8] The drawback of this recently built room was that the walls were covered with fungi growing on the mud-bricks, which were still damp. It is easy to guess that this was not in fact very comfortable, and made breathing difficult. In the high daytime temperatures that could be reached in the Syrian desert even in the spring, working in this stifling room must have been a torment.

In his report on the excavations during the following seasons at Chagar Bazar and Tell Brak in 1937 and 1938 Max again wrote in his acknowledgements that Agatha had taken all the photographs of the dig, and was an indispensable help in other fields as well.[9] This bears out the comment in Agatha's own account: 'There are a lot of photographs to be taken and developed.' In the same section she also, for once, gave a fuller account of part of her working procedure, describing the way in which she managed to clean the water she used:

Left Agatha Christie taking photographs at Nimrud

Right The Zeiss Ikon 551/6 camera used by Agatha Christie before the Second World War

Below The Leica DRP III with various lenses used by Agatha Christie before and after the Second World War

The staff is kept busy supplying me with comparatively pure water. The grosser mud is first strained off, and it is finally strained through cotton wool into various buckets. By the time it is actually used for the negatives, only stray sand and dust from the air have got in, and the results are quite satisfactory.[10]

The photographers of the nineteenth century had already spoken of the difficulty often encountered in the desert of keeping the water for developing negatives as clean as possible, free of sand and dust, complaining that the wind kept casting desert sand on the prepared plates, and the dirty waters of the Nile used to wash them made it difficult to produce clean work.[11] To avoid the worst of the heat Agatha began work on the photographs at six in the morning. Another reason for this early start was so that she could deal with the large number of negatives, which were particularly numerous at the end of a digging season. The water also became too hot later in the day, and was no use for laboratory work then.

It was probably in 1937 that Agatha took a course at the Reinhardt School of Commercial Photography in London.[12] The idea came from her daughter

Rosalind and Rosalind's friend; both girls were interested in training as photographic models and had thought of enrolling at the Reinhardt School. The course in commercial photography, however, taught photographers to make their subjects look as little like the real thing as possible. Agatha enjoyed the experimental aspect of the work; she was fascinated by the artistic freedom of photographing, for instance, only half a face, and she was also impressed by the many technical possibilities available.

Max, however, did not like the idea that on a dig Agatha might take blurred and only partially visible pictures of objects instead of accurate photographs, true to life, in the right perspective and accompanied by a scale rod. She wrote humorously: 'I sighed. I could see I had been betrayed by my artistic fancies into straying from what I had promised to do.'[13] She asked her instructor at the Reinhardt School to give her extra lessons in taking photographs in correct perspective. An interesting point in this respect is Agatha's comment that when taking the course she learned always to photograph an object several times, never just once.

The photographs from Tell Brak, taken in 1938, are of better quality than those from Chagar Bazar, and show different subjects. At Chagar Bazar Agatha mainly recorded the excavations and work on the building of the expedition house. There are no close-ups of human beings, whom she photographed only on the site of the dig and from a distance. At Tell Brak she began taking pictures of people and animals from quite close up, deliberately arranging her compositions. She assembled the domestic staff in the interior courtyard of the house, for instance, and photographed them as a complete group. She took interiors: the cook standing beside his kitchen shelves, favouring the camera with a friendly smile, and the archaeologists at supper in the dining-room. She also took several views of the expeditionary house, trying to work with perspective and construct her pictures to fill the space available. It is clear that her pleasure in photography was increasing, and she was becoming more confident in her handling of the camera. Now and then the willingness to experiment that had given her such pleasure on the course at the Reinhardt School shows through, for instance in the photograph of several food containers. Before the war she used a Zeiss Ikon (Niko, Compur) and a Leica DRP with different lenses: a wide-angle lens, a 50-mm lens and a 90-mm telephoto lens. The cameras are still in the possession of her family today.

The idea of making a film probably also originated with the Reinhardt School of Commercial Photography. It is certainly a fact that in the spring of 1938 Agatha shot a film at Tell Brak and Chagar Bazar which, interestingly, consists of alternating black and white and colour sequences, given short subtitles at her suggestion. This use of colour in an amateur film is surprisingly early, and once again is evidence of Agatha's willingness to experiment. She used a Kodak camera (SET), a USA Kodak 237 FK, which had a magazine for a 16-mm Kodachrome film 15 metres in length. If we consider that the first commercial Kodachrome films in 16-mm format did not come on the market in America until 1935, this must be among the first privately made colour films.[14] Agatha had obviously discovered the pleasure of using colour at the Reinhardt School of Commercial Photography, where she experimented with red, green and yellow filters to achieve different effects. We can date this film to the spring of 1938, since her daughter Rosalind appears in it, and she was taking part in the current campaign at Tell Brak at the time. Curiously enough, Agatha mentioned neither this film nor the one she made in Nimrud in the 1950s in her memoirs.

The film – a treasure trove to all lovers of the early amateur film – shows pictorial subjects similar to those in the photographs, but in even wider variety. Although the dig is shown in different ways, this is not so much a film of the excavations as a record of the country, of everyday life on the site and of animals. Animals – dogs in particular – were Agatha's great passion. Her love of dogs runs right through her books, her photographs and the film, in which her fondness for them is particularly clear. Several long sequences show dogs scuffling or fighting, playing, eating and sleeping. Like her autobiography, the film

A dog called Hiyou at Tell Brak (photo: Agatha Christie)

The household staff – Dimitri, Mansur, Subri, Ali, Ferhid and Michel – at Tell Brak, 1938
(photo: Agatha Christie)

also illustrates Agatha's great interest in the local people, especially their daily lives. The fact that this film shows such a wide variety of subject matter and decidedly diverse impressions of the countryside and its inhabitants is due to her highly developed sense of curiosity and her gift for precise observation. She presents her material in a manner that is both cool and humorous.

She filmed the workmen on the dig with the affection evident in her written accounts of them, but she also makes a telling and accurate record of their varying degrees of skill as they went about their tasks, and many of the situations are amusing. Indeed, the film becomes comic in almost Chaplinesque style when she shows the tedious packing of the finds in crates to be taken by lorry to the museum in Aleppo. Since the workmen had not calculated the height of the gateway of the expedition house in Tell Brak in advance, the vehicle got stuck in it and had to be reloaded.

Pay-day in the inner courtyard of the expedition house is another entertaining scene. The workmen all gathered in the small courtyard and passed the time cracking jokes as they waited. Rather than intimidating them, the camera seemed to amuse them and inspire them to further theatrical performances. Scenes of the beginning of digging and the end of the day's work, known as

Food containers from Tell Brak, 1938 (photo: Agatha Christie)

fidos, reflect the descriptions in Agatha Christie's book about the years of excavation in Syria in every detail. In the evening the workmen would throw their baskets into the air and run down the mound and all the way home, even though they sometimes had to cover several kilometres.

Favourite subjects in both book and film are the moments when the car got stuck. In the very difficult conditions when tracks were turned by rain into stretches of mud, and with the unpredictable driving abilities of the local chauffeurs, sticking in soft ground was a constant danger. Now and then the Mallowans were stranded in the desert for up to two days and had to spend the night in the car. The film shows Queen Mary being hauled relatively quickly out of a ditch full of water on a stout rope after several previous attempts. Even Rosalind is seen lending a hand on the rope, which must have been entirely beyond the comprehension of the indigenous workmen. One rather lovely sequence records an outing in a flowering meadow, with various members of the expedition picking flowers and weaving them into garlands.

In 1938 the Mallowans left Syria, and they did not return to the Orient until 1948, this time to Baghdad. Max began his excavations at Nimrud in the following year, 1949, and directed them until 1958. We have a wealth of black

Above Loading up the crates containing archaeological finds. Stills from the film made by Agatha Christie at Tell Brak in 1938

and white photographs and colour transparencies from this period in Iraq, and also another film. Both the film and the photographs record life in Iraq and on the dig.

Agatha bought herself a new camera with a flash in 1951, through an American agent, but she also continued using the Leica that had served her well in Tell Brak before the war. The first of Agatha's colour transparencies date from 1952, when she was using her new camera at Nimrud. This date can be regarded as certain, since it is confirmed by a comment in Max's memoirs. In the chapter on Nimrud he wrote that in 1951 Allen and Lettice Lane, owners of Penguin Books and friends of the Mallowans, visited the dig. They came just when the Ashurnasirpal stela had been found, but unfortunately, says Max, they had run out of colour film and could not take colour pictures of the new discovery. Obviously Agatha was not yet using colour for still photographs at this point. Mallowan adds that archaeological documentation in colour was in its infancy at the time, and they were the first to use it at Nimrud.[15] However, this comment is not correct. Walter Andrae, who had excavated on behalf of the German Oriental Society in Assur, was producing colour transparencies there as early as 1909–10, a time when they were indeed sensational.[16]

Above Driving Queen Mary through the flowering desert. Stills from the film made by Agatha Christie at Tell Brak in 1938

Left Head from the Grey Eye Temple at Tell Brak, 3500–3300 BC (British Museum, London; photo: Agatha Christie)

Lettice and Allen Lane (of Penguin Books) outside an expedition tent at Nimrud, 3 April 1951 (photo: Agatha Christie)

Interestingly, Agatha used colour photography principally for ethnological shots, landscapes and places she had visited on excursions. Her pictures of the excavations, the expedition house and the people on the dig in Nimrud are very rarely in colour. Like her written accounts, her many photographs show how fascinated she was by the variety of ethnic groups in the area and their foreign way of life. Peoples of all nationalities had already interested her before the war, and in Iraq they became her main subject for photographs and films. While her pre-war photographs had been largely confined to the workmen on the digs, in Iraq in the 1950s she took pictures of nomads, Arabs, Kurds, Yezidis – those gentle 'devil-worshippers' – and Orthodox clergy. It is interesting to note that she did not film or take photographs of indigenous women until the 1950s. For some ethnic groups, for instance Arab women, this would have been out of the question before the war, although the self-assured Kurdish women would surely not have shrunk from the camera. It is possible that

Above right A Lamassu at Nimrud, 1949? (photo: Agatha Christie)

Right Worker on the dig at Nimrud, 1950s (photo: Agatha Christie)

Agatha herself was more cautious in her approach before the war than after it. The colours of the transparencies, fortunately, have survived extremely well and retain much of their original brilliance; they have clearly been carefully conserved.

As with the pre-war accounts of excavations, Max recorded in his articles on Nimrud exactly what Agatha's contribution to the dig had been and what her responsibilities were. In his foreword to his report on the dig in 1949 he mentioned the fact that Agatha alone was responsible for the laboratory work that year, while in the following years she only helped when necessary. He also expressly mentioned that from 1950 the epigraphist Barbara Parker took all the photographs on the site.[17] Agatha herself, who gave only a brief account of her time in Nimrud, mentioned her work as photographic assistant merely in passing. Since the Mallowans were still living in a rented house with their archaeological assistant Robert Hamilton in 1949, the first year of the Nimrud excavations, and it had no dark-room of its own, photographs had to be developed in the dining-room. Max and Robert Hamilton used to go up to the first-floor rooms to talk. As they paced up and down during their

Left Boy with basket at Nimrud, 1950s (photo: Agatha Christie)

Below Boy at Balawat, 1956 (photo: Agatha Christie)

conversations, plaster was always falling off the ceiling on the pictures and into the developing dish, much to Agatha's annoyance, since it made the work much more difficult.[18] In the expedition house built in 1950 a room was specially set aside for the purpose: 'the usual dog-hole in which the wretched photographer had to develop and do loading,'[19] as Agatha wrote.

Since she was no longer responsible for the photographs of the dig she could now experiment, particularly when photographing the excavations themselves, choosing subjects which offered especially interesting scenes. At last she was free of the obligation to take photographs as accurately as possible and in the correct perspective. Photographs of the excavations, almost all in black and white, concentrate in particular on such large objects as the Lamassu creatures, taken from all possible angles, or stelae with inscriptions which were documented as the finds were conserved. Favourite subjects are workmen sitting, standing or resting in unconventional attitudes beside a pit in the excavations.

The film Agatha made of the dig at Nimrud in 1952 and 1957, set around the expedition house, again gives an extraordinarily valuable insight into the everyday life of an archaeological excavation. Unlike the earlier film, this one documents the dig itself very well. It records the finds made on the site, the workmen digging and the excavation of the well in which fine ivories were found. Technical equipment such as the light railway also appears twice in the film. A donkey with cans on its back and large pottery jars from which the workmen drink shows how the water supply had to be organized on the dig. A very long sequence records the building of a large kiln for baking clay tablets with cuneiform inscriptions, which emerged from the excavations damp and had to be fired to preserve them if they were not to fall apart. The provision of food is illustrated by scenes showing women baking and making flat bread on a hearth beside the house. The turkeys cheerfully running about provided a cheap supply of meat and also supplemented the menu on special occasions when they were cooked in more elaborate ways.

The men and women of the archaeological team are shown occupied in various different activities around the house, for instance measuring a huge food container. Almost at the end of the film, someone shot Agatha herself standing at a small table in a red dress, rather overlit. Naturally very shy, and always inclined to shun the media, she was only very occasionally to be persuaded into a television interview. This small, private film sequence is therefore a particularly valuable rarity, showing Agatha in the Orient she loved so much.

Right Visitor with small child at Nimrud, 1950s (photo: Agatha Christie)

Following page Workman uncovering pottery at Nimrud, 1950s (photo: Agatha Christie)

These photographs and films offer a glimpse into a small, self-contained world in the Middle East – a glimpse that is unique if one leaves aside scientific pre-war photographs. They bear witness to the adventure of archaeology, an image still attractive to this day. Agatha Christie succeeded in bringing that world to life before our eyes in both words and pictures. The title of her memoir of her time in Syria, *Come, Tell Me How You Live*, suggests where her main interest lay: she wanted to show the daily life of archaeologists on a dig, but at the same time she wished to demolish prejudices and persuade people to revise their opinions. Through the cool yet affectionate vision of a traveller who first visited the Orient as a tourist in 1928 and later spent long periods living and working there, we can gain a unique view of the people, the life and the landscape of what is now a partially extinct culture, in a region of the world to which access is difficult today. Since she was not a professional photographer or scholar, an archaeologist or a missionary, she could leave a more objective record than those of most western visitors to these countries.[20]

Previous page Prop for photographing objects at Nimrud (photo: Agatha Christie)

Left Barbara Parker taking photographs of the Ashurnasirpal stela, Nimrud, 1951 (photo: Agatha Christie)

Below Agatha Christie photographing pottery at Nimrud (*Jasmin* 1, 1971)

Excursion in Iraq, 1950s (photo: Agatha Christie)

Sweetmeat seller in Baghdad, 1950s (photo: Agatha Christie)

Above and below Kurds in Iraq, 1950s (photo: Agatha Christie)

Above Unearthing a Lamassu at Nimrud, 1949? (photo: Agatha Christie)

Previous double page Archaeological finds outside the expedition house at Nimrud, 1950s (photo: Agatha Christie)

Below left Light railway. Still from the film made by Agatha Christie at Nimrud in 1952/7

Below right Agatha Christie at a surveyor's table, with Tariq Madhloum on her left. Still from the film made by Agatha Christie at Nimrud in 1952/7

NOTES

1   The British Museum, Archive ANE 196.2, p. 28. The travelling expenses listed are for Max Mallowan and Cruikshank Rose only.

2   M.E.L. Mallowan and J.C. Rose, 'Excavations at Tall Arpachiyah, 1933' in *Iraq* 2 (1933), p. 1.

3   A. Faden, 'Fotografie und archäologische Forschung im 19. Jahrhundert – Voraussetzungen, Anfänge und weitere Entwicklungen', Tübingen 1991, pp. 8f. (unpublished doctoral thesis); F. Schubert and S. Grunauer von Hoerschelmann, *Archäologie und Photographie*, Mainz 1978, pp. 11ff.

4   For instance B. von Dewitz and K. Schuller-Procopovici (eds), *Die Reise zum Nil. Maxime Du Camp und Gustave Flaubert in Ägypten, Palästina und Syrien*, exh. cat., Cologne 1997.

5   M.E.L. Mallowan, 'Excavations at Chagar Bazar and an Archaeological Survey of the Habur Region of North Syria', *Iraq* 3 (1936), p. 1.

6   A. Christie Mallowan, *Come, Tell Me How You Live*, London 1999, p. 111.

7   M.E.L. Mallowan, 'Excavations at Chagar Bazar and an Archaeological Survey of the Habur Region, Second Campaign', *Iraq* 4 (1937), p. 91.

8   Christie, *Come, Tell* (n. 6), pp. 136–7.

9   M.E.L. Mallowan, 'Excavations at Brak and Chagar Bazar', *Iraq* 9 (1947), p. 8.

10   Christie, *Come, Tell* (n. 6), p. 154.

11   Schubert and Grunauer, *Archäologie* (n. 3), p.18.

12   A. Christie, *An Autobiography*, London 1981, pp. 494–6.

13   Christie, *Autobiography* (n. 12), p. 496.

14   M. Kuball, *Familienkino. Geschichte des Amateurfilms in Deutschland 2, 1931–1960*, Hamburg 1980, p. 127.

15   M. Mallowan, *Mallowan's Memoirs*, London 1977, p. 289.

16   J. Marzahn, 'Farbe in Assur. Frühe Diapositive in der Archäologie (1909–1910), *Mitteilungen der Deutschen Orient-Gesellschaft* (1998), pp. 223–39.

17   M.E.L. Mallowan, 'Excavations at Nimrud, 1949–1950, *Iraq* 12 (1950), p. 152; idem, 'The Excavations at Nimrud (Kalhu) 1951', *Iraq* 14 (1952), p. 2; idem, 'The Excavations at Nimrud (Kalhu) 1953', *Iraq* 15 (1953), p. 62.

18   Christie, *Autobiography* (n. 12), p. 542.

19   Ibid., p. 543.

20   B. Turner, 'Der Orient im Objektiv', in T. Theye (ed.), *Der geraubte Schatten. Die Photographie als ethnographisches Dokument*, exh. cat., Munich 1989, pp. 204ff.

Travelling

From Orient Express to Desert Bus: Agatha Christie's Travels in the Near East

Axel Heimsoth

In 1928 Agatha Christie, who had been planning to visit the West Indies, suddenly decided to go to Baghdad in Iraq instead. She was embarking on a whole new chapter of her life, one that would be notable not least for her many travels in the Near East with Max Mallowan, soon to become her husband. Agatha and Max used many different means of transport, and they travelled in regions where access was difficult.

The Simplon-Orient Express

The writer's first journey to the Near East in 1928, travelling alone, introduced her to the new transport link between London and Baghdad, and she used it again and again in subsequent years. She went by train, although one could already fly from England to Cairo and Baghdad at this time, but she and her husband Max Mallowan travelled by air only once before the Second World War, when they flew from Baghdad to Shiraz by way of Teheran. Not until after the war did flying become the only practicable form of travelling for the couple, and Agatha Christie never liked it, regarding it as expensive and boring.[1]

> [The Orient Express] is, undoubtedly, my favourite train. I like its tempo, which, starting *Allegro con fuoco*, swaying, and rattling and hurling one from side to side in its mad haste to leave Calais and the Occident, gradually slows down in a *rallentando* as it proceeds eastwards till it becomes definitely *legato*.[2]

Poster for the Simplon-Orient Express and Taurus Express, 1931 (Jürgen Klein collection)

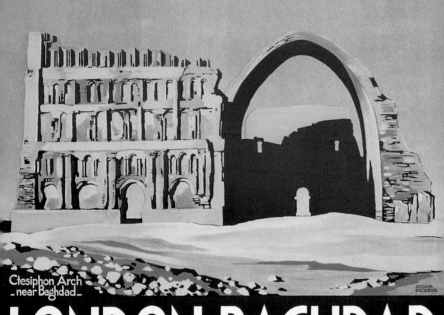

Ctesiphon Arch
near Baghdad

ROGER BRODERS

LONDON-BAGHDAD

IN 8 DAYS BY

SIMPLON-ORIENT-EXPRESS

& TAURUS-EXPRESS

Safety   Rapidity   Economy

SIMPLON-ORIENT-EXPRESS
TAURUS-EXPRESS
EUROPE
ASIE
AFRIQUE

This confession of her affection for the Orient Express shows that Agatha Christie found railway journeys a particularly appealing form of travel and her journeys on the Orient Express itself a particularly good way of moving between two such different worlds as Europe and the Orient. Train travel suited her gift for observation and gradually put her in the right mood for her distant destination.

The Orient Express, as she remarked, was the train she liked above all others. Its real name had been the Simplon-Orient Express since 1919, but it was known to both the crime novelist and the public in general simply as the Orient Express. Agatha and Max often used it and the connecting Taurus Express to reach excavation sites in Syria and Iraq. This was the golden age of the railways, when sleeping-car companies offered luxurious and expensive travel in specially equipped compartments. The most famous such company was the Compagnie Internationale des Wagons-Lits, which operated both express trains.

Luxury trains had been travelling through America and Europe since the late nineteenth century. Sleeping-car companies specially founded for the purpose offered the elite of high society a form of travel that was the epitome of exclusivity and *savoir-vivre*. What George Mortimer Pullman was to the United States, the Belgian Georges Nagelmakers was to Europe. In 1872 he founded the Compagnie Internationale des Wagons-Lits[3] (CIWL), which had its own sleeping and dining cars and luggage vans. It operated luxury trains linking the great cities of Europe. The carriages were furnished with the utmost comfort, and the cuisine had a particularly high reputation. After the rolling stock itself, specially trained staff wearing their own uniform were the second important component of the enterprise, guaranteeing it a high reputation that lasted for years. The concept of a hotel on wheels had been born.[4]

The ability to travel right across the continent in these special carriages meant that passengers did not have to go to the inconvenience of changing trains; they could sit in their own compartments from the place of departure to the point of arrival without having to think of anything but enjoying their luxurious journey. But while long-distance rail travel was no problem in the United States of America it did present a number of problems in Europe, consisting as the continent did of many comparatively small countries. The various national railway companies ran their own lines and had their own gauges, forms of headlights and rear lights, braking systems, interior lighting and heating, and service regulations.[5] The Compagnie Internationale dealt with these difficulties by signing agreements with all the railway companies along its

Poster for the Simplon-Orient Express and Taurus Express, 1930 (Jürgen Klein collection)

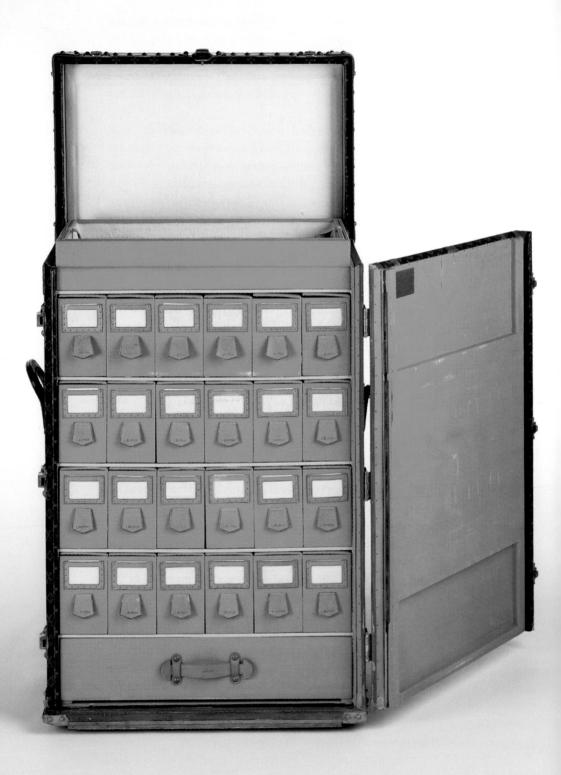

routes for the use of their railway lines, stations and locomotives, since the CIWL provided only the sleeping and dining cars and luggage vans, not the engines, which were the property of the railway companies of the countries through which the trains passed, and were coupled to the trains at every border crossing.

On her first journey to the East in 1928 Agatha Christie admired the deep and rocky ravines of Yugoslavia, the picturesque local vehicles of the country, and the peasants at the stations through which she passed on the Simplon-Orient Express. She marvelled at the foreign appearance of the locomotives, and examined them when the journey paused for any length of time, 'getting out occasionally at places like Nish and Belgrade and seeing the large engines changed and new monsters coming on with entirely different scripts and signs'.[6]

Long-distance routes through Europe also offered travellers the chance of reaching destinations that were not on the main route followed by the train. If you wanted to visit Athens, for instance, you took the Orient Express and booked a compartment in the Paris to Athens carriage. You travelled with the

Left Cabin trunk, 1930 (Louis Vuitton, Paris)

Below Medicine chest, 1920 (Louis Vuitton, Paris)

Orient Express to Belgrade, where your carriage was coupled to another train that took you on to your destination. So long as passengers had made sure that they were in the correct carriage when the coupling manoeuvres were carried out, they could remain sitting comfortably where they were.

The high standard of service offered by the CIWL[7] was evident to the passengers when they saw the trains constantly taking on fresh food at stations; only the best ingredients were used. The sheets were fine linen, and the tables were lavishly set for every meal: silver and porcelain were specially made with the company's crest on them. There were even members of staff employed to clean the silver on the trains. Such service had its price: only rich members of the upper middle class and the aristocracy could afford to travel in this way.

Right Sleeping-car compartment, carriage 3489, of 1929 (Compagnie Internationale des Wagons-Lits et du Tourisme, Paris)

Below Toilet case, 1922 (Louis Vuitton, Paris)

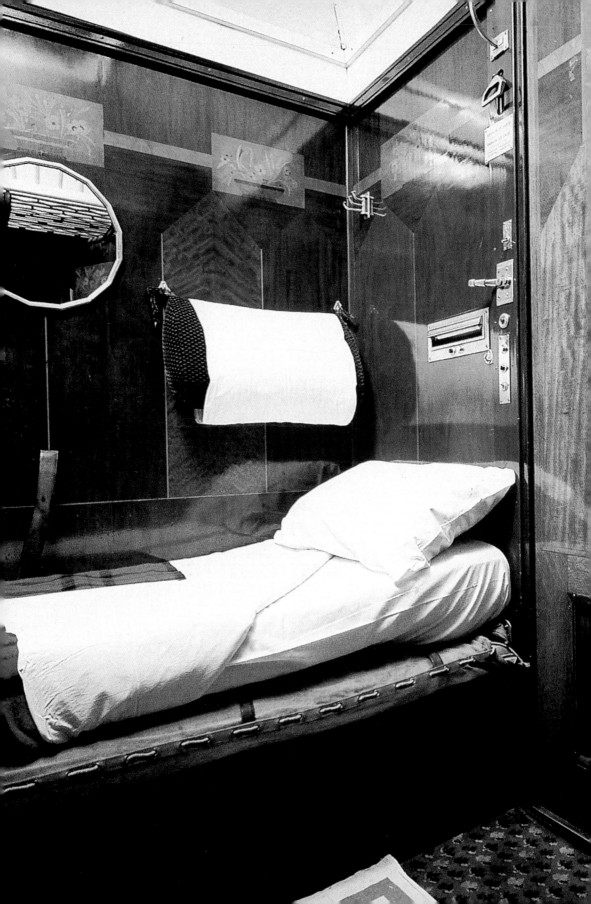

The Compagnie Internationale des Wagons-Lits had acquired luxury hotels at the main destinations and major stations along the route, running them from 1894 under the name of the Compagnie Internationale des Grands Hôtels. Like the trains themselves, these hotels enjoyed great popularity and became familiar to the passengers, who could count on the Compagnie's legendary standards of service even when they broke their journey or reached their destination.

The service also extended to acquiring all the tickets necessary for a customer's long-distance journey. Agatha Christie made her literary characters customers of the Thomas Cook travel agency,[8] which she used herself in real life.[9] We do not know what her own ticket for the journey to Ur in 1928 cost, but a Thomas Cook/Wagons-Lits travel brochure gives the price of a second-class journey of thirty-one days to Syria, Palestine and Egypt as £87 10s. Thomas Cook representatives were available to help passengers in all the larger towns and cities along the line. The business of travel agents and travel bureaux was not confined to advising travellers and selling tickets; meeting passengers from the train, taking them to their hotels and getting them to their next connection were all part of the service. The writer was glad to accept such help, particularly on her first visit to the Orient in 1928. A Thomas Cook representative collected her from the Hotel Tokatlian in Istanbul, travelled over the Bosphorus with her to the Asian side of the city, and took her to Haidar Pasha Station, where trains set off for the East: 'I was glad to have my guide with me, for anything more like a lunatic asylum than Haidar Pasha Station cannot be imagined. Everyone shouted, screamed, thumped, and demanded the attention of the Customs Officer.'[10] The Thomas Cook representative solved the problem with a tip, and Agatha Christie was able to continue her journey with no further worries.

Left Menu card of the Compagnie Internationale des Wagons-Lits, August 1925 (Jürgen Klein collection)

Below Menu card of the Compagnie Internationale des Wagons-Lits, c.1930 (Pierre de Gigord collection, Paris)

SEASON 1927-28

The Magic Heart of the East

TOURS
TO
MESOPOTAMIA
(IRAQ)

Under the Management of

THOS. COOK & SON, LTD.

When the railway network was extended, the rolling stock operated by the CIWL was also improved and enlarged. A new type of carriage was introduced in 1922, and it was to be the scene of the crime in *Murder on the Orient Express*. The first of these new S-type sleeping cars had eight compartments with single beds, and four twin-bed compartments.

The Orient Express from Paris to Constantinople (later Istanbul) was without a doubt the most famous train operated by the Compagnie Internationale des Wagons-Lits, and achieved extraordinary renown even before the First World War. It set out in 1883 on its maiden journey; in the interests of publicity all the passengers were invited guests including government ministers, diplomats and journalists. The train ran from Paris by way of Stuttgart, Munich, Vienna, Budapest, Belgrade and Sofia to Constantinople. On this and subsequent journeys the rail connections were not yet in full working order. Passengers had to leave the train in Romania, board an ordinary train to go to the Bulgarian town of Varna on the Black Sea, and they then completed the

Left Travel brochure for Mesopotamia, 1927–8 season (Thomas Cook Archives)

Below Cook's Traveller's Handbook for Palestine, Syria and Iraq, 1934

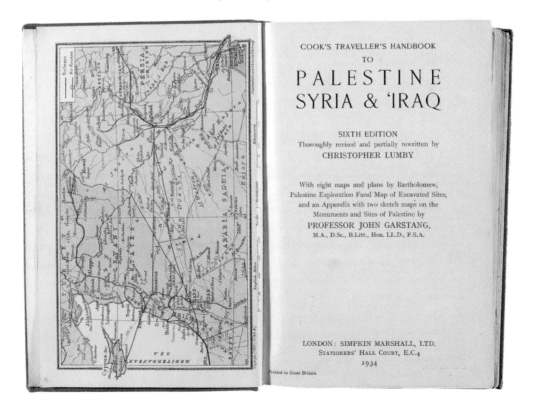

COOK'S TRAVELLER'S HANDBOOK
TO
PALESTINE
SYRIA & 'IRAQ

SIXTH EDITION
Thoroughly revised and partially rewritten by
CHRISTOPHER LUMBY

With eight maps and plans by Bartholomew,
Palestine Exploration Fund Map of Excavated Sites,
and an Appendix with two sketch maps on the
Monuments and Sites of Palestine by
PROFESSOR JOHN GARSTANG,
M.A., D.Sc., B.Litt., Hon. LL.D., F.S.A.

LONDON: SIMPKIN MARSHALL, LTD.
STATIONERS' HALL COURT, E.C.4
1934

Printed in Great Britain

last part of the journey to Constantinople on a steamboat.[11] Not all the passengers on the Orient Express were tourists and adventurers; others who travelled on the train were businessmen, aristocrats, politicians and artists, along with demi-mondaines, spies and traitors. This colourful medley of characters from the European upper classes patronized the train and made it famous.

The first Orient Express trains ran only until the outbreak of the First World War. During the war the Axis powers of Germany, Austria-Hungary, Bulgaria and the Ottoman Empire promoted the Balkan Train as a prestigious substitute.[12] After the war the victorious Allies ensured that the Orient Express, now revived, no longer ran through Germany and Austria but set off from Paris, passed through Switzerland and the Simplon Tunnel, and went on to Milan, Venice, Trieste and Zagreb. Not until it reached Belgrade did it rejoin the original Orient Express line to Constantinople. Consequently, the train was now known as the Simplon-Orient Express, although that name never replaced the old term Orient Express in the public mind. Even in Syria, Agatha Christie does not speak of the Taurus Express but uses the old name.[13]

The writer began her first oriental journey from Victoria Station in London, going by train to Dover where she made the Channel crossing on the ferry. On arriving at Calais she had to ensure that she and her luggage were in the right carriage to reach Istanbul at the end of the journey. The train went to Paris, where the locomotive that strictly speaking made it the Simplon-Orient Express was coupled to the carriages. The journey from Calais to Istanbul covered 3,342 kilometres and took three days, terminating at Sirkeçi Station in Istanbul, on the European side of the city. The Bosphorus made it necessary for travellers who wished to go further east to change trains here.

On Agatha Christie's return from her second journey to Ur in 1930 she had an amusing adventure on the Simplon-Orient Express, one in which Max Mallowan too was involved.[14] They had arrived in Athens by boat, and had to leave for England at once because Agatha's daughter was ill with pneumonia. She had only just met Max on the excavations, and he was accompanying her from Athens in the Simplon-Orient Express. They left their carriage briefly to buy some oranges, only to find on their return that, although they had been told the train would be stopping at the station for some time, it had left almost at once, along with their luggage. They decided to hire a car – at a horrendous price – with a chauffeur to drive them after it. In a frantic race they pursued the train and finally caught up with it at Domodossola, arriving in Paris as planned but almost penniless. Max's mother was waiting for them in Paris, and her future daughter-in-law was obliged to borrow all the money she had on her

Poster advertising the Golden Arrow, 1926 (Jürgen Klein collection)

Cie WAGONS LITS

CIE INTERNATIONALE DES WAGONS LITS

PULLMAN CAR

The GOLDEN ARROW
ALL PULLMAN TRAIN
DAILY BETWEEN
LONDON CALAIS PARIS

Departs: LONDON 10.45 a.m. *Arrives*: PARIS 5.40 pm.
Departs: PARIS 12 noon *Arrives*: LONDON 7.15 pm.

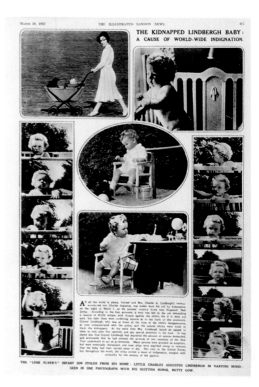

Above The Simplon-Orient Express stuck in the snow (*L'Illustration*, 23 February 1929)

Above right The kidnapping of the Lindbergh baby (*Illustrated London News*, 19 March 1932)

before continuing her journey to England, where fortunately she found her daughter Rosalind already on the road to recovery.

The most famous of all Agatha Christie's crime novels is set in the stranded Simplon-Orient Express. In *Murder on the Orient Express* the train is stuck in a snowdrift on the way from Istanbul to Paris. The novel appeared in 1934 and was based, among other incidents, on an adventure of the author's own on her way back from Nineveh just before Christmas of 1931.[15] She was travelling from Istanbul to England by the Simplon-Orient Express when the train had to stop at Pythiou in the border area between Greece and Turkey, because part of the track had been washed away by wet weather, and she used the opportunity to observe the way the passengers on the train reacted to this unexpected situation. Some of them appeared later in her novel. On her safe arrival in England she sent Max Mallowan a long letter about this adventurous journey. She wrote the novel itself on the 1933 dig at Tell Arpachiyah, dedicating it to her husband. Besides her personal experience of seeing the Simplon-Orient Express brought to a halt by the forces of nature, two other events served as the basis for the story. One was the famous occasion when the Orient Express stuck in a snowdrift in 1929. The incident caused an international furore, since it was regarded as scandalous that it took the rescue teams five days to reach the train when it was stranded in the Turkish highlands 90 kilometres from Istanbul. The second event was the kidnapping and murder of the Lindbergh baby in 1932, a crime that had attracted even more attention.

The Taurus Express

Agatha Christie was travelling in the Near East at a time when Syria, still under French administration, and the newly created state of Turkey were seeking closer technological transport connections with Europe. Railways seemed to guarantee access to trade, cultural exchange, in fact progress in general. Ultimately, however, all that came of the idea of this new departure was access to the long-distance connections offered by the CIWL. After the end of the First World War some stretches of dismantled tracks were not restored, and Syrian Railways was actually operating at a loss after 1931 while the road system was extended for internal travel. Cars were faster and cheaper than rail: in 1930 taxis took two and a half hours to cover the distance from Beirut to Damascus, while the rail journey was nine hours and cost the same amount.[16]

The Baghdad Railway, operated by Germany and the Ottoman Empire after 1899,[17] was an outstandingly good line. It was not until 1940, however, that the network was completed in the Turco-Syrian area and parts of Iraq; only then could passengers in Istanbul board a through train to Baghdad.

The governments of Turkey, Syria and Iraq (which became independent in 1932) planned to operate the Taurus Express in partnership with the CIWL on what had formerly been the Baghdad line – the train was named after the Taurus mountain range in south-east Turkey. The scheduling conference of 1927 in Florence decided to extend the Simplon-Orient Express line to Cairo, and in 1928 the CIWL attached an Istanbul-Tripoli sleeping car to a normal Turkish Railways train.[18] It ran along the stretch of the Baghdad Railway line from Istanbul, by way of Eskişehir, Konya, Adana, Aleppo and Homs, to Tripoli in present-day Lebanon. Passengers could not yet go on to Egypt because that section of track had not been built. Travellers had to take a bus from Tripoli to Haifa, and then go on by train to Cairo.

The maiden journey of the Taurus Express was from the Haidar Pasha main station on the Asiatic side of Istanbul to Nisibin, which was the end of the line at the time. In 1932 the track was extended from Nisibin to the Syrian town of Tell Ziuane in the east, and in 1935 to Tell Kotchek on the border between Syria and Iraq. Although Agatha Christie speaks in her autobiography of being obliged to stop at Tell Kotchek in the autumn of 1931, she must in fact have meant the Turkish-Syrian border station of Nisibin, since the network did not reach Tell Kotchek until 1935. Through trains were not introduced until later, in 1940, and by now few people took any interest in such an event. The original idea of establishing long-distance connections on the existing Baghdad Railway line had been dropped, and after 1935 the Taurus Express trains operated by the CIWL which had previously used the Baghdad Railway line further south passing through Konya, went by way of the capital, Ankara.

With the opening of the Taurus Express connection, travellers could leave from Haidar Pasha station for Baghdad by way of Aleppo. The line ran over Turkish soil along the Turkish-Syrian border. At the terminus of this stretch of the former Baghdad Railway line, passengers had to make do with buses operated by the Iraqi State Railway. From small railway stations such as Nisibin and Tell Kotchek a bus line ran to Kirkuk, where it was possible to catch a train to Baghdad and recover from the stress and strain of the journey in a sleeping car. The bus left Nisibin at mid-day and reached Mosul in the evening. Next morning travellers went on to Kirkuk, arriving in the afternoon in time to catch the train for Baghdad. It reached the city at seven the next morning, and those going further could get a connection to Basra or Teheran.

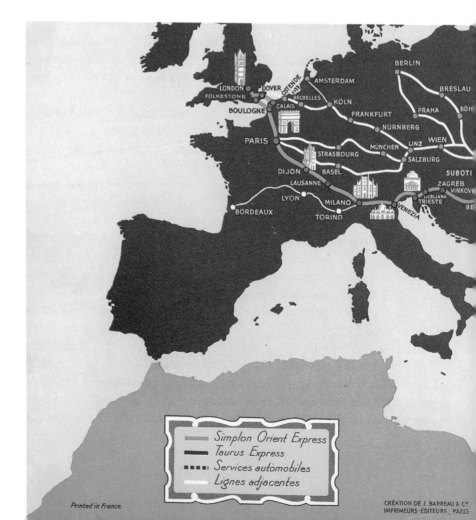

Simplon Orient Express
Taurus Express
Services automobiles
Lignes adjacentes

CRÉATION DE J. BARREAU & Cᵉ
IMPRIMEURS-ÉDITEURS, PARIS

Agatha Christie was unable to take this route on her two first journeys to Ur in 1928 and 1930, since it was not in operation until 1930.[19] In 1928 she first took the train from Aleppo to Damascus and then went on through the desert on a Nairn Line bus to Baghdad. In her autobiography she gives a colourful description of her arrival in what to her was still a strange world:

> There was a subtle difference on passing from Europe into Asia. It was as though time had less meaning. The train rambled on its way, running by the side of the Sea of Marmara, and climbing mountains – it was incredibly beautiful all along this way. The people in the train were now different too – though it is difficult to describe in what the difference lay. I felt cut off, but far more interested in what I was doing and where I was going. When we stopped at the stations I enjoyed looking out, seeing the motley crowd of costumes, peasants thronging the platform, and the strange meals of cooked food that were handed up to the train.

Travel brochure for the Simplon-Orient Express and Taurus Express (Jürgen Klein collection)

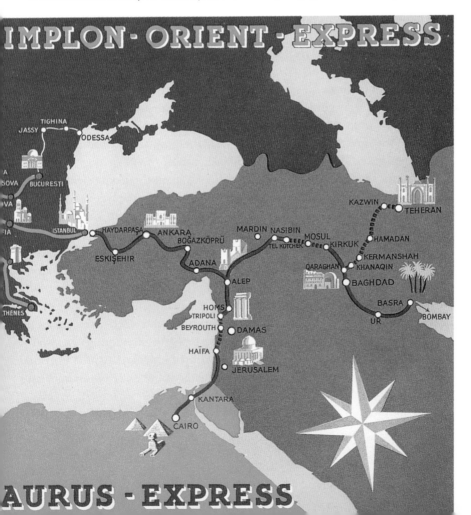

Food on skewers, wrapped in leaves, eggs painted various colours – all sorts of things. The meals became more unpalatable and fuller of hot, greasy, tasteless morsels as we went further East.[20]

The train went on from Aleppo by way of Homs to Tripoli on the coast. Since Agatha Christie was going to take the bus from Damascus to Baghdad, she caught a local train which, as she said, 'never seemed to go at more than five miles an hour', and was always stopping at something 'hardly distinguishable from the surroundings but which was called a station'.[21] After a long and tiring day's journey she finally reached Damascus. She spent three days sight-seeing in the city and its immediate surroundings before taking the bus to Baghdad. On her second journey out in 1930 she arrived in Beirut by sea from Italy and went on by the Nairn Line bus to Baghdad.

Although most of *Murder on the Orient Express* is set on the Simplon-Orient Express itself, Agatha Christie opens the story in Aleppo, where Hercule Poirot is boarding the Taurus Express for Haidar Pasha station in Istanbul. On the way through the Taurus mountains, passing the Cilician Gates, he overhears a conversation between two of the characters who will later be involved in the murder case. The magnificent landscape of the mountains has overwhelmed them both, and for a moment they drop their guard. Agatha Christie herself had been impressed by the natural beauty of the region on her first journey through the Taurus range:

Above Changing the wheel of a Nairn bus in the desert, 1935 (photo: Richard Barnett)

Above left The Taurus Express with the Borsig 2-6-0 No. 261 locomotive, October 1943
(Werner Sölch collection, Munich)

Below Travel brochure for the Simplon-Orient Express and Taurus Express, 1930 (Jürgen Klein collection)

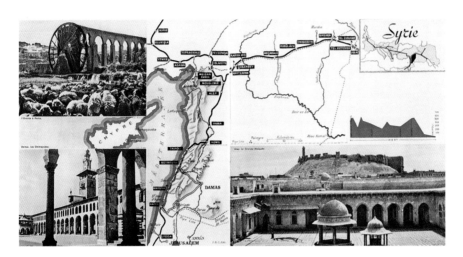

ALEP — Gare Chemin de fer Bagdad

Above Postcard of Aleppo Station, *c.*1930 (Fouad Debbas collection, Beirut)

Right Poster for the Simplon-Orient Express showing Aleppo, 1927 (Jürgen Klein collection)

Below Postcard of the Hidjaz Station in Damascus, *c.*1930 (Pierre de Gigord collection, Paris)

DAMAS (Syrie). - Vue de la Station de Hidjaz

Above Baghdad hotel voucher inclusive of transfer, breakfast, lunch and afternoon tea, 1936 (Thomas Cook Archives)

Above right Travel brochure for Baghdad, 1936 season (Thomas Cook Archives)

Then, on the second evening, we came to a halt, and people got out of the train to look at the Cilician Gates. It was a moment of incredible beauty. I have never forgotten it. I was to pass that way many times again, both going to and coming from the Near East and, as the train schedules changed, I stopped there at different times of day and night: sometimes in the early morning, which was indeed beautiful; sometimes, like this first time, in the evening at six o'clock; sometimes, regrettably, in the middle of the night. This first time I was lucky. I got out with the others and stood there. The sun was slowly setting, and the beauty indescribable. I was so glad then that I had come – so full of thankfulness and joy. I got back into the train, whistles blew, and we started down the long side of a mountain gorge, passing from one side to the other, and coming out on the river below.[22]

The inspiration for her crime novel and her approach to the writing of it relate to the railway. The details she gives for the timing of the journey on the Taurus and Simplon-Orient Express trains are so precise that she probably used a

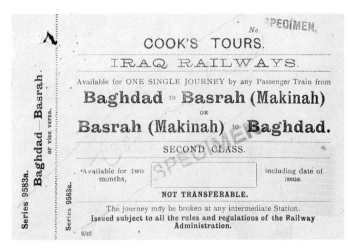

Above Travel brochure for Iraq, post-1935 (Pierre de Gigord collection, Paris)

Above right Baghdad/Basra rail ticket, 1928 (Thomas Cook Archives)

railway timetable in writing her story. She seems to have chosen not the up-to-date 1933 timetable, but its predecessor of the second half of 1932,[23] in which the time of departure from Aleppo (5.00 a.m.) and the time of arrival at Haidar Pasha (6.55 p.m.) agree with the novel. The Simplon-Orient Express left from Sirkeçi station in Istanbul at nine in the evening for several years after this.

By bus through the desert

The tourist industry establishing itself in the Near East after the First World War saw the bus as a promising new form of transport. Bus lines such as the Nairn Company were founded, and worked in co-operation with large travel agents such as the Thomas Cook/Compagnie des Wagons-Lits venture. British drivers were engaged, and the passengers were well looked after when the bus stopped for them to rest in the desert. Agatha Christie found the journey both 'fascinating and rather sinister'. Breakfast at six in the morning in the desert tasted delicious, but she found the journey through those endless expanses monotonous. She was sitting at the back of the bus, and its rocking motion made her feel sick.[24] She did not find the rest of the journey very spectacular. On the way back she made sure that she had a seat directly behind the

ABSENT
IN THE
SPRING

a novel by

Mary
Westmacott

driver, where she would not suffer so much from the rocking of the vehicle.

Since 1927 six-wheeler buses had been used for the journey across the desert. They stopped on the way at Rutbah Wells, a fort where the travellers spent the night, and a place which had been built especially to make the route secure.[25] A contingent of local police, the Guards of the Camel Corps, was stationed here.[26] Journeys through the desert could be dangerous: travellers might run out of food or lose their way, or the bus might break down and not have the right spare part available. The worst eventuality was a combination of all these possibilities, and consequently the drivers tried to be ready for anything, loading up their vehicles both inside and out with provisions and spare parts. The desert policemen were stationed in Fort Rutbah to protect travellers from attack, and had armoured cars with them. In addition, air reconnaissance might be necessary if there was any danger of attack by bandits.

Agatha Christie was to use the bus journeys to and from Damascus in her short story 'The Gate of Baghdad', one of the collection published as *Parker Pyne Investigates* (1934). In this story Parker Pyne has to solve a case of murder in a twelve-seater overland bus on its way from Damascus to Baghdad. Among the illustrious company on board are three British air force officers, whose job is to carry out air searches for missing persons kidnapped by desert bandits.

The vicissitudes of another desert bus journey inspired her novel *Absent in the Spring*, written under the pseudonym of Mary Westmacott. In the autumn of 1931 she visited her husband at Nineveh near Mosul, where he was working on Campbell Thompson's excavations. On the way a storm had diverted her ship to Beirut, and she had to go on to Aleppo on a regional train, a journey lasting sixteen hours. Since there were no lavatories on the train, she had to make use of what facilities the tiny stations along the line could offer.[27] Max Mallowan was meeting her in Mosul, so she travelled to Nisibin, where the former Baghdad Railway terminated, and planned to go on from there with the regular bus running between Kirkuk and Mosul. However, in Nisibin she heard that torrential rains had washed away the railway track in several places, and the *wadis* were full of water. She was stranded for two days at the small station.[28] The novel *Absent in the Spring*,[29] published in 1944, tells the story of an upper middle-class woman whose bus is late in reaching a desert station, so that she misses her train to Aleppo. While she waits she is forced to begin reassessing her life.

The Baghdad-to-Basra line was built as a single-metre gauge track in 1920 under British administration.[30] Ur, Agatha's destination on her first two

Jacket of the first edition of *Absent in the Spring* (The Crime Club, Collins 1944)

journeys, is on this line. The train left Baghdad West station every Monday and Thursday at 10.15, and if she had stayed on it, she would have reached Basra at seven in the morning next day. When she arrived at Ur Junction in the middle of the night, she had made a journey alternating between luxurious and Spartan conditions: one that had shown her interesting people, strange customs, and fascinating landscapes, all of which she would weave into her stories. The fascination of the Orient had cast its spell on her on her first journey to the Near East, and was never to let go.

NOTES

1 A. Christie, *An Autobiography*, London 1981, p. 540.
2 A. Christie Mallowan, *Come, Tell Me How You Live*, London 1999, p. 28.
3 Georges Nagelmakers merged his Compagnie Internationale des Wagons-Lits with the company of his competitor W. D'Alton Mann in 1872. The firm's headquarters moved from Liège to Brussels in 1876. He then bought out his partner, and thanks to international financing the capital cover of the company rose considerably. It was renamed the Compagnie Internationale des Wagons-Lits et des Grands Express Européens in 1884, to make it clear that it was no longer operating single carriages coupled to other trains, as in the past, but whole trains such as the Orient Express consisting entirely of the company's own carriages; cf. A. Mühl and J. Klein, *125 Jahre Internationale Schlafwagen-Gesellschaft. Die Luxuszüge – Geschichte und Plakate*, Freiburg im Breisgau 1998, pp. 18–20, and W. Sölch, *Orient-Express. Glanzzeit, Niedergang und Wiedergeburt eines Luxuszuges*, 4th edn, Düsseldorf 1998.
4 J. des Cars and J.-P. Caracalla, *100 Jahre Orient-Express*, Zurich 1984, p. 18.
5 Ibid., p. 26.
6 Christie, *Autobiography* (n. 1), p. 375.
7 The following information on services is from Mühl and Klein, *Schlafwagen* (n. 3), pp. 25f.
8 A. Christie, *The Mystery of the Blue Train*, London 1976, p. 48.
9 Christie, *Autobiography* (n. 1), p. 372. She tells her readers how she suddenly changed her mind in 1928 and instead of going to the West Indies exchanged her tickets at Thomas Cook's for tickets to Baghdad.
10 Ibid., p. 377.
11 W. Sölch, *Orient-Express. Glanzzeit und Niedergang eines Luxuszuges*, Reinbek near Hamburg 1980, p. 12.
12 P. Heigl, 'Der Balkan-Zug – ein deutscher Orient-Express', in V.J. Franzke (ed.), *Orient-Express – König der Züge*, Nuremberg 1998, pp. 94–103.
13 Christie, *Autobiography* (n. 1), p. 468.
14 Ibid., pp. 418–19.
15 J. Morgan, *Agatha Christie: A Biography*, London 1984, pp. 201–4.
16 E. Wirth, *Syrien. Eine geographische Landeskunde*, Darmstadt 1971, p. 349.
17 Germany asked the sultan's palace for a concession to extend the Anatolian Railway from Konya to Baghdad and Basra. See J. Lodemann and M. Pohl, *Die Bagdadbahn. Geschichte und Gegenwart einer berühmten Eisenbahnlinie*, Mainz 1988, p. 47.
18 W. Sölch, *Expresszüge im Vorderen Orient*, Düsseldorf 1989, p. 45.
19 Cf. the CIWL timetables for the years 1929 and 1930. The June 1929 timetable No. 51 London-Paris to Cairo gives no direct link to Baghdad, only to Damascus, arriving at

19.37 hours. The new Taurus Express is given under No. 65 in the June 1930 timetable. It was possible to take this train to Nisibin on the Turkish-Syrian border, arriving at 5.20 hours. A two-day bus journey then took travellers by way of Mosul to Kirkuk, where they could catch a train to Baghdad. It is not known whether this service had not yet been introduced at the time of Agatha Christie's second journey in 1930 or if she simply preferred to take the route she already knew.

20 Christie, *Autobiography* (n. 1), p. 377.
21 Ibid., p. 379.
22 Ibid., p. 378.
23 Timetable of the Compagnie Internationale des Wagons-Lits for 1 July to 1 October 1932.
24 Christie, *Autobiography* (n. 1), p. 383.
25 C. Lumby, *Cook's Traveller's Handbook to Palestine, Syria & Iraq*, 6th edn, London 1934, p. 417.
26 Christie, *Autobiography* (n. 1), p. 384.
27 Ibid., p. 468.
28 Ibid., pp. 468–9.
29 M. Westmacott, *Absent in the Spring*, London 1944.
30 Sölch, *Expresszüge* (n. 18), p. 65.

CONSTANTINOPLE - Gare des Chemins de fer Orientaux

Traces of Agatha Christie in Syria and Turkey: An Oriental Journey Seventy Years afterwards

Tom Stern

R estricted to Turkey and Syria, the quest described in this article can only shed light on a small part of the travels and excavations undertaken in the Orient by Agatha Christie and her husband Max Mallowan. The places visited were determined by Agatha Christie's texts. The journey began at a Turkish railway station and ended beside a tomb in Syria. In between lay 3,000 kilometres of roads and railway lines, excavation sites, hotels and a few remaining eyewitnesses.

How accurately can we really perceive Agatha Christie today? How have the settings she used in her crime stories changed? And how do they relate to her as a writer and an amateur archaeologist?

In many respects, then, this is an archaeological journey, inspired by the myth of Agatha Christie and her own autobiographical memoir *Come, Tell Me How You Live.*

Istanbul – Sirkeci Station

Once a terminus of the great European railways, this station now serves the suburban Istanbul lines. Its building is dwarfed by the unwieldy concrete structures full of offices and shops around it. There is no furniture left in the first-class waiting-room, which has the charm of impoverished aristocracy. A dog sleeps in a patch of light cast by the afternoon sun falling through the panes. There is a brass plate on the outer façade announcing 'Orient Express', hanging in isolation on the wall like the name of a firm. A çayçi (waiter) balancing

Above left Postcard of Sirkeci Station in Istanbul, *c.*1930 (Pierre de Gigord collection, Paris)

Left Sirkeci Station in Istanbul, 1998 (photo: Tom Stern)

Above Window of the Péra Palace Hotel in Istanbul, 1998 (photo: Tom Stern)

Above right Luggage sticker from the Péra Palace Hotel in Istanbul, *c.*1930 (Pierre de Gigord collection, Paris)

glasses of tea on a tray comes up a small flight of steps and hurries through the marble silence of the waiting-room. The cacophony of the streets of Istanbul ebbs away as the doors swing shut behind him.

The station restaurant, on the other hand, has all the lively, smoky atmosphere of male Turkish café society, full of tinkling teaspoons and hands throwing dice, reflecting modern urban life at a busy junction. Faded photographs and large oil paintings showing subjects from railway history adorn the walls, ignored but not meaningless. But Agatha, who first set foot in this station in 1928, is not remembered here.

Istanbul – the Péra Palace Hotel

The taxi stops in a narrow street, Mesrutiyet Caddesi, in front of the curved façade of a steel and glass structure similar to the old Paris Métro entrances: the Péra Palas Oteli. The hotel crest, two lions standing face to face holding a shield with an ornate letter 'P' on it, calls to mind the origin of this de luxe establishment, opened by the Compagnie Internationale des Wagons-Lits (CIWL). Heavily gathered curtains bar the view of the interior beside the main entrance, as if intent on keeping modern city life out. Entering the hotel lobby is like stepping back in time: its architecture and contents date from 1892, the year when it was founded. The list of international crowned heads and VIPs who once stayed here is as imposing and grand as the furnishings of the hotel still are today – it contains the first lift ever installed in the Ottoman Empire. Its

Above Luggage sticker from the Hotel Tokatlian in Istanbul, c.1930 (Pierre de Gigord collection, Paris)

Above right Plaque in the former entrance to the Hotel Tokatlian in Istanbul, 1998 (photo: Tom Stern)

publicity material gives prominence first to the national hero and founder of the modern Turkish state Mustafa Kemal Atatürk, and then to Agatha Christie. Her likeness adorns the hotel prospectus, and the grand saloon is named after her.

At the centre of this cult is Room 411, which bears a notice in four languages for the edification of non-initiates. The hotel room, rather small and looking out on a busy street, contains two brass bedsteads, a wardrobe and a writing-desk, the latter obviously essential, since it is claimed that Agatha Christie wrote *Murder on the Orient Express* in this room. A glass-fronted bookcase is full of her novels. A picture of the Orient Express itself adorns the wall beside the bed, and an enlarged and not particular flattering portrait of Agatha Christie suggests that anyone staying in the room should pay silent tribute. The photograph of Tamara Rand, a blonde bombshell from the Hollywood of the late seventies, seems out of place, yet she is a central figure, having led inquirers to a hiding place under the floorboards behind the door, from which a key was recovered on 17 March 1979, at 17.00 hours local time. This rusted item, the original of which is kept in a safe while interested guests are shown a copy, is said to be the key to the explanation of Agatha Christie's ten-day disappearance in 1926.

As if it was all a drama of hers! A former luxury hotel, the latest production of a major American film company,[1] a photogenic medium with an exotic name, a famous crime novelist with a gap of several missing days in her own story, a locked room with a secret hiding place, a rusty key, two million dollars, the international press, and finally a hotel strike.

But what are the actual facts? Direct evidence such as hotel registers, signatures or other such items cannot be found in the Péra Palace today – 'Unfortunately, no!' Did Agatha Christie ever stay here at all? As a passenger on

Above Postcard of the Haidar Pasha railway station in Istanbul, 1919 (Pierre de Gigord collection, Paris)

Above right Booking hall of the Haidar Pasha ferry station in Istanbul, 1998 (photo: Tom Stern)

the Orient Express run by the Compagnie Internationale des Wagons-Lits, yes, she probably did stay in the hotel on her way to and from her husband's excavations. But Room 411 is not an inviting place in which to write, and the business of the key is a whole story in itself, involving publicity-seeking hotel managers and film producers. However, that need not concern modern hotel guests in search of the legendary luxury of the hotel's past history.

Istanbul – the Hotel Tokatlian

The Istiklal Caddesi is a busy shopping street. Tramlines run through the paving of the pedestrian zone in the Taksim quarter, the most European part of Istanbul. The articles on display in the windows of the 'Deri Leather Shop' lie behind great glass panes flanking the entrance to the 'Tarihi Tokatlian ishane ve pasaji'. Only this metal plate with its Armenian proper names, in the middle of the shopping street above the neon-lit entrance and partly covered by the air-conditioning ventilators, indicates the building's former function. Now an office block and row of shops, it was once the Hotel Tokatlian. Agatha visited this hotel on her first journey to the East in 1928,[2] and consequently Poirot too stayed here before solving perhaps his most famous case on his train journey home.[3] Despite these biographical marginalia, the purpose of this building, well situated as it is for business, has always been much the same, making money – a business that calls for flexibility rather than sentimentality.

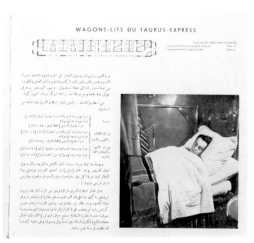

Above Information sign for the Taurus Express at Haidar Pasha Station in Istanbul, 1998 (photo: Tom Stern)

Above right Travel brochure for the Taurus Express, 1938 (Werner Sölch collection, Munich)

Istanbul – Haidar Pasha Station

The sun is refracted in the bow wave of the ferry cutting through the waters of the Bosphorus. Coming from Karaköy, it is making its way to Asia. The first port of call will be Haidar Pasha; the multi-storey sandstone station building can be seen from afar through the windows in the bows. With its round corner towers and projecting centre, the place looks like a cross between a de luxe hotel and a warehouse. The diesel engines perform two manoeuvres, making the wooden deck quiver as they bring the ferry to the jetty and the first passengers jump out on land. They stream purposefully towards a transit area with a tiled façade, its offset arches above the doors suggesting a sacred building. Islamic ornamentation and Arabic script – Arabic was still the official language on the Bosphorus in 1909 – make it clear that we have arrived in the Orient. Only the attractively restored steam locomotive painted black, gold, red and white and standing in front of the building, and a glance at the upper part of its façade, adorned in the centre by the relief image of a winged wheel, show that this is a station.

The conduct of the passengers in the booking-hall, to which Agatha was escorted over the Bosphorus by a Thomas Cook representative, is no longer reminiscent of a 'lunatic asylum', as she described it.[4] There are small queues at the windows, people are carrying their luggage about in a leisurely manner, there is no pushing and shoving, so that today the place gives a feeling

Above Luggage sticker of the Hotel Baron in Aleppo, *c.*1930 (Jürgen Klein collection)

Above right Illuminated sign for the Hotel Baron, 1998 (photo: Tom Stern)

almost of cosiness, which is not in keeping with the dimensions of the hall. Through the penetrating smell of adhesive – the flooring is being renovated – the passengers stream past the timetable which goes almost all the way up the walls, making for the station's eight platforms, not here called *peron*, as they are at Sirkeçi station, but *yol* (Turkish: way, road, method).

From this station the railway network spreads out over the huge land-mass of Turkey. But in spite of the thousands of kilometres of tracks – Haidar Pasha is both the point of departure and the terminus of the railway – today it plays only a minor role in personal transport: the bus is now the favoured means of long-distance travel.

Taurus Express

The spray of the high-pressure hose conjures up a rainbow for a few moments. Dodging the water, the travellers board the red and blue carriages of the Taurus Express. The uniformed sleeping-car attendant is waiting by Carriage No. 5 to escort the passengers and their luggage to the compartments reserved for them. These compartments do have corner cupboards with glasses and towels, and a wash-basin that can be pulled out for use, but they are nothing like the de luxe compartments of the CIWL in which Agatha travelled. However, the sleeping-car attendant will make the beds in the evening, put fresh covers on the quilts and pillows, install the ladder and wish the tired guests *Iyi aksamlar* (good night).

Above Illuminated sign for the Orient Palace Hotel in Damascus, 1998 (photo: Tom Stern)

Above right Luggage sticker of the Orient Palace Hotel, *c.*1930 (Pierre de Gigord collection, Paris)

Unspectacularly, indeed without any fuss at all, the Taurus Express slips out of the station ten minutes before its official departure time and sets out on its twenty-hour journey. Towns and landscapes merge together into impressions, reproduced in the memory as colours: cement grey for the extensive suburbs of Istanbul, a sunny blue along the Sea of Marmara, Alpine green on the long way up to the highlands, straw-yellow turning to pastel orange with the setting sun in Anatolia and becoming an all-embracing black as night falls, occasionally turning to a sea of flame where farmers are burning stubble in the cornfields.

When the scene outside fades from sight, life inside the train holds more interest. The red-carpeted corridor is the place where travellers meet, smoke and eat – for there is no dining car – and pass the time together. They exchange their life histories and family stories to the rhythm of the train's progress, and anonymous fellow passengers become agreeable neighbours. They seek for points in common, and friendships going beyond the mere wish to get the journey over and done with may develop. Fellow passengers in the train remain in the mind in more detail than the vast landscape outside. This seems to constitute the fascination of a train journey, which has little to do with its furnishings, the passengers' language and culture or the period, but probably does depend on the time that journey takes. The passengers Agatha met in 1931 on her way back from Nineveh inspired her to reincarnate their society in literary form in *Murder on the Orient Express*.[5]

Agatha travelled on the train between Istanbul and Aleppo; today the Taurus Express terminates at Adana. Even at 3.30 a.m. the humid heat weighs down on the sleepy travellers as they get their luggage out on the platform. The announcement that the next terminus will be Gaziantep station – since tunnel repairs make it impossible for the train to go further – does not conceal the bad feeling that exists between Turkey and Syria. A communicating link in the form of a train is not regarded as desirable, but still it could be the beginning of a rapprochement.

Aleppo – the Hotel Baron

Although electronically amplified, the muezzin's *al-magreb* call to prayer is difficult to hear above the concerted hooting of horns in the street. A dark, cloudless blue above the terrace announces the advent of evening and brings hope that the temperature may drop. The hotel sign, neon-lit with a yellow crown and a blue inscription on it, is switched on; it is surrounded by cables and wires. A friendly Syrian goes round the hotel guests' tables with a view to exchanging more than words, as the discreetly counted bundle of banknotes in his hand indicates: 'Fifty for one.' A red-jacketed waiter, the hotel crest on his breast pocket, comes out of the black-and-white tiled lobby on to the terrace. With the aroma of cardamom wafting around him, he serves mocha and water.

Agatha came to know and like the hotel and its proprietor Coco 'Baron' Mazloumian by 1930 at the latest.[6] The Mallowans always planned to break their journey here: 'Alep! Shops! A bath! My hair shampooed! Friends to see!'[7] The search for clues, so far consisting of laboriously tracking down artefacts, here acquires a shape and a face. Sally Mazloumian, a lady of English origin on whom the Orient has left its mark, widow of the Armenian Coco Mazloumian and 'grand old lady' of the hotel, has to cast her mind a long way back: to a cocktail party in the early 1950s, remembering Agatha Christie's blue eyes, her penetrating gaze, her cool manner to the other guests and also her expertise on the subject of lipsticks. Sally Mazloumian tells only of her own memories and cannot pass on anyone else's anecdotes. 'What a pity my husband is dead! He knew the Mallowans really well.' Armen Mazmoulian, the present hotel manager, confines his information to the history of the hotel, referring to his mother for anything about Agatha and Max. 'No, they never had a favourite room. Max may have visited the barber's opposite.'

This establishment, opened in the early 1930s with barber-shop chairs from Chicago, fifty-year-old pin-ups of Joan Tierney and a 1966 calendar, has aged with its owner. And he no longer remembers the Englishman; over the decades, after all, one customer with foam on his chin comes to resemble the next.

Darkness lies pleasantly over the terrace. 'Marlboro! Marlboro!' The black marketeers crying their wares are all part of the tapestry of sound in the street. The Hotel Baron is a place of leisure but not of repose or withdrawal from the world. This goes down well with today's guests, archaeologists and tourists with an interest in international culture. Rather worn now, without any atmosphere of legendary style about it, the place is firmly located in the modern age. It may live at ease with its past, but the manager's legal dispute with Syria – for the hotel has been nationalized – suggests that a further chapter in the history of the Hotel Baron may yet be written.

Damascus – Orient Palace Hotel

Huge banners with portraits of President Hafiz Assad and his dead son Basil conceal the façade of the Hidjaz Station. In front of it a policeman, the one unmoving form amidst a continual ebb and flow, is directing the traffic as it streams towards him. On the opposite side of Hidjaz Square a small flight of steps leads to the Orient Palace Hotel, situated in a cubic sandstone building of complicated design by the Lebanese architect Antoin Tabit.[8] Today the complex of buildings also contains the post office, a cinema and several business offices. Beyond the reception area – where the materials and styles suggest that it was renovated in the 1970s – you pass a plain glass door into large and glittering marble halls, still, as in Agatha Christie's time, poorly lit.[9] Remnants of the original furniture – the beds, cupboards and coat-stands were in Damascene intarsia work – are still to be found stored in a corner of the former ballroom, next to a piano without any strings and waiting (probably in vain) to be restored.

Sleeping boy at Palmyra, c.1870 (photo: Félix Bonfils; Fouad Debbas collection, Beirut)

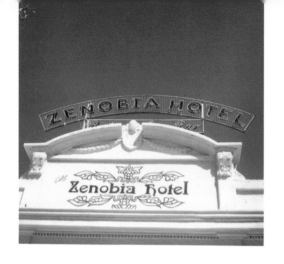

Left Signs above the entrance to the Hotel Zenobia in Palmyra, 1998 (photo: Tom Stern)

Right Road sign for Tell Brak, 1998 (photo: Tom Stern)

Far right Road sign for the village of Houtin at the foot of Chagar Bazar, 1998 (photo: Tom Stern)

Using the hotel as her base, Agatha spent three days in Damascus in 1928, and she was to spend the night there again in 1933 with Max and John Cruikshank Rose.[10] Changes of ownership – the proprietor has been Mohamed Imad since 1970 – have preserved the hotel's reputation but not its history. The hotel staff do not connect their place of employment with either Agatha Christie or Max Mallowan. Yet the hotel continues to have something cosmopolitan about it: using the old ballroom for interim storage, people from the Commonwealth of Independent States, chiefly women, make the Orient Palace Hotel their base in building up a new, privately orientated trade with Syria.

Palmyra – Hotel Zenobia

A few tourists, small figures moving through the hazy mid-day heat, stroll through the extensive ruins. The garden of Hotel Zenobia, separated from the area of erosion by a wall, lies in the shade of palm trees. This hotel, the first in Palmyra, was founded in 1919 by a French baroness and was patronized in its early days by the army troops stationed here. The ochre façade, renovated in 1990, mimics the colour of the desert of historical stone around it. The capitals of ancient columns have become garden tables, while the chairs are ordinary stacking plastic seating. Inside the neo-classical single-storey building the nose no longer catches the smell to which the Mallowans had to resign themselves: 'Mauvaise odeur, oui! Malsaine, non!'[11] Agatha is not part of the history of the hotel, her name is unknown here, the old registers have not been kept. A few pieces of old-fashioned furniture are like quotations from the early history of the place – in the same way as the patches of exposed masonry in the otherwise whitewashed walls. But none of that is of any importance when one looks at the ruined city all around. The hotel is an idea base for sightseeing.

Chagar Bazar

Cross the river Euphrates, impressive with its slowly flowing masses of water, and go on north, past the provincial town of Hasseke and towards the Turkish border. A brown and dusty plain full of harvested cornfields and cotton fields, hot and unshaded, stretches as far as the eye can see. The only hilly features of this landscape, standing out like warts on the skin, are the *tells*, or settlement mounds, rising to the sky, entirely made up of the debris from various civilizations accumulated in the course of their history.

The Mallowans surveyed this region in 1934 and chose the relatively small tell of Chagar Bazar for their first dig. The village of Houtin lies south of the mound today. It consists of some fifteen mud-brick farmhouses with about eighty inhabitants, a police station, a school and a stone house further to the east. Here, lying on a mat in a room otherwise empty but for the television set, Sheikh Marouf Kaderi, the grandson of Ahmad El Kaderi,[12] talks about his grandfather. His house stands on the spot where the ruins of the Mallowans' expedition house were still visible until the early 1970s. None of their workmen is still alive. Sheikh Marouf is not surprised by questions about Agatha and Max; archaeologists visit the tell almost every year. It is something of a place of pilgrimage. In the village, sitting in the shade of a mud-brick wall and surrounded by children, Ismael Habib, aged eighty-one, starts to talk. His Arabic is interspersed with words of Kurdish. 'No, I did not work on the dig. Only people with money worked there. Agatha Christie was popular in the village, and good-looking. It was unusual here to see a woman who could write!'

And on the tell itself, in the violet light of the setting sun, it turns out that time has not stood still. Mallowan's old excavations are still visible, particularly the deep pit dug in the northern part of the mound, but today they resemble the scars of work done in the distant past. Soon, however, there will be new studies of the mound – a second licence to dig on the site has been granted, over sixty years after the first.

Tell Brak

Tell Brak stands on the plain like a mountain of dimensions apparently not made by human hand. A flock of sheep trots slowly down the north-east side of the settlement mound, led by a boy on a donkey and raising a cloud of dust. In spite of decades of excavations, the pits dug still look as if they had been dug at desperate speed, no doubt because the spoil has never been removed.

Musa Ahmed Abdullah, *mukhtar* (mayor) of Sekman Sugar, a village 3 kilometres south of Tell Brak, sits on the floor of the assembly house. A stone staircase leads to the ante-room of this mud-brick building erected in 1958. Inside, there are niches in the whitewashed mud walls, and a baked earth hearth in one corner. The *mukhtar*, curved dagger in his belt, grinds coffee beans in a brass mortar and puts a coffee pot with a beak-like spout on the fire as he talks. Too young at the time to take part in the excavations, he describes the accident on the site in 1938 like a story that is still told in the village.[13]

Later, sitting on rugs and cushions, when the light is gentle and the heat bearable – as the result of an architectural tradition thousands of years old – Wauwi Abdulrahman and Hamid Musli Smir occupy the places of honour in the assembly room. In the oriental and biblical manner their information about their age and dates of birth does not always sound accurate, but they

Above left Expedition house at Chagar Bazar during construction, 1935 (photo: Richard Barnett)

Left Excavations at Tell Brak, 1938 (photo: Agatha Christie)

Below Hamid Musli Smir of Om Kahfa, former workman at Tell Brak, in 1998 (photo: Tom Stern)

Below right Wauwi Abdulrahman of Om Kahfa, former workman at Tell Brak, in 1998 (photo: Tom Stern)

Hamoudi ibn Sheikh Ibrahim's house in Jerablus, 1938 (photo: Agatha Christie)

must both be over seventy, and they live in Om Kahfa, 5 kilometres south-west of Tell Brak. Wauwi Abdulrahman, freshly shaven and in his best clothes, does most of the talking, with his neighbour joining in from time to time.

> At the time there was only one village around here; most people lived in tents. We worked carrying baskets at Tell Brak, taking earth from the pits to the heaps of spoil. Agatha Christie was a beautiful, strong woman. She supervised the workers. I remember her walking-stick.[14] She could unfold it and sit down on it.

His hands describe the shooting-stick, its size and its mechanism.

> Mallowan was a good-looking Englishman, a good boss, he was never angry. And there was a younger woman, too, who rode a lot and often visited the dig. We would get to the mound in the early morning, none of us had a watch, and wait for Mallowan to turn up. At the end of the day we walked three abreast behind the car to the expedition house. Those were good days! We had money, we were young!

Wauwi Abdulrahman and Hamid Musli Smir dig deeper and deeper down into the buried levels of their memories. They tell about their work, their pay, occasions when the men went on strike; they describe people and a few particularly well-remunerated finds; they talk about weapons carried on the site, and their

Hamoudi's tomb in the front garden of the new house in Jerablus, 1998 (photo: Tom Stern)

lives after the end of the working day; they even remember the simple, sparse diet of the time.

The tales these two old men tell cast light on *Come, Tell Me How You Live* from the point of view of those whom Agatha Christie described in the book, supplementing and confirming what she says. The perception of reality by all involved is bound to be subjective and different: Agatha Christie Mallowan was a European woman of almost fifty, prosperous, a writer with a special historical interest in Tell Brak, and Wauwi Abdulrahman and Hamid Musli Smir were two illiterate young Bedouin basket-boys who regarded the mound as heaven-sent, and the dig as a welcome source of money.

Jadan Albsaas al Abdullah comes in. The other two men move respectfully closer together, making room for their elder, who is almost one hundred years old. The old man answers questions about Agatha and Max with a shake of the head: 'I am not interested in any of that now. Only a hair's breadth separates me from death.'

Jerablus – the Hamoudi family

From the east, coming from Jezirah, the car drives fast over the wooden planks of the pontoon bridge, where guards are posted. Upstream, beyond islands and overgrown marshes, the steel Baghdad Railway bridge spans the Euphrates on the Turkish side of the border. Jerablus, a border town and the home of the Hamoudi family, is on the opposite bank. Passers by show the way to their house. All the local people know it.

Hamoudi ibn Sheikh Ibrahim,[15] c.1875–1953, was a figure of central importance to the British excavations of Carchemish and Ur, and his decorations show that he was also a man of political significance. He was Mallowan's foreman on the Khabur survey and during the excavations carried out there. Agatha must have met him in Ur in 1928, but he did not come to work with them on their own excavations until 1934–8. Hamoudi was part of the expeditionary team in Beirut from the first, together with his sons Yahya and Alawi.[16] Visits from the Mallowans[17] to Jerablus emphasize the connections between the sheikh and the archaeologists.

Today the Hamoudis live in a two-storey concrete house surrounded by a shoulder-high wall. An iron gate keeps intruders out and hides the front garden. In the reception room, furnished in Western style with armchairs and sofas, and with a photograph of Hamoudi accompanied by a much decorated English army officer on the wall, sit Faruk and Haldoun Hamoudi, two of the sheikh's grandsons. Over tea and 'crush' they talk about their grandfather, but it is soon clear that Agatha and Max are not remembered clearly any more, and even the grandfather is a vague iconic figure to them. Hamoudi's tomb in the front garden is evidence of his prominent position; the private burial place, with the status of a place of pilgrimage, nourishes his myth and his family's reputation – but the real history behind it all is now forgotten.

NOTES

1 *Agatha* (UK 1978), produced by Warner, directed by Michael Apted, with Vanessa Redgrave, Dustin Hoffmann and Timothy Dalton.
2 A. Christie, *An Autobiography*, London 1981, p. 376.
3 A. Christie, *Murder on the Orient Express*, London 1994, p. 19.
4 Christie, *Autobiography* (n. 2), p. 377.
5 J. Morgan, *Agatha Christie: A Biography*, London 1984, p. 201–4.
6 Christie, *Autobiography* (n. 2), p. 413.
7 A. Christie Mallowan, *Come, Tell Me How You Live*, London 1999, p. 76.
8 Antoin Tabit also designed the King David Hotel in Jerusalem and the St George Hotel in Beirut.
9 Christie, *Autobiography* (n. 2), p. 379.
10 Ibid., pp. 379–80.
11 Christie, *Come, Tell* (n. 7), p. 39; M. Mallowan, *Mallowan's Memoirs*, London 1977, p. 104; The British Museum, Archive ANE 196.2, p. 235.
12 Christie, *Come, Tell* (n. 7), pp. 62–3, 70–71, 112, 121, 127–8.
13 Ibid., pp. 189–95.
14 The word used here by Wauwi Abdulrahman for 'stick', *bakura*, is from the colloquial language of northern Syria; 'stick' in classical Arabic is *assa*.
15 Mallowan, *Memoirs* (n. 11), pp 37, 43.
16 Christie, *Come, Tell* (n. 7), p. 35.
17 Mallowan, *Memoirs* (n. 11), p. 162.

Agatha's Arabs: Agatha Christie in the Tradition of British Oriental Travellers

Reinhold Schiffer

No, 'Agatha's Arabs' does not entirely fit as a title. True, Arabs form the bulk of the local population in Christie's books set in the Near and Middle East, but many other ethnic groups turn up, such as Egyptians, Turks, Kurds and Armenians. We see Christie sorting a motley Eastern crowd into religious communities, Muslims, Devil Worshippers and Christians of the rarest Syrian orthodoxies. Furthermore, we come to know Agatha Christie's British characters, her living friends and acquaintances in the East and those created in her head, the fictional men and women of her oriental stories.

A distinction between fictional orientals and Europeans on the one hand and real ones that saunter through the autobiographies *Come, Tell Me How You Live* (1946) and *An Autobiography* (1977) on the other is not very helpful because Christie herself did not always draw the boundaries distinctly. Characters from her real life appear wearing the flimsiest of veils in novels, while her own experience has permeated the workaday Orient of her fiction. Apart from the title, the detective novel *Murder on the Orient Express* (1934) has hardly an oriental feature; on the train travellers do not drink a single cup of Turkish coffee. The two autobiographies and the crime novels *Death on the Nile* (1937) and *They Came To Baghdad* (1951) provide the scenes of her oriental theatre. The autobiography of 1977 sketches impressions briefly and somewhat indistinctly; *Come, Tell Me How You Live*, in contrast, offers a closely observed, lively, humorous, loving and serene picture of the Orient. It is the principal text on which my discussion of Christie's handling of oriental themes is based.[1] Her views on the large variety of Eastern peoples and customs coalesce into a distinct image when a mirror is held up to them. Such a mirror is most usefully made of British ethical values and maxims of conduct in the Orient. Which of these maxims, I shall ask, did Christie share with earlier travellers, mostly of the nineteenth century, and which not?[2]

Above Flock of sheep in Iraq, 1950s (photo: Agatha Christie)

Previous double page Excavation workers at Ur, 1920s (photo: Max Mallowan)

Naturally, every individual thinks as he or she thinks, but he or she does not think independently of education and social position. In Christie's case the social background quite evidently influenced her ethical standards. The family was well off, they owned handsome villas such as Ashfield; her father lived, as long as it was possible, the life of a wealthy man who did not have to work for his living but felt, beyond his wealth, committed to the ideal of a gentleman. He was friendly, humorous, generous, retiring, not overly intellectual, yet the friend and acquaintance of such famous writers as Henry James and Rudyard Kipling. Agatha was a carefree child; nurses and cooks took care of her. Like her father, she retained throughout her life, even as a famous and very rich author, a certain shyness in the company of strangers. In brief, Victorian upper middle-class values prevailed in her parents' home, and she never radically broke away from these values. This is evident in her attitude towards morality and politics.

Christie remained a morally conservative woman. Her defence of the death penalty for criminals comes as no surprise. She has no forgiving phrases about criminals being conditioned by society, no excuse for human beings who turn towards evil of their own free will. Why, she asks, should killers not be executed? And she answers in terms of innate good or evil: 'We have taken the lives of wolves, in this country; we didn't try to teach the wolf to lie down with the lamb – I doubt really if we could have.'³ This belief explains why in *Murder on the Orient Express* Hercule Poirot allows the twelve murderers of Samuel Ratchett to get off scot-free, despite having proved their guilt. Ratchett, alias Canetti, extinguishes a whole family by kidnapping and murdering the daughter, whereupon the wife has a miscarriage and dies, whereupon the husband shoots himself. The monster Ratchett had escaped the law and was not to be removed from the face of the earth except by self-administered justice.

Christie regards evil in human beings as hubris that will throw them into the abyss as Satan was thrown. When Victoria Jones, one of the good characters in *They Came to Baghdad*, suddenly detects Satan, the corrupter of the world, in Edward Goring, a glamorous young air force officer, a quotation from Milton runs through her head: 'Lucifer, Son of the Morning, how art thou fallen.'⁴ Edward's world conspiracy is thwarted by an alliance of the good, which knows of no ethical distinction between British and oriental men and women. Sheikh Hussein el Ziyara of Kerbala attends the decisive peace

Stereoscopic cameras in Syria, 1930s (photo: Agatha Christie)

Right Gertrude Bell shown with Arabs on the jacket of the German edition of her *Daughter of the Desert*, Scherz Verlag 1993

Far right Gertrude Bell in 1909 in front of her tent in Babylon (E.W. Andrae and R.M. Boehmer, *Bilder eines Ausgräbers. Walter Andrae im Orient 1898–1919*, Gebrüder Mann Verlag 1992)

conference in Baghdad. His very appearance lends him authority; he is tall, deep-voiced, a patriarch. His reputation as holy man and poet looms large in the Muslim world. The sheikh does not speak a single political word; he draws attention to his friendship with Henry Carmichael, a life-long friend of the Arabs; he places his trust in new British friends because they are intimate with classic Arab poetry and able to quote a line by the poet Mutanabbi. At this momentary encounter Christie establishes a cultural and moral harmony between Arabs and Britons; she does not emphasize the political dimension of a disarmament conference. Neither is the fact made a theme that in the Iraq of 1950 (the year in which the novel is set) there might be reasons for internal unrest. The police, so the British archaeologists in the country assure their visitors, have the situation in hand. Symptomatically, Christie's archaeologists turn out to be entirely apolitical beings. Dr Pauncefoot Jones, heading the dig at Tell Aswad, is not even deflected by violence from an ardent contemplation of his shards, and of those alone.

Searching for a political perspective on the Middle East in Christie, the wife of an archaeologist excavating in Syria, would be futile. She sedately accepted the French mandate over Syria in the 1930s; we find no trace of protest against what would today be termed imperialist and colonialist suppression of the Syrians. On the other hand Christie did not sing a paean about European civilization, to which orientals would have to be introduced before they became truly human. Europeans in the country, the officers of the French mandate military force, were helpful, polite, fond of good meals and capable of keeping peace in the villages. They knew, as well as the British, the lax disposition of Arabs towards hard work, but they coped better by retaining half a wage in arrears and so making the labourers stick to their jobs. Christie's husband Max Mallowan, British gentleman that he was, refused to play these tricks at his dig. Agatha approved. Christie's restraint in political judgement, her amicable yet at the same time manifest self-distancing from her object, the Orient, places her in opposition to most British travellers in the Near and Middle East.

Christie's position stands out in bolder relief when compared to that of Gertrude Bell. In *The Desert and the Sown* (1907) Gertrude Bell shares some of her Syrian experience with Christie, yet a sharper contrast is hardly thinkable. Bell, too, lived as a woman among Arabs in Syria for several years; she also busied herself with archaeology; she also travelled hazardously through the waste lands of the country. But Bell journeyed alone, her male protection consisting of her own servants; travelling some twenty years earlier than Christie, she made no use of a motor vehicle, instead she sat in the saddle for days and weeks; additionally, she spoke Arabic fluently. Bell belonged to that generation of British travellers who felt a deep love for the Arabs (sometimes, indeed, their motives are best kept veiled), who regarded their stay in the Orient as an existential adventure and who saw their dealings with oriental people as a mission. T.E. Lawrence in *The Seven Pillars of Wisdom* (1926) appears to have voiced that sympathy most successfully.

To return to pragmatic differences between Bell and Christie, when Bell, wearing women's clothing, met Arabs, she insisted on not being treated

Max Mallowan pushing a stranded car in Iraq, 1920s

by the sheikhs like some female creature subordinate to males. Several times she encountered mortal danger and rescued herself through her own circumspection. In contrast, Christie's team suffered and overcame minor dangers. They were caught in sand storms; their car, more than once, got stuck in the mud of a river bed. In such situations Agatha Christie, the British lady, naturally did not dirty her hands but watched her men manoeuvre the vehicle out of the mess. In *They Came to Baghdad* Victoria, the heroine, stumbles into an adventure against her will; she is abducted and escapes from a village into the desert; she behaves, admittedly, courageously, yet by no means as if capable of survival. Rescue does not come about through her own strength, but through the agency of a cool brain belonging to Richard Baker, her admirer. Christie's women, so it seems, cope quite practically, quick-wittedly and sensitively in a half-oriental, half-Europeanized context, but when overtaxed by the perils of country and politics, they prefer to lean on a strong male arm. Once more in contrast, Bell did her own manipulating in the East.

In 1915 Bell joined the British Arab Bureau in Cairo; her secret service task was stirring up the Arabs against the Turks. In Iraq she worked as Oriental

House servants furnishing the expedition house at Ur, 1920s (photo: Max Mallowan)

Dancing worker on the dig. Still from the film made by Agatha Christie at Nimrud in 1952/7

Secretary at the Embassy in Baghdad; in the 1920s she played the *éminence grise* behind the enthronement of King Faisal. Bell loved the Arabs, but the nomads of the desert more than their cousins in the cities. She admired dignity, calm, hospitality, rank. Servants she treated amicably and condescendingly, sheikhs she met as an equal, if not as a secret superior. She shared this secret but unshaken belief in her own superiority with many oriental travellers. It rested on the conviction that fundamentally orientals never reach maturity. 'The Oriental is like a very old child,' she exclaims.[5] The singular betrays Bell. It is de-individualizing and levelling. It reveals a conception of oriental peoples that denies them change and development. An oriental is an oriental – no differentiation is being made as to historical circumstances or the social position of an individual.

In *Orientalism* (1978) Edward Said justly attacks this ahistorical and essentialist definition and castigates its adherents as devotees of orientalism. He defines orientalism as a variety of European ethnocentrism, as systematic cultural and political exploitation of the Orient from a position of (assumed) strength and superiority.[6] To early orientalists, in Said's sense, all orientals were children, whether Turks, Arabs or Kurds. They were ancient, venerable children, to be sure, but compared with progressive Europeans they were infants, who on occasion had to be administered happiness against their own will. The generation travelling in the Near and Middle East during the 1920s and 1930s was the last capable of believing in the White Man's Burden, more precisely in the task of bringing the blessings of civilization to the 'childlike' nations of the Orient. Ideologically, that generation was the heir to Victorian imperialism. Christie's attitude is better understood against a late Victorian and Edwardian background. Here, then, are some of the judgements on oriental men and women passed by travellers during the heyday of imperialism, the second half of the nineteenth century.

William Ramsay, classical philologist, theologian and in his time the greatest expert on the historical geography of Asia Minor, belonged undoubtedly to the true friends of Anatolian Turks. Yet he concluded in *Impressions of Turkey during Twelve Years' Wanderings* (1897) that, in the calm seclusion of their village existence, Anatolian farmers did not grow up into adults: 'Intellectually, they are only children.' In *To and from Constantinople* (1873) Hubert Jerningham, diplomat and scholar, equally spoke of the childlike nature of the Turks: 'Just as children desire to possess every kind of knowledge without ever striving to obtain it, so the Turks wish instinctively to emulate the Christians, but are too lazy and too proud to work toward that end.'[7] Concerning oriental women – I merely quote verdicts on Ottoman women – the view predominated that these beings represented infants, no more, no less. James Dallaway, chaplain and physician to the British Embassy in Constantinople, declared in *Constantinople Ancient and Modern* (1797): 'Throughout Turkey, in every rank of life, the women are literally children of a larger growth.' Decades later, in *The Crescent and the Cross* (1845) Elliott Warburton, popular travel writer on the Orient, still struck the same note: 'The women have all the insipidity of children without their innocence and sparkling freshness.'[8]

At least Jerningham and Ramsay dispensed with the prevalent polemical explanation that the cultural backwardness of orientals was primarily due to Islam. An infant state of mind, backwardness and Islam entered into an unholy alliance when it came to offering a smooth explanation of the cultural superiority of Europeans over orientals, a cultural superiority that, for its part, was never questioned. Two such nineteenth-century explications, as full of pathos as they were blind to reality, will suffice. Robert Semple, Scot, agriculturist and commercial traveller, stated in *Observations on a Journey through Spain and Italy* (1807): 'It is impossible to be a true Mussulman and a lover and cultivator of those arts and sciences which adorn and exalt mankind.' Much later the geologist William Hamilton, in *Researches in Asia Minor* (1842), judged in a similarly condescending spirit, despite his knowledge of Sultan Mahmut's great reforms: 'The bigotry and intolerance ever presented themselves as an insuperable bar to their [the Turks'] moral or political improvement.'[9]

So far, only some polemicists have had their say. An extensive analysis of nineteenth-century travellers would point out men and women who met oriental customs and manners in a tolerant, friendly, even admiring fashion. Furthermore, militant orientalists (Said's ilk) did by no means meet unanimous approval at home. In 1842 the *Athenaeum* reproached Hamilton for his attack on the Turks. It castigated 'dislike of reason', 'political ill-humour' and 'self-indulgent dogmatism'. The *Edinburgh Review*, in 1843, felt compelled to charge Hamilton 'with extreme prejudice in thus stigmatising the Turkish character'.[10] Nevertheless, the majority of nineteenth-century travellers in the East believed oriental people incapable of cultural progress, and this was chiefly due to Islam demanding total submission to the will of God. In brief, God's gifts must be accepted by man, may His will be done – *Inshallah*. Strictly speaking, such resignation was not miles apart from Christian humility; yet what was called virtue in Christians, in Muslims was given a bad name – fatalism. Europeans saw the difference in this: men and women were free to follow a Protestant work ethic, i.e. to work strenuously for their earthly bliss (and, hopefully and indirectly, for their heavenly bliss); leaning back, however, and waiting for God's will to be done would, decidedly, not do. In Islam Christians

The Patriarch of Babylon, with Max Mallowan standing in the door, Nimrud, 1953 (photo: Agatha Christie)

Above Boat on the Tigris, 1950s (photo: Agatha Christie)

Below Children at Balawat, 1950s (photo: Agatha Christie)

identified acceptance with fatalism and fatalism with apathy. William Hunter, a legal man belonging to the ranks of inglorious but by no means mute orientalists, fumed in *Travels through France, Turkey* (1792): 'The firm belief of predestination ... is, perhaps, the most powerful political machine, that stupidity ever submitted to ... It deprives man of all the energy and sublimity of his character.' John Cam Hobhouse, Byron's friend and companion on their tour through Albania and the Dardanelles between 1809 and 1810, was no less certain that Islam had in the past prevented, and would in the future prevent, any change in the state of an individual and consequently in the character of the Turkish people.[11] Still, the verdict on Muslim fatalism was never unanimous; the more the nineteenth century progressed, the more often Muslim love of repose, Muslim contentment with one's fate, were seen as beneficial and refreshing when compared with the restlessness of Europeans. Accordingly, Julia Pardoe, an intelligent and friendly observer of life in Istanbul, highly praised the rural Turk in *The City of the Sultan* (1837). He was 'a creature of calm temperament ... who labours in his vocation with a placid brow and a quiet heart'.[12]

When we return to Agatha Christie and her characters, we find a similar state of things: Arab fatalism plays no small role, and European reaction to it is divided. In *They Came to Baghdad* Henry Carmichael understands fatalism as a desirable philosophy of life. He yearns to be a man of 'Eastern and not of Western blood'; he no longer wants to weigh the chances of success or failure but wishes to 'throw responsibility on the All Merciful, the All Wise. *Inshallah*'. Invoking the name of Allah, he feels 'the calmness and the fatalism of the country overwhelming him' and he welcomes the experience.[13] Among all of Christie's fictional figures Carmichael shows the greatest attachment to, and respect for, the oriental character.

In *Come, Tell Me How You Live* the live characters are a divided lot concerning oriental fatalism, and they have numerous occasions for philosophizing about it. Two instances stand out. The first case is more ridiculous than tragic. A labourer suffers from constipation and is given an enema at the hospital. He finds this humiliating and would have preferred to die. The episode serves Christie for her own reflection on the significance of human life. Like Carmichael she regards fatalism – which she prefers to call submission to the will of God – as something entirely positive. In the West, she thinks, life has a high value, whereas in the Orient it does not. Birth and death are ineluctable; the coming of death depends on Allah's will; submission to God is required. Submission, for its part, overcomes the fear of death that dominates Western thought. A trifling objection must be allowed. Submission to God's will is all very well as long as people are deciding their own fates. But is fatalism acceptable when people resign themselves to the death of another human being?

This question is raised in the second instance. The sheikh owning the land on which Mallowan's excavation takes place one day sends his harem to Christie, so that she can give medical aid to the principal wife and several subordinate wives. The principal wife suffers from a septic eye, which ought to be treated as soon as possible. Urgency is impressed on the husband, too. 'This summer, says the Sheikh, or at any rate in the autumn. There is no hurry. All will be as Allah directs.'[14] If his favourite horse had fallen ill, the critic surmises, the sheikh would have acted more speedily. Christie offers no comment on the man's unmoved mind.

Her refusal to condemn fatalism is underlined by two further episodes. Overhearing a conversation between her husband and the sheikh, she realizes that discourse on both sides fails to be modern. They argue by parables and exempla, as does the New Testament. Christie ponders over the parable of the Good Samaritan, who picked up a man beaten by robbers on the road to Jericho, took him home and nursed him like a child. Love of one's neighbour and mercy are, so to speak, dependent on the medical infrastructure of a country. Where police, ambulances and hospitals exist in sufficient numbers, individual help is no longer urgent. Among the peoples of the desert, however, the commandment of mercy is still valid; mercy must be shown to a human being fallen into distress far remote from other aid. One of the archaeologists, Robert Macartney ('Mac'), combines a fatalistic argument with British love of animals in a singularly cold-hearted fashion: since in the Orient people die like flies anyway, the point in time of a person's death matters little. But were he to encounter a horse in distress, he would do everything to save it whereas he would do nothing for a human being.

At this point an interim appraisal may come in useful. First, Christie's autobiographical experience of the Orient does not contain mad adventures; instead it speaks of common, trivial, often exasperating things and occurrences. This is not meant as a criticism of her tale; on the contrary, her pictures of ordinary lives deep in the countryside are made all the more credible by a narrative in a low key. Conversely, the crime novel, as genre, demands extraordinary irruptions into ordinary human lives, murder and manslaughter. In Christie's crime novels extreme incidents such as these are only weakly linked to the oriental setting. The Orient Express might as well have got stuck in Switzerland; murders might have been committed on a steamer on the Rhine rather than the Nile; Edward Goring's world conspiracy did not strictly demand Baghdad as a setting, though an oriental colouring will have helped the reader's expectation of a cloak-and-dagger story.

Cook with Christmas cake at Ur (photo: Max Mallowan)

Sailing boat on the Nile in Egypt, 1931 or 1933 (photo: Max Mallowan)

A second characteristic has also emerged. Christie by and large renounces political analysis; her own comment on possible profound differences between Europeans and orientals remains discreet and guarded. Such restraint of the self is very marked in the autobiographies and less so in the novels. In her fiction characters give free rein to their prejudice concerning foreign nations and the Orient. They do not represent the opinion of their creator, but, since they are conceived as flat characters anyway, they are given permission to utter ethnocentric and slightly derogative clichés. At the same time Christie exercises poetic justice. Almost no national character, as embodied in the protagonists, is exempt from ridicule. A small selection follows. On the Orient Express the Hungarian count cuts a dashing figure, straight out of an operetta; the Italian is fleshy, dark skinned and, like all Italians, fond of the dagger; the English servant is as buttoned up as Jeeves in the novels of P.G. Wodehouse; and the Greek doctor constantly has carnal thoughts of his mistress. In the eyes of clever Miss Debenham even Hercule Poirot is a laughable little man, a figure whom nobody would take seriously. Poirot's initial humbling is part of Christie's narrative technique; at the beginning of a detective

Snake charmer in Egypt, 1931 or 1933 (photo: Max Mallowan)

novel it is only fit that Poirot, the dandy, be underestimated. Colonel Arbuth-not moreover classifies him under 'damned foreigners'.

Xenophobia is a speciality of Christie's British travellers. In *They Came to Baghdad* Victoria Jones is gripped by an 'Anglo-Saxon intolerance of foreigners' and turns most pushy when confronted with tenacious resistance in the office of Dr Rathbone. Christie comments: 'Before an imperious Briton who means to get his or her way, barriers nearly always fall.' In *Death on the Nile* Tim Aller-ton is expressly exempted by his mother from 'the ordinary Britisher's dislike, and mistrust of, foreigners. Tim was very cosmopolitan.'[15] Coming from Vic-toria's and Mrs Allerton's lips, the phrase 'foreigners' is nothing if not ironical, because it is they who are staying abroad, whereas the Egyptians, respectively the Iraqis, have every right to be called the true inhabitants of the country.

Considerable psychological distancing from the 'natives' goes hand in hand with sociological differentiation. 'Natives' are not kept at arm's length indiscriminately, but graded according to ethnicity, social rank and age. All three factors determine the degree of acceptance. In her fiction and autobi-ographies Christie handles sheikhs and old men gently and with respect for

Above Camel herd in Iraq, 1920s (photo: Max Mallowan)

Left Children at Ur, 1920s (photo: Max Mallowan)

their dignity; with women, particularly with Kurdish women, she is friendly. Dealers, beggars, begging children come off worst. In *Death on the Nile* Hercule Poirot and Rosalie Otterbourne react defensively to souvenir peddlers and children, the riff-raff. Poirot tries in vain to drive off the human cluster of flies; Rosalie walks through the rabble as if sleepwalking; in a slight attack of hysteria she even pretends to be deaf and blind. Otherwise Rosalie behaves like a normal lady tourist, down to a superficial knowledge of Egyptian antiquities. The nineteenth century described her type as 'young ladies with pink parasols that glide about the Pyramides'.[16] Mrs Allerton, one of the engaging characters, sadly deplores Egyptian children that grin, posture and demand *bakshish*. They had been watching her for two hours and were now closing in on her. Her shout, a claustrophobic reaction, would drive them away, but they returned and stared and stared, their 'eyes [were] simply disgusting and so [were] their noses'. It is more than curious that Agatha Christie herself describes oriental children in exactly the same terms. In Brak the wife of a water carrier and her children want to thank the Mallowans for a favour and crowd around them. Trying to escape is useless. The children's noses are 'in a

Above Flock of sheep in Iraq, 1950s (photo: Agatha Christie)

Right Water carriers at Ur, 1920s (photo: Max Mallowan)

disgusting condition'. Christie asks herself, 'Why should it be only the human young whose noses run when left in a state of nature?'[17]

A more serious, yet not unrelated problem is this. Why do Christie's British friends and fictional characters so often shy away from bodily contact with oriental people? I give an example from Christie's circle of friends. The sheikh of the Mallowans greets his guests in the oriental manner by embracing and kissing on both cheeks. Whereas Max Mallowan and Robert Macartney find nothing strange in that, Colonel Burn, a member of the excavation campaign of 1937, struggles in panic against being kissed by the repulsive old man. In vain, when the company is about to depart, the sheikh shouts, 'Farewell, brother' and embraces and kisses him. The colonel turns plum colour.[18] In *Death on the Nile* the travellers also complain that they find no peace, not a single spot where they would be unmolested.

Such fear of close physical contact with orientals and tenacious insistence on bodily and social distance are commonly found in earlier British travellers. The fear was not entirely unreasonable in two situations that they could hardly avoid. First, in the interior of an oriental city physical distance from man and beast was easily lost. Second, social distance was also endangered at every encounter with oriental hosts. There follows an instance of either kind of risk; Izmir exemplifies the oriental city, Turkish villagers the peculiarities of hospitality.

Oriental cities were generally regarded by Europeans as labyrinths. Losing one's way in them, even if not actually perishing, created anxiety and revulsion. Since a traveller was not able to 'read' a city, he condemned it as

Pipe-smoking men in Kurdistan, 1931 or 1933 (photo: Max Mallowan)

'unreadable'. In Izmir streets were narrow, barely three yards wide, without pavement, and stinking sewage flowed down the middle. Most streets had no names, houses had no numbers, there was no artificial lighting. In *Greece and the Levant* (1834) Richard Burgess, tutor to Lord George Paget on his Grand Tour, complained: 'The interior of Smyrna is a labyrinth of narrow, ill-built streets … a Babel of confusion of tongues assails the ear.'[19] Other elements added to the feeling of physical insecurity. On market days the streets became near impassable. Chaos increased when camels, in lines of 200 or 300 animals, marched slowly through them, led by a donkey. Travellers were in constant danger of being knocked down or pushed aside. Protest was useless, because Europeans were not understood by either locals or animals. Open spaces did not exist. The cumulative effect of unpleasant circumstances created a claustrophobic mood in which British visitors felt hemmed in and soiled by the contact with human beings and animals. Sightseeing in Izmir in 1871, Mrs Baillie proved to be a sensible Victorian lady, yet she had been jostled so constantly by porters, donkeys and mules that she was only too glad to escape from the labyrinth.[20]

In the countryside travellers experienced the removal of physical and psychological distance under different circumstances. Local people, having no other design upon strangers than the wish to press hospitality upon them, were nevertheless regarded as a nuisance. Indeed, the hospitality of Anatolian peasants was above blame. In 1907 Gertrude Bell commended the Turkish peasant as more hospitable than any other oriental; throughout the nineteenth century Turcophile travellers had sung the same praise. Yet a large number of travellers reacted to village hospitality with varying degrees of moroseness.

This was so because there were two sides to an encounter of foreigner and villager. The peasants were suddenly confronted with an object of intense curiosity and therefore unwilling to allow private space to their guests. The Europeans were presented with food and accommodation by the locals, but resented being pushed into an unwanted proximity. In the early twentieth century travellers such as Wilfred Blunt, T.E. Lawrence and Richard Burton might long to be close to the desert Arabs, the kindred spirits of their imagination, but travellers in the nineteenth century were far from seeing a brother in the Anatolian peasant. Hobhouse and Lord Byron stayed cool and unmoved when in 1810 rural Turks near Ephesus offered them a guest-room and made fun of their preparations for the night. Hobhouse's account reads like that of a striptease. With astounded smiles the peasants watched the two travellers taking off garment after garment, apparently waiting for the foreigners to take off their skins, too, and finally burst into laughter. The next morning the same villagers sat in their places, smoking pipes, sipping coffee and waiting for a repeat performance, 'with', comments Hobhouse, 'nothing rude or uncivil in their manner'.[21] A quick glance at the Mallowans reveals a similar aloofness. In Beirut the Hamoudi family rushes into the couple's bedroom early in the morning, and they all regard the visit as the most natural thing in the world. In Anatolia visitors commonly reacted negatively.

Throngs of rural humanity aroused a feeling of claustrophobia rather than of brotherhood. Near Ushak Francis Arundell, chaplain to the Levant Company in Izmir, and his travelling companion Dethier, the Belgian consul in the town, became very jittery when at least forty villagers pushed into their room measuring twelve feet square. Yet these two were no novices but, as *Discoveries in Asia Minor* (1834) proves, experienced archaeological travellers. In Cappadocia villagers were a great pest. They overstepped, the geographer William Ainsworth writes in *Travels and Researches in Asia Minor* (1842), all

Bedouin tent in Iraq, 1950s (photo: Agatha Christie)

limits of an acceptable thirst for knowledge. Ainsworth had come across char-
coal burners who greeted him and his companions with the 'most malicious
grins and more than suspicious looks'. They crowded into the small guest-
room and fingered every object. The Britons kept a sharp look-out for their
possessions.[22] In all probability Ainsworth was right to be upset, because,
although rare, minor thefts did occur. Pistols and tobacco, for example, were
wont to vanish from European baggage. There was yet another reason for
keeping rural people at arm's length. Scholarly travellers and such harbouring
literary ambitions as a rule had only the evening to record daily events in their
diaries, so a room crammed full with peasants was no help. Charles Fellows,
the famous discoverer of Lycian monuments and a staunch friend of the rural
Turk, mentions in *A Journal Written during an Excursion in Asia Minor* (1839)
how difficult it was to write his diary in a room filled with Turks. These had sat
down with the friendliest intentions, smoked their pipes and watched every
movement of his lips and hands intently. His scribbling must have looked like
hard work to illiterate men. Fellows had enough understanding to detect good
manners behind ostensible rudeness. Every time he looked up, curiosity
yielded to natural politeness, and the peasants averted their eyes. He explains
that these people did not have the slightest notion of the luxury of being solitary. They were sociable to an extraordinary degree because they depended on
each other for entertainment. So they watched their European until mid-
night.[23]

One more motive for the aversion of British visitors to crowds at close
quarters remains unspoken but is to be deduced indirectly. At home the majority of travellers occupied the social position of gentlemen. They were familiar
with a calibrated empty space around them, indeed they demanded a graded
emptiness, and so in the house servants, children and wives kept their respec-
tive and respectful distance to the master. In Anatolia the gentlemen, to their
large surprise, noticed that between their Turkish peer group, i.e. justices, government officials and landowners, and their humble clients a socially calibrated empty space simply did not exist. One reason for such egalitarianism
may be seen in the Islamic commandment of universal brotherhood. But that
thought did not enter the minds of our British travellers in their overcrowded
rooms. If a low peasant, surrounded by a pungent odour of garlic, appeared to
disregard foreign superior status and approached them as a brother, the gentlemen translated their indignation into action and threw the brother out.

Despite all momentary indignation British travellers were generally
well inclined towards rural Turks. As to the good or perverted character of

The epigraphist Dr Legrain dressed as an Arab, Ur expedition house, 1927/8 (photo: Max Mallowan)

Above Arab playing a stringed instrument, Iraq, 1920s (photo: Max Mallowan)

Left Arab girl by the expedition house at Nimrud, 1950s (photo: Agatha Christie)

Yezidis in Iraq, 1954 (photo: Agatha Christie)

orientals, they drew a distinct dividing line between people in the country and those in the cities, and another one between settled farmers and nomads. The more citified the oriental, the more perverted his character; the more rustic his life, the purer it appeared. John Macdonald Kinneir in *Journey through Asia Minor* (1818) praises Turkmen nomads for their many virtues, which were to be sought in vain in the degenerated Turks in the cities. Julia Pardoe joins the hymn on rural Turks, who were intuitively cultured, polite and dignified. Lt. Thomas Spratt, of the Royal Navy, assisted Fellows in the excavations at Xanthos, and in *Travels in Lycia* (1847) he confesses that his visit to Lycia had taught him the traits of the true Turkish character – openness, politeness and honesty. In the country that character was unspoilt by the vices of the capital and noticeable in 'a race comparatively pure'.[24] Lady Anne Blunt, in *A Pilgrimage to Nejd* (1881), holds that pure-bred horses and pure-bred Arabs have nobler features than creatures of mixed blood.[25] Although the belief in pure blood warranting excellent quality is best restricted to those breeding dogs and horses, but objecting to it means arguing against a late Victorian notion.

The high esteem in which British travellers held nomads as being the purest, least adulterated orientals stemmed from a romanticizing enthusiasm for pastoral simplicity, for the dignity and beauty of ancient ways of life that can be traced back to biblical times. The Bible as paradigm of contemporary oriental existence was most powerful in Victorian times and later. In effect orientals were presented as members of a world unchanged for centuries and hence unchangeable; in other words they were lifted from the world of here and now and set down in a fictional never-never land made up from such texts as the Bible and the *Arabian Nights*. There they sit and vainly wait for progress. Christie does not altogether eschew the biblical paradigm, as when she ponders on the conversation between Max Mallowan and the sheikh that is interspersed with parables and exempla, but biblical life is no significant key to the oriental life she observes around her. She deals much more extensively with how the present local population lives, with differences in character and dress between members of the various ethnic groups on their dig. Thus she continues an old tradition of travellers who were always eager to order and classify the motley oriental crowd. At the excavation she meets Kurds, Turks, Arabs and Armenians. The Armenians are given a bad name. True, they are the most intelligent among the labourers, but also the most seditious. Instead of keeping peace, they quarrel continuously and so unite Kurds and Arabs against them. Christie's servant Aristide suffices to exemplify the distinct traits of his 'race'. He is Armenian and hence thrifty, indeed miserly. The small town of Amuda is for the large part inhabited by Armenians; it is an unattractive place, stinking of sheep's cadavers, swarming with flies and the most unmannered children. The inhabitants appear to be as bored as they are malicious. Nineteenth-century urban Armenians, too, had a reputation for being clever, hence they were excellent business people, and they were thought to possess great physical strength and a stolid temperament. They were, in Julia Pardoe's unkind phrase, 'the buffaloes of the East'.[26] As to the Arab character, Christie finds it distinguished by liberality and fatalism. The Arab labourers on the dig have a pre-modern and pre-capitalist attitude towards time, labour and money. Since male dignity means so much to them, there has to be a debate whether working on an excavation is a job compatible with Arab dignity or not. Their first look at money is one of suspicion; saving it does not enter their minds because working more and earning more than is required for maintenance during the next few days or weeks is also undignified.

Arab women are by nature shy, modest and subservient to men. In *They Came to Baghdad* Victoria Jones stumbles, when kidnapped, upon Arab village women. She, inventive young European woman that she is, confirms their 'very simple mentality'. Arab women wear the veil, and Christie's verdict on this garment is entirely and surprisingly positive. For one thing, the veil offers protection to women in a society dominated by men. Victoria, too, knows its protective power: 'A virtuously veiled Arab woman, however ragged and poor, had … all possible immunity.' Secondly, the veil tempts Christie herself into daydreams that may have biographical origins. Agatha, having had to fight shyness for so many years, envies oriental women wearing the veil; the veil lends invisibility by taking away identity. Having your face veiled 'must make you feel very private, very secret … only your eyes look out on the world – you see it, but it does not see you.'[27] On a train journey somewhere in the middle of Anatolia Christie strikes up a conversation with an American lady. They watch Turkish women that do not wear the veil working in the fields. Atatürk had abolished the veil, remarks the American, and so given freedom to women. Christie refuses to be drawn into a debate that, she feels, is demeaned by the use of symbols. As hard work had not changed for the women, the new right of going without the veil did not, presumably, mean much to them.

In Turkey today the acrimonious discussion is by no means over as to whether the veil represents an oppression of women by Islam or whether wearing no veil indicates secular emancipation. In the nineteenth century the debate was less vicious. In Istanbul the religious meaning of the veil became half forgotten, and it changed into a mere comfortable garment, occasionally an instrument of coquetry. The higher the social position of a woman, the less inclined she was to wear the veil. In the country, however, women obeyed the tradition of the veil, irrespective of their religion and ethnic community. Only nomad women, particularly Kurds, went without it. This situation had not changed in Christie's day. On the dig her sympathy belongs to Kurdish women. She takes pleasure in their multi-coloured clothes, and she finds them gay, erotic, flirtatious, self-confident and by no means subjected by their menfolk. One Kurdish woman shows rare enterprise: she poisons her three husbands, but her initiative, alas, is punished at the gallows in Mosul.

Christie's aversion to ideological and religious hotheads is also evident in her description of Yezidis, the Devil Worshippers. The Devil Worshippers are friendly people, their religion is a mixture of Islamic mysticism and earlier beliefs. Their sanctuary in the mountains, the burial place of Sheikh 'Adi, possesses calm and beauty as no other place in the world. Christie movingly writes: 'Sheikh 'Adi is a place I shall never forget – nor shall I forget the utter peace and satisfaction that possessed my spirit there.'[28] These are strange words from a lady traveller who, in general, abhors all hyperbole. They also throw light on her idea of an ideal oriental landscape. Other travellers had admired the vastness and dangers of Arabian deserts, the utmost loneliness of the high plains in Turkey and Iran, and by describing sublime landscapes, they meet their reading public's expectation of a romanticized Orient. Though Christie evades sublime expectations, the sanctuary of the Devil Worshippers lies in a pastoral landscape; it is surrounded by deep silence; a path runs through a grove; water trickles from a spring; the temple is surrounded by trees; every part breathes quiet, cool peace. Such an oriental spot, if it can be considered in painterly terms at all, resembles the landscapes of Claude Lorrain and Nicolas Poussin. The objection might be raised that Christie describing a landscape as ideal is far from characteristic. Her description, I would answer, is characteristic in another sense, namely that she once more demonstrates her independent manner of writing. She avoids moral and political partisanship (and so waives analysis along such lines); she shuns long-established verdicts on the Orient (and does so without a trace of anxiety); she describes from an amicable and closely observing distance.

NOTES

1   Agatha Christie, *An Autobiography*, London 1977, and *Come, Tell Me How You Live*, London 1999.
2   Reinhold Schiffer, *Oriental Panorama: British Travellers in 19th Century Turkey*, Amsterdam, 1999.
3   Christie, *Autobiography* (n. 1), pp. 453f.
4   Christie, *They Came to Baghdad*, London 1944, p. 221.
5   G. Bell, *The Desert and the Sown*, London 1985, preface, no pagination.
6   E. Said, *Orientalism*, New York 1978, p. 19 and passim.
7   W. Ramsay, *Impressions of Turkey during Twelve Years' Wanderings*, London 1897, p. 21; H. Jerningham, *To and from Constantinople*, London 1873, pp. 335f.
8   J. Dallaway, *Constantinople Ancient and Modern*, London 1797, p. 27; E. Warburton, *The Crescent and the Cross*, I, London 1845, p. 96.
9   R. Semple, *Observations on a Journey through Spain and Italy to Naples; and thence to Smyrna and Constantinople*, II, London 1807, p. 217; W. Hamilton, *Researches in Asia Minor, Pontus and Armenia*, I, London 1842, p. 355.
10 *The Athenaeum* 785 (1842), pp. 987, 988; *The Edinburgh Review* 77 (1843), p. 460.
11 W. Hunter, *Travels through France, Turkey, and Hungary*, II, London 1803, p. 57; J.C. Hobhouse, *A Journey through Albania and Other Provinces of Turkey in Europe and Asia*, II, London 1813, p. 912.
12 J. Pardoe, *The City of the Sultan*, II, London 1837, p. 208.
13 Christie, *They Came to Baghdad* (n. 4), p. 45.
14 Christie, *Come, Tell* (n. 1), p. 136.
15 Christie, *They Came to Baghdad* (n. 4), p. 98; *Death on the Nile*, London 1985, p. 98.
16 *The Quarterly Review* 76 (1845), p. 126.
17 Christie, *Nile* (n. 15), p. 85; *Come, Tell* (n. 1), p. 169.
18 Christie, *Come, Tell* (n. 1), p. 177.
19 R. Burgess, *Greece and the Levant*, II, London 1835, p. 75.
20 E.C.C. Baillie, *A Sail to Smyrna*, London 1873, pp. 212f.
21 Hobhouse, *Journey through Albania* (n. 11), II, p. 654.
22 F.V.J. Arundell, *Discoveries in Asia Minor*, I, London 1834, p. 134; W. Ainsworth, *Travels and Researches in Asia Minor*, I, London 1842, p. 95
23 C. Fellows, *A Journal Written during an Excursion in Asia Minor*, London 1839, pp. 82, 150f.
24 J. Macdonald Kinneir, *Journey through Asia Minor, Armenia and Koordistan*, London 1847, p. 59; Pardoe, *City of Sultan* (n. 12), II, p. 32; T. Spratt, *Travels in Lycia, Milyas and the Cibyratis*, II, London 1847, p. 5.
25 A. Blunt, *A Pilgrimage to Nejd*, London 1985, pp. 8f.
26 Pardoe, *City of Sultan* (n. 12), II, p. 382.
27 Christie, *They Came to Baghdad* (n. 4), p. 179; *Come, Tell* (n. 1), p. 183.
28 Christie, *Come, Tell* (n. 1), p. 110.

MURDER IN MESOPOTAMIA

AGATHA CHRISTIE

A NEW POIROT STORY

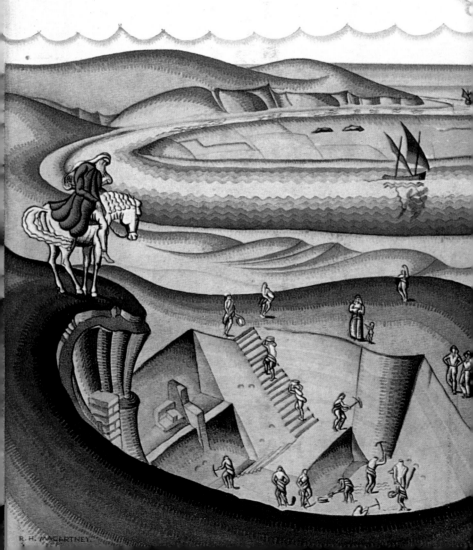

R. H. MCCARTNEY

Detective Novels

'The Glamour of the East':[1] Some Reflections on Agatha Christie's *Murder in Mesopotamia*

Nadja Cholidis

> You would have made a good archaeologist, M. Poirot.
> You have the gift of re-creating the past.
> Eric Leidner in *Murder in Mesopotamia*[2]

If one compares the problems that lie at the root of both detective investigation and archaeology, the scene of a crime has much in common with an archaeological site. Without intensive study of the when, how and why of the case, the criminal would not be discovered, nor would the condition and significance of an archaeological site be properly assessed. In her novel *Murder in Mesopotamia*, first published in 1936, Agatha Christie linked her archaeological knowledge to the classic detective story, inspiring later generations of crime writers to create two new variants: the historical detective story whose action is set in the past and, developing out of this, another genre that focuses more strongly on archaeologists and their work.

When Agatha Christie travelled to Baghdad alone in the late autumn of 1928, you could not talk of her having any great interest in ancient oriental cultures. After her divorce from her first husband Archibald Christie she wanted to put the past behind her with a journey to some distant foreign land and make a new start. Her ideas of the Near East were not very clear, but they did include the alluring prospect of going much of the way on the Simplon-Orient Express, which ran from Calais to Damascus by way of Constantinople. She made the last part of the journey on a bus, which in those days took two days

Jacket by Robin Macartney for the first edition of *Murder in Mesopotamia*, the Crime Club, Collins 1934

The ziggurat at Ur
(photo: Georg Gerster)

Katharine and Leonard Woolley on pay-day at Ur, 1920s (photo: Max Mallowan)

to reach its destination of Baghdad and stopped overnight on the way. Baghdad disappointed her at first: 'Geographically I might be in Baghdad, spiritually I was in England still.'[3] Only a few days later she went on to Ur, where extensive excavations were then in progress directed by the British archaeologist Leonard Woolley (1880–1960). The discovery of the Royal Cemetery there had aroused international interest. Woolley's wife Katharine, who had just been reading Agatha Christie's *Murder of Roger Ackroyd*, gave their famous guest from England a warm welcome. Once immersed in daily life on a dig, Agatha Christie greatly enjoyed her stay in these exotic surroundings: 'I fell in love with Ur, with its beauty in the evenings, the ziggurat standing up, faintly shadowed, and that wide sea of sand with its lovely pale colours of apricot, rose, blue and mauve changing every minute.'[4]

In March 1930, a few days before the end of the seventh season of digging at Ur, she arrived for a second visit. Her meeting with Max Mallowan,

Katharine and Leonard Woolley on the site at Ur, 1920s (photo: Max Mallowan)

fourteen years her junior, who had been assistant to Woolley on the dig since 1925, was of fundamental importance to her and changed her life. At Katharine Woolley's express wish, he was to show their famous guest round the sights of the area before she began her journey home. Both of them found this excursion, which lasted several days, extremely pleasant and entertaining, and after Agatha's calm conduct when their car broke down in the middle of the desert, Mallowan knew that his travelling companion would be just the wife for an archaeologist.

The eighth season of excavations on the site, in 1930–31, was to be the last that Mallowan spent at Ur. Katharine Woolley turned out to have reservations about the presence of his wife; now that he and Agatha were married, the famous writer became a potential rival to Katharine for the attention of the other participants on the dig. As neither of them could contemplate a long separation, the Mallowans joined Reginald Campbell Thompson's dig in Nineveh in the autumn of 1931, before Max began on his own first excavation at Arpachiyah in 1933.

Murder in Mesopotamia, featuring Hercule Poirot, hinges on the murder of the wife of the director of the dig. The requisite suspense is created by the fact that the murderer can only be one of the team members, who bear an obvious likeness to the members of the expedition at Ur. Although the Mallowans were friendly with the Woolleys – Agatha's book of short stories, *The Thirteen Problems*, was dedicated to them in 1932 – she did not forget that Katharine had been opposed to her marriage and her presence at Ur.

In the crime novel the highly regarded leader of the expedition becomes an American of Swedish descent, Dr Eric Leidner. His modest manner, friendly nature and touching concern for his wife win the reader's sympathy. Behind the façade of the successful scholar, however, hides the figure of Frederick Bosner, Louise Leidner's first husband, who is thought dead. The complicated circumstances leading up to the crime, which is triggered by Louise's adultery with Richard Carey, an assistant on the dig, gives Hercule Poirot an opportunity to put his powers to the test. Agatha Christie had Leonard Woolley's relationship with Katharine in mind when she sketched the character, as well as his engaging manner and his enthusiasm for his work. While the parallels between Katharine Woolley and the murder victim have frequently been pointed out, the similarity between Leonard Woolley and Dr Leidner has passed almost unnoticed in archaeological circles.

Louise Leidner is presented as an ambiguous personality who both fascinates and subtly dominates those around her. In her second marriage to Dr Leidner the supervision of the expedition house is her responsibility. The similarities between her and Katharine Woolley, which probably passed unnoticed only by Katharine herself, are more than obvious: both women had the same kind of character, had married twice and had lost their first husbands in unusual and indeed almost tragic circumstances.

In trying to describe Katharine Woolley (1888–1943) appropriately, anyone who did not know her can give only an approximate idea of her character and may not do her justice. As her personal papers were destroyed after her death at her own request, there are very few sources available. The usually subjective accounts of her contemporaries outline the picture of a dominant woman. The eroticism emanating from her on the one hand and her sexual frigidity on the other are perhaps the clearest illustration of the element of contradiction running through her life. Katharine Woolley was very well read, and could be a charming and amusing companion if she liked. Although she had considerable artistic talent she lacked the self-confidence to recognize it. Undoubtedly her unconventional attitudes and her vitality, combined with beauty and brains, had an extremely fascinating effect on those around her.

Katharine and Leonard Woolley with the excavation team at Ur, 1920s

The inner turmoil hidden behind her personal magnetism, however, was widely misunderstood and aroused considerable hostility. Her first husband's spectacular suicide only six months after their wedding may well have exacerbated her problems. Her marriage to Leonard Woolley, whom she had first met at Ur in 1924, did more than restore her sense of material and emotional security; her work on the site as a widowed and very attractive woman had been regarded as 'fast' at the time, giving rise to moral reservations about her character. These were now at an end. Although there had been problems in the marriage from the first, both partners had tried their best to find a *modus vivendi*. Katharine fully supported her husband's work, kept public interest in it alive and did what she could to help with the considerable expenses involved. The photographs showing her on the site still convey the impression of an elegant, confident woman who knew how to show herself to good advantage.

Until the first half of the twentieth century it was very unusual for women to take part in archaeological excavations at all, and only personal connections allowed them to do so. Most archaeological expeditions were made up of men who wanted to test their powers and make a name for themselves in a foreign country. The world of the Orient, its primitive and often Spartan conditions and its sometimes rough and ready customs held considerable attractions of their own, but it was difficult to reconcile the aura surrounding the early pioneers of archaeology with the ideal image of women current at the time. A slow change began to take place only after the First World War. Against such a background Katharine Woolley's work on the dig must have impressed Agatha Christie, and once Max Mallowan was in charge of his own excavations, it was natural for her to go with him and provide active support.

But to return to *Murder in Mesopotamia*: the story is told in retrospect by a nurse, Amy Leatheran, a capable young woman of thirty-two. She is engaged to look after Louise Leidner, but that is only the ostensible reason; without knowing it, she is intended to help the murderer set up the necessary alibi by determining the time of death. Agatha Christie gave the nurse some features of her own character and some that are purely fictional, for unlike her Amy Leatheran takes no interest in archaeology. She helps Louise Leidner to mend some broken pots, but the point of doing it at all is a mystery to her: 'Are they really worth keeping?'[5] she enquires. (Agatha Christie did sometimes base a character on herself, for instance one of her detectives Ariadne Oliver, whom she invented in 1934.)

The reader encounters Max Mallowan in the figure of the American David Emmott. Although this character plays only a subsidiary part, he marries the doctor's daughter at the end of the story. Christie's tendency to marry off her heroines at the end of their adventures is evidence of both her romantic vein and the value she set on the personal happiness she herself had found in her second marriage to Max Mallowan (1904–1978).

Marie and Joseph Mercado are reminiscent of two American missionaries, a married couple whom Agatha Christie had met in Diwaniyah in 1930 on her sightseeing excursion with Max. She had noticed how nervous they both were, and found the husband's conduct quite disturbing – he was tearing a handkerchief to shreds under the table. Agatha Christie could not resist devising a literary version of him. In *Murder in Mesopotamia* the couple's nervous agitation is explained by the fact that the husband is addicted to drugs and his wife fears that his addiction will be discovered. According to her notes, Agatha Christie also wanted to include the Campbell Thompsons in her story, although it is not clear whether she used them as individual characters rather than a married couple (Dr Reilly, Anne Johnson?) or rejected the idea in the end.

Raoul Menier, who slips into the role of epigraphist to replace the sick Father Lavigny, turns out to be a thief and a fraud. Any similarity to the Jesuit father Eric Burrows from Ur lies only in their vocation and their sceptical view

Left The epigraphist Father Burrows at Ur railway station, 1920s (photo: Max Mallowan)

Below The expedition house at Uruk, 1933–4

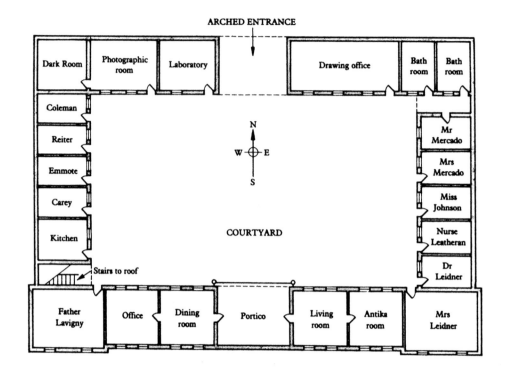

Plan of the expedition house at Tell Yarimjah (Agatha Christie, *Murder in Mesopotamia*, first edition, the Crime Club, Collins 1934)

of the finds made on the excavation. In the late nineteenth and early twentieth centuries the attraction of the scene of the biblical stories had induced several monks and churchmen to take up the study of cuneiform script and travel in the Orient. Father Lavigny's remark that Louise Leidner is a 'dangerous woman' derives from a remark about Katharine Woolley made by the Arabist Gertrude Bell, a comment probably passed on with some glee in archaeological circles.

Anne Johnson is presented to the reader as an intelligent, strong-minded, middle-aged woman. Her secret love for Dr Leidner is unrequited and causes great agony of conscience in her when she uncovers his secret. The few clues available do not allow us to decide whom Agatha Christie had in mind as a model – perhaps Freya Stark, perhaps someone else. The bold oriental traveller Freya Stark was in fact one of the few women who could assert herself in the presence of Katharine Woolley and who enjoyed her respect. But perhaps Agatha Christie was chiefly concerned to create a counterweight to Louise Leidner, Marie Mercado and Amy Leatheran.

Less flattering is the description of the photographer Bill Coleman and the new assistant Carl Reiter. Their appearance and clumsy behaviour are constantly giving Louise the opportunity to make sharp remarks. Amy Leatheran ends her story nursing Bill Coleman back to health after an attack of appendicitis (Mallowan's own illness prevented him from being present when Agatha Christie visited Ur for the first time in 1928); the comment that she has 'got quite fond of him' may suggest the beginning of a romance.

Agatha Christie's novels present several variations on the classic 'locked room' crime, transferring it to such unusual settings as an aircraft in flight, a train caught in snowdrifts or an island. In describing the expedition house in *Murder in Mesopotamia* she was probably thinking of the accommodation for the German expedition in Uruk, which, arranged round an interior courtyard and with a flat roof, offered just the setting she needed. Over the years this originally simple building had become a self-contained unit adapted to its various purposes, and it was extended several times. It is not surprising, then, that the south wing of the fictional expedition house at Tell Yarimjah has also been extended. The furnishing of the rooms, which Agatha Christie describes in

Pottery bowl from Tell Arpachiyah, Tell Halaf period, 5500–5000 BC, diameter 26 cm (British Museum, London)

detail on occasion, still corresponds to the basic equipment of many expedition houses. Now, as then, practicality is the main concern, with local accessories such as printed fabrics, kelims or metalwork products from the bazaars contributing to the atmosphere (cf. the essay by Joan Oates, 'Agatha Christie, Nimrud and Baghdad').

Amy Leatheran's first impressions of Baghdad, recorded in a letter to a nursing colleague, suggest the conditions Agatha Christie encountered on her first journey to the Orient. The English way of life pursued here and in the British colony of Hassaniyah is an important and recurrent element in her crime stories, and despite the foreign environment is meant to create an atmosphere of familiarity. According to the description of the route, Tell Yarimjah must be on the banks of the Tigris, a day and a half's journey from Baghdad. The tedious car journey from Kirkuk to the camp on the excavation site is reminiscent of the survey carried out by the Mallowans in Syria in 1934.

Agatha Christie's free reconstruction of the history of the settlement covers three major chronological periods – the Halaf period, the Akkadian period and the New Assyrian period – corresponding to the dating of the excavated sites at Ur, Nineveh and Arpachiyah. The 'deep cut' mentioned suggests the stratigraphic study made by Max Mallowan when he uncovered important information about the early history of northern Mesopotamia on the site at Nineveh in 1931 and in Arpachiyah two years later: with the aid of pottery sherds found in the different levels, he was able to establish for the first time a chronology of the ceramics of the period. Some of the vessels and sherds mentioned in the novel relate to the pottery of the Halaf period (sixth to fifth centuries BC), notable in particular for the painted motif of stylized bull's heads, which is mentioned several times. Cleaning deposits of mud from the vessels with hydrochloric acid, as Leidner and Mercado do, was a common practice at the time. From the modern viewpoint it is of dubious value, since the acid may attack the structure of the material itself if the sherds contain any lime.

The early Akkadian necropolis in the novel contains several grave goods that Agatha Christie saw in real life at Ur. The golden dagger with its lapis lazuli inlay on the handle is reminiscent, for instance, of the dagger found in 1927 that had belonged to a richly furnished royal grave of the Meskalamdug period (c.2500 BC). Woolley described the technique of studying a grave in an interview with the BBC as: 'the clearing of a grave may be a long job … obviously a necklace is much more interesting if it is re-strung in its original order, and tells us more about the fashions of dress than would an arbitrary arrangement of beads collected promiscuously from the grave; but to obtain that the excavator

Dagger and sheath from Ur, gold and lapis lazuli, 2600–2500 BC (*Illustrated London News*, 26 November 1927)

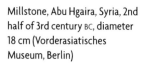

Millstone, Abu Hgaira, Syria, 2nd
half of 3rd century BC, diameter
18 cm (Vorderasiatisches
Museum, Berlin)

may spend painful hours stooping or lying over the body, he cuts and blows
away the earth so delicately as to leave the loose beads undisturbed.'[6] When
Hercule Poirot and Amy Leatheran come upon David Emmott they find him
at work in this uncomfortable position, knife in hand.

The description of the Assyrian royal palace may have been suggested
by the few remains uncovered by Campbell Thompson at Nineveh in 1929 and
1930. Agatha Christie must have seen them in 1931. The inconspicuous
remains of the walls give her a chance to add some comments on the nature of
mud-brick architecture. Besides the finds mentioned above she speaks of ter-
racottas, cylinder seals and clay tablets. The murder weapon used on Louise
Leidner was an old millstone or quern with a hole through the middle.

Murder in Mesopotamia is notable for its exotic setting, the unusual
murder and the depiction of an interesting and sharply observed set of suspects: a former spy as head of the dig, a drug-addicted assistant and a thief dis-
guised as a monk on the one hand, three very different women characters on
the other. Agatha Christie had a full hand of trumps with these ingredients and
played them well, constructing an exciting story. Her interest was not just in
depicting human depravity and the question of who or what set off the act of
violence, but in describing everyday life on an archaeological expedition. Her
great gift for observation and her sensitive feeling for a dramatic situation were
extremely useful to her. She depicts atmosphere and character in a few sentences, using literary invention: the figure of Dr Leidner may be based on
Leonard Woolley, but the criminal aspect is entirely fictional. Although Agatha
Christie's detective stories usually follow the same pattern – a greater or
smaller number of suspects, a setting cut off from the outside world and a dra-

matic finale in which the murderer is publicly revealed – she always succeeded in leading the reader astray. The revelation that in this case the grieving husband has himself committed the crime must have come as a great surprise to the book's original public.

The careful tempo of the narrative also allows those who are not familiar with conditions in the Near East to follow the background descriptions easily; an entertaining style is a constant feature of Agatha Christie's books. This particular drama of love, hate and betrayal was probably written in Chagar Bazar in Syria. Agatha Christie herself found the environment there, the daily life of a dig and the fact that there was no need to waste time on social obligations all very congenial, although she was not unaware of the human tensions and problems to be found on excavations. The odd atmosphere at the end of the 1930 season at Ur, of which she made use in *Murder in Mesopotamia*, was not due solely to the dominating presence of Katharine Woolley. The enormous stress of a season of digging, the characteristics of the individuals involved, the various ways in which their actions were restricted, and not least the rigorous living conditions must have affected the mood within the team. Perhaps the amusingly sharp little remarks directed at the archaeological profession by Agatha Christie in *Murder in Mesopotamia*, *Death in the Clouds* and *They Came to Baghdad* were not entirely fictional, but contain reminiscences of her own experiences on a dig.

NOTES

1 A. Christie, *Murder in Mesopotamia*, London 1994, p. 185.
2 Christie, *Mesopotamia* (n. 1), p. 215.
3 Christie, *An Autobiography*, London 1981, p. 386.
4 Christie, *Autobiography* (n. 3), p. 389.
5 Christie, *Mesopotamia* (n. 1), p. 44.
6 C. Leonard Woolley, *Digging up the Past*, London 1930, pp. 112–13.

BIBLIOGRAPHY

J. Kamm, *Gertrude Bell, Daughter of the Desert*, London 1956
A. Christie, *An Autobiography*, London 1977
A. Christie, *Murder in Mesopotamia*, London 1994
M. Mallowan, *Mallowan's Memoirs*, London 1977
M. Mallowan, 'Memories of Ur', in *Iraq* 22 (1960), pp. 1–17
J. Morgan, *Agatha Christie: A Biography*, London 1984
D. Sanders and L. Lovallo, *The Agatha Christie Crime Companion: The Complete Guide to Agatha Christie's Life and Work*, New York 1984
H.V.F. Winstone, *Woolley of Ur: The Life of Sir Leonard Woolley*, London 1990
C. Leonard Woolley, *Digging up the Past*, London 1930.

AGATHA CHRISTIE

SIGN OF A GOOD
DETECTIVE NOVEL

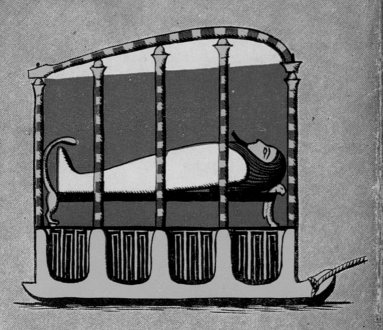

DEATH COMES
AS THE END...

Agatha Christie and her Use of Ancient Egyptian Sources

Waltraud Guglielmi

1. *Death Comes as the End*

Death Comes as the End (1945) has the most unusual setting of all Agatha Christie's detective stories. While the antiquities of Egypt, particularly the temples of Wadi el-Sebua and Abu Simbel, were merely part of the background of a Hercule Poirot story in *Death on the Nile* (1937),[1] the action of the later title actually takes place in Thebes at the time of the early Middle Kingdom (2081–1938 BC).

The story of how it came to be written is described in the autobiographies of both Agatha Christie and her husband. In 1943, during the war, Stephen Glanville (1900–1956), a professor of Egyptology and friend of the Mallowans, urged her to write a detective story set in ancient Egypt.[2] Although she had already done a good deal of research into Egyptian history for her play *Akhnaton*, and had enjoyed reading James Henry Breasted's *The Dawn of Conscience* (1933; see p. 367), she hesitated at first. She knew she did not want to write a novel about a real historical character; her sure instinct for plausibility told her that it would be presumptuous of her to do so, and the result would not ring true. Only when Glanville found her sources that dealt with everyday life did she embark on her book.[3] These texts were the Hekanakhte Papers, a collection of early Middle Kingdom letters still unpublished at the time, and known only in an approximate translation by B. Gunn. Their use in a novel before publication met with some criticism in a review by an Egyptologist.[4]

The papyri contained the letters of a man who served as the funerary priest of a high official, keeping himself and his large family on the yield from the estates granted him in return for his services, from his own property and

Cover of first edition of *Death Comes as the End*, the Crime Club, Collins 1945

AGATHA CHRISTIE

Rächende Geister

Sie glaubt, mit
der Lüge nicht
leben zu können.
Doch mit der
Wahrheit über die
mysteriösen Todes-
fälle kann sie's
erst recht nicht...

Paperback edition of the German
translation of *Death Comes as the End*,
Scherz Verlag, 24th edition, 1996

from newly leased land. The papyri suggested that his home was near Thebes. When he was away in the north, carrying out his duties in Memphis, he wrote to his eldest son, who had been left in charge of the house and the family in his absence. We discover that the household consists of five sons, his mother, his daughter, and a new wife bearing the title of *hebesit* – a term that does not imply the dignity of 'mistress of the house' – and who is not recognized by the family. The sons are expected to do their share of work in the fields, and are constantly being reprimanded and urged to work industriously with such remarks as: 'This is not a year for a man to be negligent towards his master, or his father, or his brother' (Hekanakhte, Letter I). The father's favourite is one of the younger sons, who does not have to work on the land and is allowed to choose his own tasks. The well-being of his new wife is much on the man's mind, and he warns his family against treating her with too little respect. Apart from very detailed directions relating to their work and stipulating, for instance, how many sacks of grain the sons must produce, the letters also contain a list of the rations of grain allotted to individuals. He answers accusations of allowing too little food by pointing out that, since the inundation of the banks of the Nile has not reached high levels, people elsewhere are starving ('Why, they have begun to eat men and women here!' 'The entire land is dead with famine'), while they are still doing very well because he is toiling away to feed them, and that 'half-life is better than dying altogether' (Hekanakhte, Letter II). He shows great respect for his mother, but is not well disposed to another female relative, and says he does not want to see her in his house when he returns. The letters break off rather abruptly.

These papyri stimulated Christie's imagination, since they presented a lively picture of a family of different characters and the conflicts between them, and probably also because they concentrated on only a small area of events, leaving plenty of scope for imaginative reconstruction. She wanted to paint as faithful a picture as possible of everyday life at the time, and kept asking Glanville questions, which he obviously answered at length. The result of this close collaboration was not just a 'normal' detective story with seven bodies, but a vivid and convincing book about the life of a family in early Middle Kingdom Egypt. Agatha Christie can claim credit for inventing this genre of crime novel, with the murder set in the past but avoiding the high-flown style of the nineteenth-century historical novel. It is in vogue again today, as can be seen from the success of detective stories set in the Middle Ages or ancient Rome. We have only to think of Umberto Eco's ambitious *The Name of the Rose*,[5] the detective stories of Ellis Peters, or the novels for young people by John Maddox Roberts.

Egyptologists can also derive great pleasure from tracking down the various sources that Christie adapted and integrated into her text with such expertise. It makes them feel a little like detectives themselves. If sources are noted or deviations from them mentioned in this article, it is merely in order to document the author's empathy with the period or her freedom in making use of the texts and other sources. It would be inappropriate to use the yardstick of historical exactitude to judge a book that so convincingly conveys the atmosphere of the Hekanakhte letters and of everyday life and the cult of death in ancient Egypt.

Her sources were primarily the Hekanakhte letters themselves,[6] which not only appear as 'letters' in the novel but are sometimes used word for word to depict the characters of the father and other dramatis personae. This unique private correspondence comes from the tomb of Meseh, which was excavated in Deir el-Bahari in 1921–2 by the Egyptian Expedition of the Metropolitan Museum of Art, headed by Herbert E. Winlock.[7] Together with Max, Agatha Christie had visited the Valley of the Kings herself in 1933. The tomb (Theban Tombs No. 516 B) is among the rocks of Necropolis 500, in the courtyard of the tomb of Ipy (Theban Tombs No. 315), who was vizier to King Nebhepetre Mentuhotep II, from which T.G.H. James, an editor of the papers, concluded that Hekanakhte was funerary priest ('*ka* servant') of the vizier Ipy himself. However, this is speculation: Hekanakhte does bear the title of funerary priest, but there is no indication of what master he served. We do not know how the letters found their way into the corridor in Meseh's tomb. Since the seal on one papyrus is unbroken, showing that the letter was placed in the tomb unread, it has been assumed that the messenger supposed to deliver the documents was intercepted en route and the letters thrown away. The steep and dangerous path up to the tomb in the rocks, which is used as a short cut down to the Valley of the Kings beyond it and plays a major part as the crime scene in the novel, was identified by John Romer and is now called the Agatha Christie Path.[8]

Because of the place where it was found, the correspondence was dated to the reign of the founder of the Middle Kingdom, Nebhepetre Mentuhotep (2008–1957 BC), and his successor Sankhkare Mentuhotep III (1957–1945 BC), or slightly later.[9] Two letters were written in the course of a single summer, and Christie used the Egyptian method of dating by seasons in the titles of her chapters. There are also suggestions that she had in mind the politically chaotic conditions of the First Intermediate Period before her eyes, when the country had not yet been reunified and general uncertainty prevailed.

She completely changed the names of the people in the letters, although they were drawn largely from her ancient source. With the exception of the beautiful new young wife, the cause of the conflict, who is called Iutenheb in the letters but in the novel is Nofret ('The Beautiful One'), the names are not descriptive of the characters, although in other novels Agatha Christie did play games of this kind with proper names to make them suggest appropriate backgrounds and qualities.[10] Hekanakhte, the father and writer of the real-life letters, becomes Imhotep in the novel, the name of King Djoser's architect, while his mother Ipi is called Esa by Christie, and the name of Ipy is given to the father's favourite and youngest son. The idea seems to have been to use stylized and euphonious names. Nofret, on the other hand, is the real name of a daughter in the letters. Another carefully chosen name is that of Ashayet, the dead first wife of the head of the family, which was also the name of one of the queens of King Nebhepetre Mentuhotep II. Agatha Christie also used the names of two embalmers called Monthu and Hori who had been found mentioned, with their materials, on vessels in a neighbouring 18th-Dynasty tomb.[11] In the novel the embalmers become Montu and Opi, while Hori is the name given to the steward of the estate, who turns detective. Such details show that Christie had read her sources very closely.

The quotations from the Hekanakhte Papers themselves can be easily enough recognized, since she uses only letters I–III, but she makes a kind of collage of them. The first letter written by her character Imhotep opens with the greeting formula from Hekanakhte III (1–2), but when he goes on to greet

Hekanakhte papyri, 1st letter, recto, 11th Dynasty, *c.*1950 BC (Metropolitan Museum of Art, Rogers Fund and Edward S. Harkness gift, 1922)

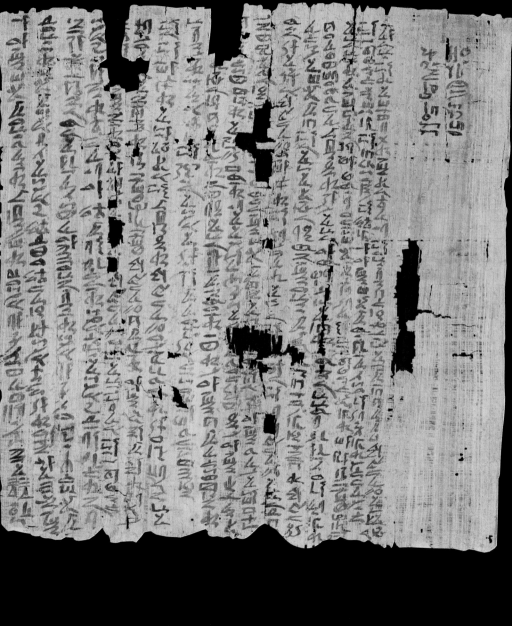

Hekanakhte papyri, 1st letter, verso, 11th Dynasty, *c.*1950 BC (Metropolitan Museum of Art, Rogers Fund and Edward S. Harkness gift, 1922)

his mother the wording comes from II (1–2), and the injunctions to his family to work industriously are taken from II (30).[12]

Christie drew almost as extensively from the maxims of Ptahhotep, the most famous collection of precepts in ancient Egypt. Even the title of the novel, *Death Comes as the End*, is a quotation from the Eighteenth Maxim, which concentrates on the dangers of consorting with women. This text is put into the mouth of Imhotep's mother, the wise and experienced Esa, when she tells her son that he has been foolish to bring a young wife into the household of his extended family, which already consists of a daughter, three sons, daughters-in-law and grandchildren: "'Men are made fools by the gleaming limbs of women, and lo, in a minute they are become discoloured cornelians ...'" Her voice deepened as she quoted: "'A trifle, a little, the likeness of a dream, and death comes as the end ...'"[13] In the copy from the Eighteenth Maxim (277–288) in the variant of British Museum papyrus 10509 it runs:[14]

If you want friendship to last
inside a house you enter –
as son, or a brother or a friend –

Postcard of the Valley of the Kings, Egypt, c.1930 (Fouad Debbas Collection, Beirut)

THÈBES
Tombeaux des Rois

Above Deir el-Bahri, Egypt

Left The Temple of Hatshepsut, Deir el-Bahri, Egypt (*The Traveller's Gazette*, October 1928; Thomas Cook Archives)

> whatever your rank may be –
> beware of approaching the women!
> The place where this is done cannot be good.
> A body shimmering like faience makes a man foolish,
> but it is soon turned to carnelian.
> It [the pleasure] is a little trifle, the likeness of a dream
> and death brings the end.

Less obvious is another reference in Esa's remarks:[15] '"Fine words," said Esa. "Fine words." She cackled. "But a good discourse can be found with slave girls over the millstone."' This derives from the First Maxim of Ptahhotep (52–9), warning against the vanity of those who think they know everything:[16]

> Do not be proud because you are wise!
> Consult with the ignorant as with the wise!
> The limits of art are unattainable;
> no artist is fully equipped with his mastery.
> Good discourse is more hidden than malachite,
> yet it is found with the maidservants at the millstones.

The Temple of Hatshepsut, Deir el-Bahri, Egypt, 1931 or 1933 (photo: Max Mallowan)

Another quotation from Ptahhotep used by Esa in the course of a long conversation is barely recognizable:[17] 'Who can tell what goes on in the human heart?' In Ptahhotep (134) the passage runs: 'One can not know what is in the heart.'

Imhotep's mother Esa can be said to embody the traditions of wisdom in Egyptian literature. This is clear in the final episode, when she is trying to clarify her suspicions.[18] She first suggests, in the form of a free 'quotation', that in view of the certainty of death it is wise to live for the moment as intensely as possible: 'Do you not hear it at every feast? Eat, drink and be merry for to-morrow you die?' The idea derives from the *carpe diem* theme of Egyptian harpers' songs, which in turn derives from Ptahhotep. She continues by warning, 'Trust no one!' and repeats it, adding, 'You know nothing … None of us know anything. That is our danger.' The sense of this is very much in line with the teaching of King Amenemhat (I, 3), and we may suspect that Christie used this source too:[19]

> Concentrate against subjects who prove non-existent,
> in whose respect no faith can be placed!
> Do not approach them when you are alone!
> Trust no brother! Know no friend!
> Make for yourself no intimates – this is of no avail!

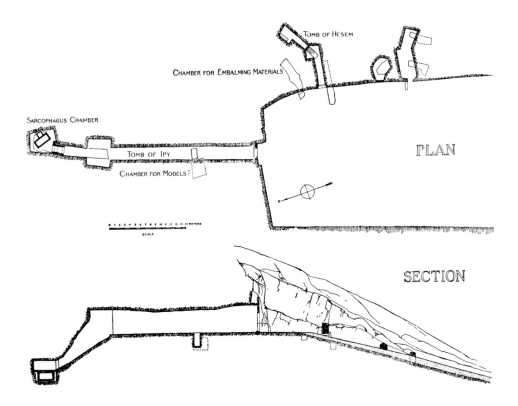

Plan and section of the vizier Ipy's tomb in the cliffs of Deir el-Bahri, Egypt (*Bulletin of the Metropolitan Museum of Art 1922, part II, The Egyptian Expedition 1921–1922*)

Agatha Christie pinned down the ancient Egyptian attitude to life with an unerring instinct. The harper's song and love-song sung in her book by the young scribe Kameni from the north are taken from the Harris 500 papyrus in the British Museum. Both harper's song and love song are in fact anachronistic, since no love poetry has been found from before the 19th Dynasty, but they suit the character of a young man in love. Christie uses her sources to strike a lyrical note. It does not matter whether she was inspired by the love song or whether the young man's character was in her mind first and sent her in search of appropriately expressive texts. The introduction of the love song and its repetition later seem natural rather than contrived:[20]

'I will go to Memphis,' sang Kameni, 'I will go to Ptah, Lord of Truth. I will say to Ptah, "Give me my sister tonight … The dawn breaks through her beauty. Memphis is a dish of love apples set before the fair face …"'
He kept his eyes on her, singing softly: 'Her arms are full of branches

of the persea, her hair is weighed down with unguent. She is like a Princess …'

Here Christie combines the sixth song, performed by the young man, with the ninth, sung by the girl in the original. Both songs begin with the same phrase: 'I am sailing north …'[21]

> I am sailing north with the current,
>   to the oar-strokes(?) of the captain,
> my bundle of reeds on my shoulder:
>   I'm headed for Ankh-Towy.
> I'll say to Ptah, the Lord of Truth:
>   'Give me (my) sister tonight!'
> The river – it is wine,
>   its reeds are Ptah,
> the leaves of its lotus-buds are Sekhmet,
>   its lotus-buds are Yadit,
> its lotus-blossoms are Nefertem,
>   … joy,

Wooden toy lion, New Kingdom, c.1500–1200 BC (British Museum, London)

The earth has grown light through her beauty.
Memphis is a jar of mandragoras
   set before the Gracious One.

I am headed to the 'Love Garden'
   my bosom full of persea (branches),
      my hair laden with balm.
I am a [noblewoman],
   I am the Mistress of the Two Lands
      When I am [with you].

Using her collage technique, Agatha Christie works into the novel not only the Hekanakhte Papers and literary texts such as the maxims and love songs but also draws on letters to the dead and everyday objects, as well as the description of the design of a tomb, the grave goods placed there and the offerings made to the dead. Archaeological details taken from an excavation report are so skilfully merged into the story that it is not always easy to say where reality stops and Christie's imagination takes over. She makes sensitive use of the belief in ghosts, which helps to camouflage the murderer and spreads vague fears among the characters, fears to which the clear-thinking Esa and Hori are opposed, although they do agree to write a letter to the dead Ashayet, who had belonged to an influential family. The Egyptians, like many other peoples, were convinced that the dead could influence the lives of their living relations for good or ill. Letters to the dead in the First Intermediate Period were frequently written on pottery vessels and placed in tombs as offerings, as was probably the case with the bowl now in Berlin which also provided material for Agatha Christie.[22] After a prayer for the dead its text runs:

Thou wast brought here to the city of eternity without there being any discontentment of thine against me. If it so be that these wounds are being inflicted with thy knowledge(?), behold the house with thy children is in fresh (?) misery. If it be that (they) are inflicted in spite of thee, thy father is great <in> the necropolis. If it be that an accusation is in thy body, forget it for the sake of thy children.

In the English version by Agatha Christie,[23] the letter to the dead from the Berlin bowl is combined with the extensive Leiden Papyrus containing a 19th-Dynasty letter to the dead from a reproachful widower to his dead wife.

Concrete objects have been carefully studied, too, and some are modelled on items in the British Museum, for instance the toys belonging to the heroine Renisenb's little daughter, a lion with jaws that will open and shut (BM

අගතා ක්‍රිස්ටි ගේ

නදීතෙර කුමරිය

දයාසේන ගුණසිංහ

EA 15761) and a ball. A bracelet with golden lions, preserved among the jewellery of princesses of the Middle Kingdom,[24] becomes Nofret's triple necklace in the novel. The chamber with the embalmers' utensils corresponds exactly to what was found on the excavation.[25] And the piece of linen marked with a name probably goes back to this event, although such items were often found. Many of the descriptions and metaphors in the book are inspired by Egyptian tomb paintings and papyri, for instance when the dead husband sails his boat in the Field of Offerings[26] or the tomb is swept after the burial.[27]

Through the unusual and carefully researched setting of this book Agatha Christie succeeded in breaking the mould of the classic 'whodunnit' detective story, in which almost all elements concentrate on the components of the puzzle – that is to say, the identity of the murderer – by giving it a historical and cultural setting and thus making it what, in the eyes of an Egyptologist at least, is a 'realistic' historical novel.

2. Akhnaton: A Play in Three Acts

Agatha Christie wrote her historical play *Akhnaton* in 1937, after a voyage down the Nile and a meeting with Howard Carter in Luxor.[28] Carter, who had discovered the tomb of Tutankhamun in the Valley of the Kings in 1922, spent ten years working on the recovery and preservation of the finds. As with Thomas Mann's tetralogy of novels on the subject of Joseph and his brethren,[29] there was a long gap of time between the writing of Agatha Christie's work and its publication. *Akhnaton* was not brought out by Collins until 1973, and has never had a stage production.[30] When a major exhibition took place in London in 1972 to celebrate the fiftieth anniversary of the finding of the tomb of Tutankhamun – an exhibition that later went all round the world and set off what might be described as Tutankhamun mania similar to that aroused by the discovery of the tomb itself – Agatha Christie felt that the moment had come for the publication of her play and that the public was now open-minded enough to accept its subject: the Amarna period in ancient Egypt and the well-known royal figures of Tyi (Tiye), Akhnaton, Nefertiti, Tutankhamun, Ay and Horemheb.

There were several Egyptologists among Agatha Christie and Max Mallowan's friends. In writing the play, she had the assistance of Stephen Glanville,[31] and later, when it was published, the support of Iorwerth Eiddon Stephen Edwards, who had been Keeper of Egyptian antiquities at the British Museum since 1965. He was therefore involved in the preparations for the Tutankhamun exhibition and wrote its catalogue, *Treasures of Tutankhamun*

Cover of Sri Lankan edition of *Death Comes as the End*

Postcard of the Old Cataract Hotel in Aswan, Egypt 1930s (Fouad Debbas collection, Beirut)

(1972).[32] Christie's dedication and letter of thanks to Edwards of 16 May 1973 are evidence of their collaboration. Her husband Max Mallowan regarded *Akhnaton* as the best of her plays, and she herself thought highly of it, but none the less it remained largely unknown.

In terms of literary and cultural history the play should be seen in the context of the discovery of Akhnaton in the 1920s and 1930s, when the Pharaoh was glorified as a religious innovator and became the hero of several novels and plays.[33] The most important of these were Thomas Mann's *Joseph and his Brothers* and Franz Werfel's adaptation of the Hymn to the Sun. The monotheistic religion of belief in the Aten, as expressed in this great hymn, was regarded as the forerunner of Christian ideas. Christie's picture of the king is strongly influenced by Arthur Weigall's *The Life and Times of Akhnaton, Pharaoh of Egypt* (1910) and James Henry Breasted's *The Dawn of Conscience* (1933). Breasted was one of the first to recognize the great historical significance of Akhnaton and his religion in the development of biblical monotheism; he thought that the concept of a universal deity creating and nurturing all mankind arose in Heliopolis as the religious counterpart of the Egyptian empire in the New Kingdom, and he regarded Akhnaton's monotheism as being based on this doctrine.[34] Christie adopted this idea herself and personified it in the figure of the royal tutor Ay who brings up Akhnaton in the religion of the Aten, the disc of the sun, with the knowledge and consent of his mother Tyi.[35] Weigall presents Akhnaton as a pacifist cocooned in the unrealistic and idyllic world of Amarna and his newly founded residence of Akhetaten ('Horizon of the Aten'), living there in accordance with the tenets of his new doctrine of the religion of light and truth, but ignoring political events in the Middle East outside Egypt and thus destroying the Egyptian empire. In the end Akhnaton fails as a ruler both at home and abroad, for his pure iconoclastic doctrines are not accepted by the people. The priests of Amun and their polytheistic ideas gain the upper hand, Akhetaten is abandoned and destroyed, and the Middle Eastern provinces – including Byblos with the Pharaoh's faithful vassal Ribaddi – break away or are ruined. This view of the Amarna period was a persistent one and is reflected, for instance, in Philip Glass's opera *Akhnaten* (one of a trilogy of operas, the other two being on the subjects of Buddha and Gandhi), which had its première on 24 March 1984.[36] The faithful Ribaddi became a stock character himself, and also fea-

Agatha Christie in front of the head of Ramesses II, in the Ramesseum at Thebes, Egypt 1931 or 1933 (photo: Max Mallowan)

tures in *Echnaton: Ein Trauerspiel* (Akhnaton: A Tragedy) by Walter Erich Schäfer, where he waits in vain, fighting on the walls of Byblos, for the arrival of his Egyptian allies.

In his late work on Moses and monotheism, published in 1939, Sigmund Freud sees Moses as an Egyptian who brought the religion of Akhnaton to the tribes of Israel. Jan Assmann, following the Acts of the Apostles 7: 22, regards Moses the Egyptian as a figure of traditional oral history, and studies the antagonism between Jewish monotheism and the traditional idol-worship of

Statues of the god Amun and his female partner Amaunet in the temple of Karnak, Egypt 1931 or 1933 (photo: Max Mallowan)

Cover of *Akhnaton*, William Collins & Sons 1973

the Egyptians.[37] Akhnaton's belief in the Aten has also sometimes been interpreted as anticipating the Enlightenment in its ideas of reform and natural philosophy.[38] In Egyptological research, assessments of the king himself still range between the extremes of hero or heretic.[39]

It was not only the tragic figure of Akhnaton, the idealist who failed, that Agatha Christie's contemporaries found fascinating; they were also greatly interested in works of art from the Amarna period, especially the painted bust of Nefertiti found in 1912 during excavations by the German Oriental Society.[40] The intimate scenes known to us from tomb paintings and altars, showing members of the royal family kissing and caressing each other, the liveliness and quasi-expressionism of such pictures and their natural style represented a freedom from convention hitherto unknown in Egyptian art and departing from its earlier principles.

How does Agatha Christie deal with her powerful subject, a theme covering a whole epoch? Does she try to avoid clichés by looking below the surface? In depicting her main characters, she accepts the ideas of Weigall and Breasted but produces free variations on them – for instance, making Akhnaton himself the sculptor who created the bust of Nefertiti – while on the other hand she keeps very close to the historical facts as they were known at the time, and she was strongly influenced by the pictorial representations. This historically faithful approach, and her knowledge of detail, makes her play very interesting for Egyptologists.

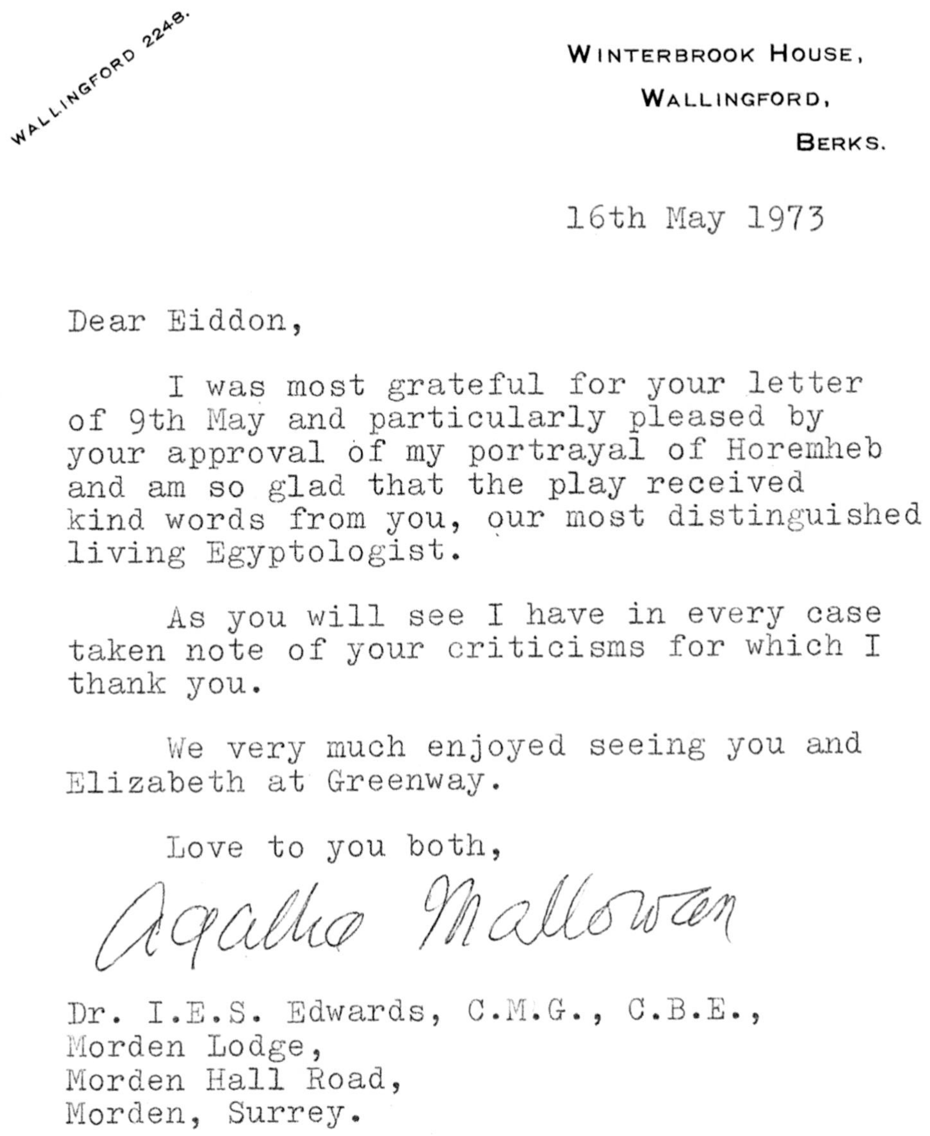

WALLINGFORD 2248.

WINTERBROOK HOUSE,
WALLINGFORD,
BERKS.

16th May 1973

Dear Eiddon,

I was most grateful for your letter
of 9th May and particularly pleased by
your approval of my portrayal of Horemheb
and am so glad that the play received
kind words from you, our most distinguished
living Egyptologist.

As you will see I have in every case
taken note of your criticisms for which I
thank you.

We very much enjoyed seeing you and
Elizabeth at Greenway.

Love to you both,

Agatha Mallowan

Dr. I.E.S. Edwards, C.M.G., C.B.E.,
Morden Lodge,
Morden Hall Road,
Morden, Surrey.

Above Letter from Agatha Christie to the Egyptologist Eiddon Edwards, 16 May 1973

Far left Manuscript notes for *Akhnaton*, 1937

Left The dedication and acknowledgements in *Akhnaton* to the Egyptologist Eiddon Edwards,
28 April 1973

Bust of Nefertiti from Amarna, painted
limestone, 1345 BC, height 50 cm
(Ägyptisches Museum und
Papyrussammlung, Berlin)

The drama has three acts and ten scenes, with an epilogue, and features twenty-two main characters and a number of extras. It covers a period of seventeen years from the death of Amenophis III, that is to say the entire reign of Akhnaton (1353–1335 BC). The characters, including the smaller parts, are all based on real historical figures such as the sculptor Bek, although some are known to us only by name, for instance the high priests of Amun, Meriptah and Ptamose, and the dwarfs Para and Reneheh in the retinue of Nefertiti's sister Nezzemut. Christie shows an astonishing knowledge of detail, derived from her wide reading. The main figures among the idealists are Akhnaton and Nefertiti, together with Akhnaton's tutor and godfather Ay, who has brought him up to believe in the sun god Re. The political realists include the shrewd queen mother Tyi, who is torn between maternal love, hatred for the priests of Amun and concern for the country, and dies when she discovers the spy Ptahmose in Amarna; Horemheb, the upright but materialistic general, devoted to the king, a man of action who finally, when faced with the alternatives of choosing between his country and his king, leaves Akhnaton to restore order in the land; Nezzemut (Mutnodjmet), Nefertiti's ambitious and unscrupulous sister, who wants to be queen herself and sets her sights on the soldier and future king Horemheb; and finally the deposed high priest of Amun, Meriptah, who is working underground against monotheism in Thebes. A neutral figure is the architect and sculptor Bek,[41] who has great influence because he designs Amarna in Akhnaton's new artistic style. Akhnaton himself remains a curiously two-dimensional character, although he is depicted as an artist, idealist and dreamer, a mystic and a consistent pacifist who imposes his ideas with increasing rigour, while Nefertiti is a naïve beauty who is devoted to him, but at heart does not understand the full meaning of his faith, more particularly his opposition to the idolatry of the old religion. Court life is presented as an idyll of 'never-ending happiness',[42] in contrast to the political reality, which is marked by human greed, conflicts, famine and the loss of Egypt's empire.

The language in which Christie chooses to deal with this material is especially interesting, and so is the skill with which she integrates the sources into her text. She makes use of the hymns chiefly to convey the king's religious and ethical claims, and turns to the Amarna letters and the decree of Horemheb in the passages dealing with political reality. In spite of the tragic dimensions of her subject, Christie avoids elevated diction and writes in a simple style. Her aim is to exploit the forceful language of her sources and yet to suggest something close to real life. She develops directly those aspects of the existing material that she, as a modern writer, wants to express, but exercises strict control over that material through the structure of the dramatic dialogue. As far as possible she avoids emotionalism and rhetoric, even when the sources themselves are highly emotional, but she does not quite succeed in achieving irony and a sense of poetic distance. Perhaps the rhetoric and propaganda in her source texts militated against stage performance of the play, rather than the fact that a production would have been very expensive. The difficulty of presenting the Akhnaton story in dramatic form, where all the ideas and concepts – monotheism, iconoclasm and idolatry, new artistic styles and tradition, foreign politics and the importance of the temple of Amun – could be depicted only through the actions and speeches of individuals and not directly described as in an epic, suggests why Thomas Mann's novel was much more successful.

Christie uses the Great Hymn to the Sun from the tomb of Ay, which is sometimes thought to have been composed by the king himself, in almost literal translation. This hymn to the new god, the Aten or disc of the sun to which all life owes its existence, is of great poetic beauty and was chief among the sources used. It is always cited as a poem, a prayer composed by Akhnaton

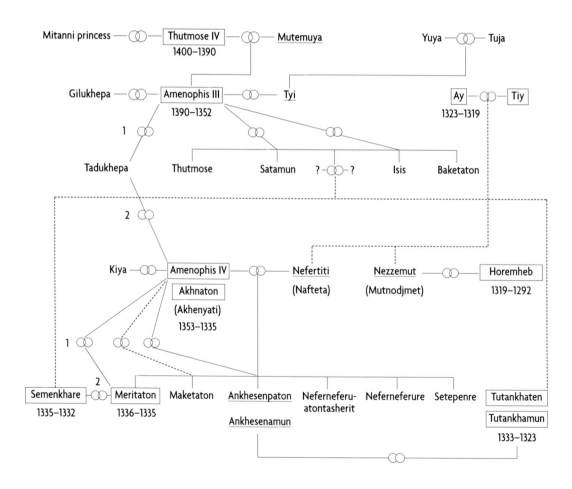

Left Family tree of Thutmose IV

Right Small head of Queen Tyi, wife of Amenophis III, yew-wood, *c.*1370 BC, height 21 cm (Ägyptisches Museum und Papyrussammlung, Berlin)

himself. An ingenious device on Christie's part was to divide it into various units of meaning, using them to express the king's striving for artistic expression. At the beginning of the play she describes sunrise, a passage that in the original runs:[43]

> 'All cattle rest upon their pasturage,
> The trees and the plants flourish,
> The birds flutter in their marshes,
> Their wings uplifted in adoration to thee.
> All the antelopes dance upon their feet,
> All creatures that fly or alight,
> They live when thou hast shone on them.'

The first scene closes with the idea that the god is both revealed and concealed:[44]

> Though thou art far away, thy rays are upon earth;
> Though thou art in the faces of men, thy footsteps are unseen.

The description of the care taken by the god in creating living beings follows the birth of mankind in the original text:[45]

> 'When the fledgling in the egg chirps in the shell,
> Thou givest him breath in the midst of it to preserve him alive.
> Thou hast made for him his term in the egg, for breaking it.
> He cometh forth from the egg to chirp at his term
> he goeth about upon his two feet
> When he cometh forth therefrom.'

And in the long verses describing the god's maintenance of the world, Christie keeps very close to the original:[46]

> 'The world subsists in thy hand,
> Even as thou hast made them.
> When thou hast risen they live,
> When thou settest they die;
> For thou art length of life of thyself,
> Men live through thee.'

Stela by Bek, chief sculptor to Akhnaton, quartzite, c.1350 BC, height 67 cm (Ägyptisches Museum und Papyrussammlung, Berlin)

Christie refers frequently to the king's claim to be the only intermediary of the god, expressed in the hymn in the words, 'There is no other that knoweth thee / Save thy son Ikhnaton,' and she also refers to his father-son relationship with the Aten.[47]

In the moving scene at the end where he is abandoned by Horemheb, Akhnaton speaks the words of sunset as the god moves away:[48]

'When thou settest in the western horizon of the sky,
The earth is in darkness like death.
They sleep in their chambers,
Their heads are wrapped up,
Their nostrils are stopped,
And none seeth the other,
While all their things are stolen,
Which are under their heads,
And they know it not.

'Every lion cometh forth from his den,
All serpents, they sting.
Darkness broods,
The world is in silence.'

Christie adapted the divisions of this hymn, which is very long in the original and has often been compared to Psalm 104 and St Francis of Assisi's *Canticle of the Sun*, to the progress of the action; presumably she would have felt that otherwise it would be too much of a lyrical and declamatory monologue. She occasionally uses material from other hymns for Akhnaton's speeches, for instance the hymn from the tomb of Ahmes and Merire, from which she takes the poetic circumlocution for the concept of eternity:[49] 'until the swan is become black and the raven white, until the mountains rise up and walk and water flows up-hill!' She eloquently conveys the traditional ideas of the Egyptian kingdom by using verses from the Poetic Stela of Thutmose III, the great conqueror's song of victory, thus creating a strong contrast with the fervent tone of the hymn to the Aten. Intuitively, she chose the very song that was tradition-creating for the Egyptians themselves:[50]

I have come, causing thee to smite those who are in their marshes,
The lands of Mitanni tremble under fear of thee.
I have caused them to see thy majesty as a crocodile,
Lord of fear in the water, unapproachable.

Hands of a couple, from Tell el-Amarna, sandstone, c.1345 BC,
length 9 cm (Ägyptisches Museum und Papyrussammlung, Berlin)

Above Fragment of a painted palace floor from Tell el-Amarna, painted stucco, *c.*1345 BC, width 150 cm (Ägyptisches Museum und Papyrussammlung, Berlin)

Right 'The Walk in the Garden', relief, painted limestone, 1345 BC, height 24 cm (Ägyptisches Museum und Papyrussammlung, Berlin)

For the account of the founding of Akhetaten she sometimes repeats word for word and sometimes summarizes the extensive text of the Border Stela, combining older and more recent versions.[51]

Christie used the cuneiform correspondence found in the state archives of Tell el-Amarna for many different purposes, quoting it almost literally in the first scene as the account of the envoy of the Mitanni king Dushratta (Tushratta), who is bringing the statue of Ishtar from Nineveh to cure the sick Amenophis III.[52] Later it is used in Dushratta's demand for gold, with the remark that in Egypt 'gold is as common as dust', which leads to the confrontation with the High Priest of Amun.[53] In the second act we have 'urgent letters have come from from Ribaddi of Byblos', which Horemheb hopes will induce the king to take military action.[54] Later, she usually puts the words of the Amarna letters into the mouth of Horemheb as he sets out the political situation abroad for the king. The area of Egyptian influence has diminished with the expansion of the Hittites, he explains, because the former allies of Egypt are rebelling or are becoming pro-Hittite.[55] Horemheb literally 'quotes',

Stela, domestic altar showing Akhnaton, Nefertiti and the disc of the Aten, limestone, c.1345 BC, height 32.5 cm (Ägyptisches Museum und Papyrussammlung, Berlin)

reading aloud the desperate letter from the people of Tunip, besieged by Aziru, and he also quotes from a letter of his friend Ribaddi who says of Simyra that it is 'like a bird in a trap'.[56] He then mentions the cities of Askalon, Geser and Lachish, which have defected from Egypt, and reads out an appeal for help from Abdikhibas, the ruler of Jerusalem.[57] It is when Ribbadi and his family perish that Horemheb makes his decision.[58]

To illustrate the power and influence of the god Amun and his priest-hood in Karnak, there is a reference in the first scene to the choice of Thut-mose III by an oracle of Amun in the temple of Karnak, as well as to a cruel act described on the Amada Stela of Amenophis II,[59] and to a passage from a prayer to Amun-Re, the 'vizier of the poor, who takes no bribes from the guilty'.[60]

The description of such draconian measures as cutting off noses and deportation to Sile, which Horemheb intends to use against the encroach-ments of the tax collectors but which Akhnaton forbids, and the reorganiza-tion of the country's administration in the epilogue all owe much to the Decree of Horemheb;[61] Agatha Christie usually combines several passages and quotes them as required:

> When the overseer of the cattle of Pharoah … goes about to attend to the loan-herds in the whole land, and there be not brought to him the hides of the […] which are on the lists … As for any citizen of the army, (concerning) whom one shall hear, saying: 'He goeth about stealing hides', beginning with this day, the law shall be executed against him, by beating him a hundred blows, opening five wounds, and taking from him by force the hides which he took.

In later sections the king warns his officials not to take bribes, and threatens them with death if they disobey:

> Now, as for any official or any priest (concerning whom) it shall be heard, saying: 'He sits, to execute judgment, and he commits a crime against justice therein;' it shall be against him a capital crime. Behold my majesty has done this, to improve the laws of Egypt …

The account of Horemheb's restoration of the idols and temples is taken almost literally from the coronation inscription of the statue group in Turin.[62] It is noticeable how vividly and precisely formulated all the original texts are.

A great deal of material gleaned from Agatha Christie's reading has gone into certain details that can only be briefly mentioned here: they range from the apologia of the creator god in the Middle Kingdom Coffin text (spell

1130), questioning the sense of suffering and divine justice (the 'accusation of the god') while the god defends himself by saying that he created all men equal,[63] through the installation of the vizier (Rekhmire 107–11), given word for word in Breasted's translation,[64] and the Treatise of the Memphite Theology,[65] to a saying from the Instruction of Ankhsheshonqi (20,9).[66]

The works of art of Amarna play an important part and were a source of inspiration for Agatha Christie. Some references to actual items are skilfully included in the text: the famous painted bust of Nefertiti (Berlin 21300), which in the play is created by Akhnaton himself and is to outlast all other portraits and statues of her,[67] the famous Amarna hands,[68] which the king intends to model – they too are presented as the hands of Nefertiti – the floor paintings and the paintings of the Maru-Aten with their curious natural scenes.[69] The reliefs of the dwarfs Para and Reneheh, Nezzemut's dwarfs, which appear in many tombs as figures with deformed feet,[70] intrigued Christie to a particularly high degree and inspired her to invent her complicated murder plot. Para is described as a witch and soothsayer from Punt, who prophesies to Nezzemut that Horemheb will become king.[71] In the last scene Nezzemut gets Para to prepare a poisoned drink for Akhnaton, which she then gives to Nefertiti; she, believing it is a medicine, gives it to the sick Akhnaton to drink. This scene, in which the potion is carefully administered, may be modelled on a scene on the back of Tutankhamun's throne or on a depiction in a tomb. The so-called Walk in the Garden, a limestone relief, was Christie's model for a relief planned by the sculptor Bek.[72] Her play also includes accounts of the appearance of Tyi and her visit to Amarna,[73] the gauzy robes which Nezzemut wears to flirt with Horemheb and which seem indecent to the people, and the raising of worshippers' arms at the name of the Aten, all of which can be found in Amarna art. Depictions of the king kissing are found several times on reliefs and domestic altars, and there is evidence for the existence of an unfinished statue of the subject. The detailed stage direction in Act II, Scene 2, is based on the representation in the tomb of Merira II showing the tribute paid by foreign countries in the year 12.[74] Christie skilfully combines it with the passage in the Great Hymn where the Aten's care for the whole world is conveyed to foreigners by the image of the 'Nile in the sky'.[75]

But in spite of her wide reading and her study of the sources, in the end Agatha Christie makes her material into a murder story. That may be something to do with her preference for exciting entertainment and her modest view of herself as a writer of light literature. However, the play was meant to be taken in more than one way. Unlike most dramatic presentations of Akhnaton, which tend to be over-written and grandiloquent, hers is entertaining to read, conveys a life-like and interesting picture of history drawn from the sources, and offers Egyptologists the pleasures of detection.

Agatha Christie's working method in *Akhnaton* is different only in degree but not in principle from a scholar's approach to historical facts. In writing it, she was usually drawing on the latest research of her time, although some of it has now been superseded, for instance by the new material from the Amarna *talatat* blocks, building blocks of stone reused in other structures as fill-in. In particular, the romantic love of Akhnaton for the lovely Nefertiti and their wedded bliss are European fantasies. The harem of Amenophis III contained many women, including several foreign princesses, and we know that the Mitanni princess Tadukhepa was taken into Akhnaton's harem, so we cannot suppose that Akhnaton had only one wife. Since the 1960s and 1970s scholars have known of a concubine called Kiya who had a daughter, and who has sometimes been identified with Tadukhepa.[76] Today it is thought that the picture of the Pharaoh's loving family life is a substitute for the mythological groups of the old religion, with the triad of the sun disc Aten, Akhnaton and Nefertiti replacing the old divine family triads on domestic altars. Since stelae have been found in Nubia describing a campaign against the enemies of Akhnaton, we know that he was no pacifist. And the king's failure in foreign policy as it is described in the Amarna letters is now regarded in part as rhetorical exaggeration, and has been reassessed. None the less, Christie did depict the main events of the reign of Akhnaton in a manner that was true to the historical facts.

NOTES

1   The Pyramids of Giza are the setting for the short story 'The Adventure of the Egyptian Tomb' in *Poirot Investigates* (1924).
2   A. Christie, *An Autobiography*, London 1977, pp. 495ff. On Stephen Glanville: ibid., p. 490; M. Mallowan, *Mallowan's Memoirs*, London 1977, pp. 177f.; W.R. Dawson and E.P. Uphill, *Who was Who in Egyptology*, 3rd edn by M.L. Bierbrier, London 1995, pp. 168f.
3   A. Christie, *Death Comes as the End*, London 1945, in which it is easy to find echoes of the Egyptian quotations, the letters, the 18th Maxim of Ptahhotep and the love songs.
4   J. Capart in *Chronique d'Egypte* 21 (1946), pp. 224f. The first partial translations by Gunn appeared in Winlock, *Bulletin* (n. 7). On this and the whole complex of ideas of the afterlife, and the way in which ancient Egypt has been regarded, see the still unique book by S. Morenz, *Die Begegnung Europas mit Ägypten*, Zurich 1969, p. 237 n. 124. Attitudes are more liberal today; a note on the book by T.G.H. James, *The Hekanakhte Papers and Other Early Middle Kingdom Documents*, New York 1962, in *Ancient Egyptian Bibliography* 1962, no. 62290, already contains a reference to Agatha Christie, as does R.B. Parkinson, *Voices from Ancient Egypt: An Anthology of Middle Kingdom Writings*, London 1991, p. 102.
5   Eco also makes use of Graeco-Egyptian sources from the Papyri Graecae Magicae (PGM); for instance, the description of the birth of Psyche from the laughter of the creator deity is from the so-called Eighth Book of Moses (PGM XIII, pp. 343–646); see H.D. Betz, *The Greek Magical Papyri in Translation*, Chicago 1986, pp. 185f.
6   James, *Hekanakhte* (n. 4). These papyri are now in the Metropolitan Museum of Art, New

York, and a radical new edition is about to be published: J.P. Allen, *The Heqankht Papyri*, PMMA 27, Metropolitan Museum of Art, New York, 2001.

7   Account by H.E. Winlock in *Bulletin of the Metropolitan Museum of Art 1922, part II, The Egyptian Expedition 1921–1922*, New York 1922; idem, *Excavations at Deir el-Bahri 1911–31*, New York 1942, pp. 47–67.

8   J. Romer, *Valley of the Kings*, London 1981, pp. 134f.

9   The papyri have been redated to the early Twelfth Dynasty by J.P. Allen (see n. 6).

10   Cf. D.-G. Erpenbeck, 'Namengebung in Agatha Christies Detektivromanen', in G.C. Rump, *Sprachnetze*, Hildesheim 1976, pp. 87–117.

11   Winlock, in *Bulletin* (n. 7), p. 34.

12   The jigsaw puzzle of Agatha Christie's quotations and references is distributed throughout the novel, and it would be beyond the scope of this essay to place the individual components in order.

13   Christie, *Death* (n. 3), p. 27.

14   Translation after R.B. Parkinson, *The Tale of Sinuhe and other Ancient Egyptian Poems* (Oxford 1997), p. 256.

15   Christie, *Death* (n. 3), p. 50.

16   Translation after Parkinson (n. 14), p. 251.

17   Christie, *Death* (n. 3), p. 110. As this phrase also occurs in the Tale of the Eloquent Peasant, it could be a proverb or colloquial saying.

18   Ibid., p. 125.

19   Translation after Parkinson (n. 14), p. 206. According to its title, this teaching was composed by King Amenemhat I (1939/8–1909 BC) for his son Senusret I.

20   Christie, *Death* (n. 3), pp. 43, 75.

21   Papyrus British Museum 10060; the papyrus is damaged in many places; see M.V. Fox, *The Song of Songs and the Ancient Egyptian Love Songs*, Madison 1985, pp. 11f., 15, 372, 374 (recto 2.5–2.9; 3.12–3.13); German translation by E. Hornung, *Gesänge vom Nil*. In the fifth song 'beauty' presumably refers to Hathor's, the goddess of the sky and of love, rather than the girl's.

22   H. Gardiner and K. Sethe, *Egyptian Letters to the Dead*, London 1928, pp. 5f., pls 5, 5a, pp. 8ff., pls 7, 8.

23   Christie, *Death* (n. 3), p. 125.

24   A. Wilkinson, *Ancient Egyptian Jewellery*, London 1971, pl. 6.

25   Winlock, in *Bulletin* (n. 7), p. 40 (fig. 31, plan).

26   Christie, *Death* (n. 3), p. 88.

27   Ibid., p. 36. This ceremony, known as the 'obliteration of footprints', came at the end of the ritual of the Opening of the Mouth.

28   According to Max Mallowan, *Mallowan's Memoirs*, London 1977, pp. 219ff.; A. Christie, *An Autobiography*, London 1977, p. 335; see also J. Morgan, *Agatha Christie: A Biography*, London 1984, pp. 213, 226, 370–1; J.C. Trewin, 'A Midas Gift to the Theatre', in H.R.F. Keating, *Agatha Christie, First Lady of Crime*, London 1977, pp. 135ff.

29   A. Grimm, *Das Sonnengeschlecht. Berliner Meisterwerke der Amarna-Kunst in der Sprache von Thomas Mann*, Mainz 1993, pp. 4ff., and *Joseph und Echnaton, Thomas Mann und Ägypten*, exh. cat., 2nd edn, Mainz 1993, pp. 58–68.

30   O. Mummert in *Neuer Theater-Almanach, Theatergeschichtliches Jahr- und Adressen-Buch*, year 9, Berlin 1940, p. 518, has an entry under 'London, Daly's Theatre' to the effect that new works included Agatha Christie's *Akhnaton*, but it had not yet been produced.

31   Glanville positively 'fed her' with Egyptian and cuneiform material, according to Mallowan, *Memoirs* (n. 28), p. 221.

32   I.E.S. Edwards (1909–96) was Keeper of Egyptian Antiquities in 1955–74; he published several works on epigraphy and history, including *The Pyramids of Egypt*, 1947. His

obituary by J. Malek in *The Independent* (Wednesday 9 October, 1996) describes the Tutankhamun exhibition as 'the crowning glory of his keepership'.

33 In Egyptological literature the work is mentioned only in G.T. Martin, *A Bibliography of the Amarna Period and its Aftermath*, London & New York 1992, no. 343, and T. Schneider, *Lexikon der Pharaonen*, Munich 1996, p. 102. Martin lists many novels and plays under nos 73, 128, 374 (film), 688f., 764, 1174, 1274, 1295, 1331, 1597, 1612f., 1677, 1700, 1707 and 1722. On the rediscovery of Akhnaton, see E. Hornung, *Echnaton, Die Religion des Lichtes*, Zurich 1995, pp. 9–27.

34 *The Dawn of Conscience*, New York 1933, pp. 272–302. Christie seems to have taken many translations from J.H. Breasted, *Ancient Records of Egypt* (referred to below as BAR) I–V, New York 1906, reprinted 1962.

35 A. Christie, *Akhnaton*, London 1973, pp. 34f.

36 The libretto is by Philip Glass with Richard Ridell, Shalom Goldman and Robert Israel: *Akhnaten* (opera), 1987, complete recording on CBS Masterworks MdK 42457 (CDs). A play by Wilhelm Schloz was published in 1968, *Amenophis des Vierten Revolution um Gott*, Stuttgart. It focuses on the conflict between the priests of Amun and belief in the Aten.

37 J. Assmann, *Moses der Ägypter. Entzifferung einer Gedächtnisspur*, Munich 1998, pp. 47–72, 250–260 ('Echnatons Unterscheidung: Die Wahrheit des Lichts und die Lüge des Mythos'). Assmann sees Akhnaton's monotheistic revolution as the first expression of counter-religious feeling in human history.

38 J.P. Allen, 'The Natural Philosophy of Akhenaton', in W.K. Simpson (ed.), *Religion and Philosophy in Ancient Egypt*, New Haven 1989, pp. 89–101.

39 A seminar held in New York in 1990 was entitled 'Hero or Heretic'.

40 At first in the possession of James Simon, who financed the excavations, it was not introduced to the general public until 1922; see R. Krauss, 1913–1988, '75 Jahre Büste der Nofretete/Nefret-iti in Berlin I', in *Jahrbuch Preussischer Kulturbesitz* 24, 1987 (1988), pp. 87–124.

41 Christie, *Akhnaton*, pp. 40, 50, 59, 64, 70f., 133; p. 74, Bek: 'I, your first pupil', cf. Breasted, BAR II (n. 7), § 975: 'whom his majesty himself taught' (rock image in Aswan).

42 Christie, *Akhnaton*, p. 69.

43 Ibid., p. 20; Breasted, *Dawn* (n. 34), p. 283; Great Hymn to the Aten, see J. Assmann, *Ägyptische Hymnen und Gebete* (subsequently ÄHG), Zurich 1975, no. 92, v. 46–52, and Miriam Lichtheim, *Ancient Egyptian Literature : A Book of Readings; Volume II : The New Kingdom*, Berkeley 1976, pp. 96–100.

44 Christie, *Akhnaton*, p. 27; Breasted, *Dawn* (n. 7), p. 282; Assmann, ÄHG (n. 16), no. 92, v. 25f.

45 Christie, *Akhnaton*, pp. 29f.; Breasted, *Dawn* (n. 34), pp. 283f.; cf. Assmann, ÄHG (n. 43), no. 92, v. 68–75; the 'embryology' of mankind: 'Creator of the germ in woman / Who makest seed into men / Making alive the son in the body of his mother' is quoted in Christie, *Akhnaton*, p. 38, in a scene of conflict as Nefertiti expresses her wish for a son. The passage in Christie, ibid. p. 39, corresponds to Assmann, ÄHG (n. 16), no. 92, v. 115f.

46 Christie, *Akhnaton*, pp. 52f.; Breasted, *Dawn* (n. 34), p. 286; cf. Assmann, ÄHG (n. 16), no. 92, v.125 to end of text.

47 Breasted, *Dawn* (n. 34), p. 286; Assmann, ÄHG (n. 43), no. 92, v. 122–124.

48 Christie, *Akhnaton*, pp. 138f.; Breasted, *Dawn* (n. 34), p. 282; cf. Assmann, ÄHG (n. 43), no. 92, v. 27–36.

49 Christie, *Akhnaton*, p. 114.; Breasted, *Dawn* (n. 34), p. 306; Assmann, ÄHG (n. 43), no. 95, v. 46–47.

50 Christie, *Akhnaton*, pp. 20f.; Breasted, BAR II (n. 34), p. 265, § 659; Assmann, ÄHG (n. 43), no. 233, v. 60–67; Christie, *Akhnaton*, p. 30, combines verses 57–67. B. Mathieu, 'Etudes métriques egyptiennes III', in *Revue d'Egyptologie* 45 (1994), pp. 139–53.

51 Christie, *Akhnaton*, pp. 50ff.; both versions, with a precise description of the layout of the place, the tombs and boundaries have been revised in W.J Murnane and C.C. Van Siclen III, *The Boundary Stelae of Akhenaten*, London 1993. W.J. Murnane, *Texts from the Amarna Period in Egypt*, Atlanta 1995, contains a new translation of the Amarna texts up to the time of Horemheb.

52 Christie, *Akhnaton*, pp. 10f., Amarna Letters, EA 23; on the translation of the 383 letters so far known, see W.L. Moran, *The Amarna Letters*, Baltimore & London 1992; EA 23, pp. 61f. Christie was by no means 'shaky on the historical side', as her biographer Janet Morgan (n. 1) thinks, p. 213, but was concerned with a question still not satisfactorily explained today: when was the image of Ishtar (Saska) sent to Egypt for the first time. The letter to Teye (EA 26) emerges in the play as a greeting to Tyi, see Christie, *Akhnaton*, p. 16; Moran, op. cit., p. 84.

53 Christie, *Akhnaton*, p. 28, literal quotations from EA 19 ('Love and Gold').

54 Ibid. p. 86; for a general survey of the extensive dossier on Ribaddi see Moran, *Letters* (n. 52), p. 383 (EA 68–95, 101–138). Rib-Hadda of Gubla / Byblos was finally driven from Byblos by Kings Abdi-Asirta and Aziru of Amurru, a kingdom in Lebanon, and perished.

55 Christie, *Akhnaton*, p.95, letter of the Burna-Buriyash of Babylon, EA 8; Tushratta detains Egyptian messengers, EA 28; Christie, op. cit., p. 102: Itakhama (Aitukama) of Kadesh, like Aziru, adopts a policy of sitting on the fence. The latter is then invited to Egypt and held prisoner, EA 169.

56 Christie, *Akhnaton*, pp. 111f.; EA 59, Moran, *Letters* (n. 52), p. 131; 'Tunip, your city, weeps, and its tears flow, and here is no grasping of your hand. We have gone on writing to the king, our lord, the king of Egypt, for 20 years, and not a single word of our lord has reached us.' The modern title of EA 74 runs in the same way but refers to the situation of Ribaddi in Byblos, 'Like a bird in a trap', see Moran, op. cit., pp. 142ff. Christie is very free with the place-names in both letters.

57 EA 287, 10–19; EA 286, 289, and end of EA 288, Moran, *Letters* (n. 52), p. 331: 'If there are no archers this year, may the king send a commissioner to fetch me, along with my brothers, and then we will die near the king, our lord.'

58 Christie, *Akhnaton*, pp. 136f.

59 Ibid. p. 25; Breasted, BAR II (n. 34), p. 797 (the seven princes of Takhsi were hung head down from the bows of the royal ship and displayed on the enclosure wall of Karnak and Napata).

60 Christie, *Akhnaton*, pp. 22f., 125; cf. Breasted, *Dawn* (n. 34) p. 316; Assmann, ÄHG (n. 43), nos. 174, 188; cf. Christie, op. cit., p 84.

61 Christie, *Akhnaton*, pp. 83, 87, 156; Breasted, BAR III (n. 34), p. 27, § 57.

62 Christie, *Akhnaton*, p. 155 (epilogue); Breasted, BAR III (n. 34), p. 32, § 64.

63 Christie, *Akhnaton*, p. 140. Ay replies to Akhnaton's question about the origin of wrongdoing in the world: 'It is, I think, because it is in their hearts so to do'. The original runs: 'I have made *every man like his brother*, and I have forbidden that they do evil, (but) it was their hearts which undid that which I had said.' (Breasted, *Dawn* [n. 34], p. 221).

64 Ibid., p. 89. Tyi insists that when Akhnaton receives foreigners he should make a magnificent entrance in his royal regalia. Breasted, BAR II (n. 34), § 669: 'a prince is a prince of whom one is afraid ... Be not known to the people; and they shall not say: "He is (only) a man."'

65 Christie, *Akhnaton*, p. 34 (Ay).

66 Ibid., p. 31, Tyi: 'The cunning of the serpent accomplishes more than the roaring of the lion' is an adaptation of a quotation: 'The hissing of the serpent is more significant than the braying of the donkey.'

67 Ibid., p. 63, last act, p. 150.

68 Ibid., pp. 37, 65, 110, 147; Berlin 20494. Christie several times makes use of pictorial motifs

that also appear in Thomas Mann, most of them from Heinrich Schäfer's *Amarna in Religion und Kunst*, Leipzig 1931; see Grimm, *Sonnengeschlecht* (n. 29), p. 49.

69   Christie, *Akhnaton*, p. 38.

70   Known in Egyptological literature as 'mocking viziers'; see W. Guglielmi, 'Humor in Wort und Bild auf altägyptischen Grabdarstellungen', in H. Brunner, R. Kannicht, K. Schwager, *Wort und Bild. Symposium des Fachbereichs Altertums- und Kulturwissenschaften zum 500jährigen Jubiläum der Eberhard-Karls-Universität Tübingen 1977* (1979), pp. 181–200, esp. p. 185; V. Dasen, in *Dwarfs in Ancient Egypt and Greece*, Oxford 1993, pp. 147f., links them with the youthful form of the sun god, and points to the similar outline of the scarab.

71   Christie, *Akhnaton*, pp. 45–9, pp. 61f. (relief of the sculptor and spy Ptahmose), pp. 143–9. Dwarfs traditionally came from the south, from Nubia and Punt. They were employed to provide entertainment and as 'dancers before the god'. People from the south were often suspected of sorcery. Agatha Christie merges both ideas here in the character of Para.

72   Ibid., p. 74; the couple in the garden are generally thought to be Akhnaton's son-in-law Semenkhare and his daughter Meritamun; cf. Grimm, *Sonnengeschlecht* (n. 29), p. 63.

73   Berlin 21834; head of Tyi; Christie, *Akhnaton*, pp. 77f.; tomb of Huya, see C. Aldred, *Echnaton, Gott und Pharao Ägyptens*, Bergisch-Gladbach 1968, figs 203, 104.

74   Christie, *Akhnaton*, p. 91; Aldred, *Echnaton* (n. 73), fig. 44.

75   Breasted, *Dawn* (n. 34), p. 285; Assmann, ÄHG (n. 34), no. 92, v. 79, 83, 96–9.

76   L. Green, 'Who was Who', in D. Arnold, *The Royal Women of Amarna*, Metropolitan Museum of Art, New York 1996, pp. 7–15; J. van Dijk, 'The Noble Lady of Mitanni and Other Royal Favourites of the Eighteenth Dynasty', in idem, *Essays on Ancient Egypt in Honour of Herman Te Velde*, Groningen 1997, pp. 33–46.

The Maker of "The Grey Cells of M. Poirot."

With her daughter, Rosalind; Agatha Christie, the great detective-story writer.

At the telephone.

At her writing table.   At work with her type-writer.

In her drawing-room: the author of the series of detective stories we begin this week.

With "Tutankhamen cushions": Agatha Christie and her little girl.

CREATOR OF THE MOST INTERESTING DETECTIVE SINCE SHERLOCK HOLMES: AGATHA CHRISTIE.

Agatha Christie (who is in private life Mrs. Archibald Christie, the mother of a charming little daughter, Rosalind) is the brilliant writer of detective fiction, and creator of Hercule Poirot, the most fascinating character any novel-reader could wish to meet. Her first book, "The Mysterious Affair at Styles," introduced Poirot, the detective who, by the aid of what he calls "those brave little grey cells" of his brain, unravels the strangest tangles of crime. A series of stories dealing with Poirot's further exploits has been written for "The Sketch," and opens this week—on the page opposite. The tales are a thrilling set of detective yarns which equal anything ever published in that style.

PHOTOGRAPH BY ALFIERI, SPECIALLY TAKEN FOR "THE SKETCH."

The Detective and the Archaeologist

Barbara Patzek, Regina Hauses and Andreas Dudde

About the only *work* ever done in a Christie novel is archaeology.[1]

gatha Christie is an expert practitioner of the 'simplicity' of crime fiction;[2] she presents memorable images that have not been watered down by any attempt at profundity. Other notable characteristics of the classic detective story – viewed as a parlour game in which introspection and deeper meaning have no part, since interest is focused on the criminological riddle – are that it is straightforward, vivid and accurate. The rules of the game include traditional, easily recognized features and references to famous predecessors or to the contemporary social scene. Christie is also an expert in characterization; the social and intellectual types represented by the people in her books harmonize neatly. Finally, she is a master of presentation: her characters, plots and *bons mots* are nearly always solidly based in their own historical and social world. The same may be said of the analogy between detective and archaeologist to be found in her crime stories, although only in connection with her star detective Hercule Poirot and her less famous private eye Parker Pyne.

Poirot, as an early twentieth-century gentleman, is often on his travels.[3] Like Christie and other members of her social class, he is accustomed to going abroad but often suffers from seasickness and the other disadvantages of foreign climates, foreign customs and the foreign mentality. Although these discomforts can sometimes injure his vanity, he preserves an ironic attitude towards them. Poirot is an educated member of the upper middle classes, a stratum of society that recognized foreign travel as culturally valuable. Yet Poirot is also an outsider in this class. He speaks with a French accent, although he is not a 'real' Frenchman but 'only' a Belgian. His elaborate Gallic manners

Agatha Christie, 'The Maker of "The Grey Cells of M. Poirot"', *The Sketch,* 7 March 1923

make him stand out among the English, and he comes up against typical British prejudice. He is more intelligent than the average member of his society and, unlike most Britons, is flexible in adapting and applying his ideas.

Archaeologists are outsiders too in Christie's crime novels. They tend to wear thick glasses and are seldom elegant or handsome; they do not have the social polish of the upper class, but thanks to the social prestige of their academic discipline they are accepted as scholars, and regarded as skilful intercultural mediators.[4] Since they are unpretentious, are acquainted with more than one culture and can apply analytical methods, they move as easily between foreign cultures of the present day and their own as they do between the past and the present. They are also absorbed by their scholarship. The analysis and historical reconstruction of the past occupy their minds so much that such incidents in the present day as a murder committed in an aeroplane leave them unmoved. Poirot is as familiar with this unworldliness as was Agatha Christie Mallowan, herself the wife of an archaeologist. 'You are not, perhaps, acquainted with many archaeologists?' Poirot says to Inspector Japp in *Death in the Clouds*, published in 1935. 'If these two were having a really absorbing discussion on some point at issue – *eh bien*, my friend, their concentration would be such that they would be quite blind and deaf to the outside world. They would be existing, you see, in five thousand or so BC. Nineteen hundred and thirty-four AD would have been non-existent for them.'[5]

One must assume that this observation, like most of the character sketches of archaeologists in Christie's detective stories, is based on her husband Max Mallowan, the incarnation of the objective, scholarly archaeologist interested in ancient cultures for their own sake, a man aware that he would learn more from an excavation about the everyday life of peoples of the past than about single events and single personalities.[6] Mallowan's first archaeological position was as an assistant on Leonard Woolley's dig at Ur, where Christie met him. Woolley's purpose was to uncover the historical basis of the Deluge and the history of the Chaldaeans, the ancestors of Abraham.[7] The cuneiform tablets found by Layard were of great importance to him, and indeed had an almost numinous aura, since when they were translated, an event which aroused much public interest, they proved to contain a Babylonian version of the biblical story of the Flood. Woolley's ambitious attempt to discover levels that could be shown, from this ancient text, to date from the time of the Deluge itself grew into a major archaeological project, using the most modern methods then available for dating finds and exploring early historical periods that were of great interest in themselves, quite apart from the biblical story.[8]

Peter Ustinov during the making of the film *Death On The Nile* (photo: Lord Snowdon)

Christie actually makes Poirot explain his detective methods by analogy with the uncovering and interpretation of archaeological finds. The general view of archaeology seems to have changed: it was no longer sensational archaeology that impressed but its empirical methods. In *Death on the Nile* (1937) Poirot explains his methods:

> Once I went professionally to an archaeological expedition – and I learnt something there. In the course of an excavation, when something comes out of the ground, everything is cleared away very carefully all around it. You take away the loose earth, and you scrape here and there with a knife until finally your object is there, all alone, ready to be drawn and photographed with no extraneous matter confusing it. That is what I have been seeking to do – clear away the extraneous matter so that we can see the truth – the naked shining truth.[9]

The dig to which Poirot is referring here – the excavations in the novel *Murder in Mesopotamia* (1936) – is fictional, but it is based on the dig at Ur. In Woolley's popular scientific work *Digging up the Past* (1930) the way an archaeologist deals with such finds is described in words and images parallel to Poirot's quotation. The point is not just to clean the object, but to uncover historical facts by recording the precise state of the culture around it at the time when it went into the earth, so that its present condition can allow as much information as possible to be deduced about that historical moment. Similarly, Poirot succeeds in reconstructing the moment when a crime was committed. There is no doubt that the pedantic detective likes the archaeologist's rigorous methods.

Agatha Christie included other experiences in her novels that illustrate the fruitful relationship between the detective story and archaeology. The heroine of *They Came to Baghdad* (1951) also gained some experience on a dig in southern Mesopotamia. Christie writes:

> The baskets of broken potsherds had at first excited her astonished derision ... Then as she found joins, stuck them and propped them up in boxes of sand, she began to take an interest. She learned to recognize shapes and types. And she came finally to try and reconstruct in her own mind just how and for what these vessels had been used some three thousand odd years ago. In the small area where some poor quality private houses had been dug, she pictured the houses as they had originally

Paperback German edition of Anne Hart's *Agatha Christie's Hercule Poirot*, Scherz Verlag 1994

AGATHA CHRISTIE'S

Hercule Poirot

Sein Leben und seine Abenteuer

Nach Originaldokumenten
verfaßt von Anne Hart

Katharine and Leonard Woolley on the excavations at Ur in the 1920s (C.L. Woolley, *Digging up the Past,* London 1930)

stood and the people who lived in them with their wants and possessions and occupations, their hopes and their fears.[10]

After analysing the finds, the archaeologist's task is to reconstruct their historical context. When Woolley was showing people round his dig, according to
the critical Mallowan, he used to make the ancient world almost visible before
his astonished visitors' eyes, from no more than the remaining foundations.[11]

Historical evidence, though fragmentary, can provide a complete picture through archaeological finds and any additional historical information
thus acquired. Similarly, real objects were finding their way into the historical
novel at the time when Agatha Christie was writing, to convey authenticity
and the atmosphere of the past.[12] There are two different ways in which the
detective story and archaeology can be linked: first, they both enquire into
causes – the empirical establishment of a past sequence of events at the time
when they took place – and second, detective and archaeologist alike are tracking down or divining the past, building up an image of it through research or
enquiry in order to discover new aspects. The converse of this last process

occurs in the thriller or horror story in which the past really does enter the present – a mummy comes to life, for instance, like Frankenstein's monster in Mary Shelley's classic tale. The finding of the religious legend of the Deluge on an ancient cuneiform tablet written by a historical people whose language had been revived was felt to be an almost numinous experience. No doubt a similar effect was produced by the publication of those ancient Egyptian ghost stories which may have seemed relevant to the early twentieth-century excavations in the Valley of the Kings.[13]

The link between detective story, thriller and archaeology in Christie's works arises not just from her own life but indicates this general context. A short story written in the early 1920s, 'The Adventure of the Egyptian Tomb' (1924), predating her travels in the Orient and her marriage to Max Mallowan in 1930, shows that Christie was following the general trend of her time, when there was great interest in scientific archaeological work undertaken for serious historical purposes, and at the same time the literary figure of the

German edition of Leonard Woolley's book *Digging up the Past*, Leipzig 1932

detective with his unusual and empirical skills was becoming increasingly popular. This short story, which is in the nature of a thriller, is based on the sensation created by the opening of the grave of Tutankhamun in February 1923 and the sudden death of one of its two excavators, Lord Carnarvon, in April of the same year.[14] In 1923, when Christie was just establishing herself as an author and ensuring that she could earn a regular income from her writing, she published short stories in the *Sketch*, the *Weekly Times* and the *Evening News*.[15] These tales were on a variety of subjects and varied in their literary merit; they were probably written at great speed. One of them, the short story mentioned above, derives from the sensational discovery of the tomb of Tutankhamun and the atmosphere of mystery surrounding it. Like her contemporaries, Christie took a lively interest in Howard Carter and Lord Carnarvon's archaeological expedition, which had been going on for seven years before its sudden and spectacular discovery was made, and she shared the enthusiasm for Egypt which it aroused.[16] But she was not yet a person of sufficient influence to be among those invited to hear Howard Carter's lecture at the British Museum on 22 September 1923.[17]

The detective couple who appear in her short story are the famous Poirot and his early companion Captain Hastings, modelled on Conan Doyle's even more famous pair Sherlock Holmes and Dr Watson. The Poirot / Hastings duo had contributed to the great success of Christie's first crime novel, *The Mysterious Affair at Styles* (1920), and she had Conan Doyle's Sherlock Holmes in mind when choosing the kind of character her detective would be. Conan Doyle himself had taken the idea of such a figure from the first literary detective of all, Auguste Dupin in Edgar Allan Poe's *The Murders in the Rue Morgue* (1841). The literary policeman or detective is initially encountered drawing deductions from clues, in other words establishing the value of circumstantial evidence as it is accepted by modern jurisdiction. Circumstantial evidence of guilt derived from clues can lead to the reconstruction of the crime: police procedure, like archaeology, benefited by the empirical methods of proof devised in the nineteenth century and the technology involved in them, for instance photography and its ability to copy and record clues which on the face of it might not have seemed significant at first. Sherlock Holmes's methods of objective and intellectual deduction constituted something of a challenge to real-life criminology of his creator's time. The taking of fingerprints for purposes of identification was introduced into British police procedure around 1880;[18] one may compare the way in which Conan Doyle credited Holmes with publishing a number of curious facts in the author's favourite journal, the *Strand Magazine*, including a 'little monograph' on the 140 different kinds of tobacco ash. Conan Doyle himself was not far from associating archaeological and detective methods in his stories.[19]

Above Cover of a German translation of *Death on the Nile*, Scherz Verlag, first hardback edition, 1978

Above right German paperback translation of *They Came to Baghdad*, Scherz Verlag, 22nd edition, 1991

Agatha Christie's own short story concerns the case of two archaeologists who have died immediately after excavating an Egyptian royal tomb, and the reaction caused by their deaths in London.

> The more sensational newspapers immediately took the opportunity of reviving all the old superstitious stories connected with the ill luck of certain Egyptian treasures. The unlucky Mummy in the British Museum, that hoary old chestnut, was dragged out with fresh zest, and quietly denied by the Museum, but nevertheless enjoyed all its usual vogue.[20]

Poirot is summoned to the excavations to prevent another murder and clear up any ideas of superstition. To the disappointment of Hastings, however, he does not set about providing a rational explanation of the uncanny events, but takes 'the force of superstition' seriously. Unlike Conan Doyle, Christie dwells on the effects of deception in her stories and novels,[21] rather than concentrating on the meticulous empirical enquiry into the causes of a crime.

The fascination of the scene of a dig in a foreign country also plays a considerable part in her short story: 'A wonderful place … and wonderful work. I can feel the fascination. This desert life, this probing into the heart of a vanished civilization. Surely, Poirot, you too must feel the charm?'[22] says Hastings enthusiastically just at the moment when his friend is beginning to clear the case up. Poirot's explanation, after he has come up with the surprising solution, is that ancient Egyptian magic had nothing to do with the case – the clues had been thrown together without any regard for history. Rather, it was to be supposed that there was a natural human instinct to believe in the supernatural: 'Once get it firmly established that a series of deaths are supernatural, and you might almost stab a man in broad daylight, and it would still be put down to the curse, so strongly is the instinct of the supernatural implanted in the human race.'[23] Naturally the *corpus delicti* is then given to a chemist for investigation, and it is explained that by research into such matters the whole story

Lord Carnarvon (left) and Mr. Howard Carter (right), whose wonderful discoveries are the reward of some sixteen years' research in the Valley of the Kings. The story of the preliminary investigation of the inner chamber is given on another page.

A photographic impression of the daily scene at Tutankhamen's tomb since the first news of the discovery was announced in *The Times*. Large numbers of visitors have crowded around the tomb-entrance watching the work of Mr. Howard Carter and his party of experts.

MR. BONAR LAW'S GRANDSON CHRISTENED. — Sir Frederick and Lady Sykes photographed yesterday after the christening of their infant son, Bonar, in the Crypt of the House of Commons. Lady Sykes is the daughter of Mr. Bonar Law.

Dr. Gow, Headmaster of Westminster School from 1901 to 1919, whose death is announced.

THE SEALED ENTRANCE TO THE KING'S MAUSOLEUM. — Yesterday afternoon the secret of King Tutankhamen's tomb was revealed by the breaking-down of the sealed doorway (shown above), guarded by two life-size figures of the Pharaoh. The King's mausoleum presented a scene of stupendous magnificence, a graphic account of which appears elsewhere in *The Times* to-day. A second chamber, leading out of this sepulchral hall, was also discovered, and, like the two ante-chambers already found, it is full of funerary furniture. [*The Times* World Copyright, by arrangement with the Earl of Carnarvon. Photograph by Mr. Harry Burton, of the Metropolitan Museum of Art, New York.]

Members of Lord Carnarvon's party who were present yesterday at the breaking down of the sealed wall to the Pharaoh's burial chamber, preliminary to the formal ceremony to-morrow. These photographs taken at Luxor recently show: Sir William Garstin (left), who has been prominently associated with the development of modern Egypt; Lady Evelyn Herbert, Lord Carnarvon's daughter, who was the only woman present; Dr. Alan Gardiner, the editor of the *Journal of Egyptian Archaeology*, who is a member of the expedition.

Two Egyptian ladies leaving Tutankhamen's tomb after a preoccupation with the contents of the ante-chamber and for the opening of the burial chamber beyond. Mr. Carter has of visitors over the tomb.

Lady Ribblesdale and Mr. Stephen Vlasto arriving in Queen of the Belgians, General Lord Allenby and Lady the many distinguished people who will attend the formal

MONTE-CAR

The rendezvous of Aristocracy

THE MEAN TEMPERATURE IS 59 DE THE MOST EVEN OF THE SOUTH OF ON ACCOUNT OF ITS SHELTERED PO

could be reduced *ad absurdum* to Egyptian magic and religion. Science and archaeological research eventually prove the absurdity of the deception that was the murderer's *modus operandi*.

A study of press reports in 1923 points up a direct connection with these ideas in the publication record of the opening of the tomb of Tutankhamun and its consequences. *The Times* in London, outbidding the *New York Times*, had obtained exclusive rights to the story of the opening of the tomb and the finding of the grave goods it contained. The official opening of the tomb on 17 February 1923 took place some time after it had actually been discovered – the process was described as a 'serio-comedy' by one of the journalists present.[24] Howard Carter had in fact taken a preliminary look inside the tomb on 26 November 1922, and it was then sealed again. Just before the great public event *The Times* of 8 February gave a dramatic account of the eager anticipation preceding the alleged 'first opening' of the tomb: 'Daily the sphinxlike sealed door, with its twin guardian images of the king, stares them in the face, and they have already amazingly curbed their curiosity. They must also, in some degree, consider the rest of the world, and from present symptoms … it seems that half the world will go mad, from sheer suspense, if the crucial step is much longer postponed.'

A large staff of experts took part in the official opening of the tomb and in the subsequent recording of the finds there. Emphasis was laid on the fact

Left Lord Carnarvon and Howard Carter, the excavators of Tutankhamun's tomb, *The Times*, 18 February 1923

Below Contents of Tutankhamun's tomb, *National Geographic Magazine*, February 1923

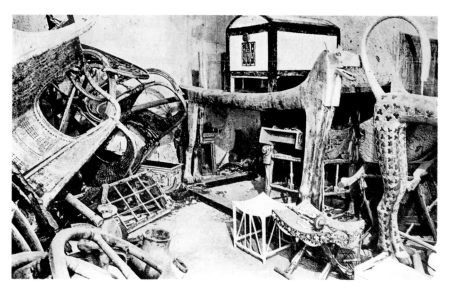

Above Removing objects from Tutankhamun's tomb, *National Geographic Magazine*, February 1923

Right Queen Elizabeth of Belgium visiting the tomb of Tutankhamun (above right); spectators at the official opening of the tomb on 18 February 1923 (below right); *National Geographic Magazine*, February 1923

that the latest scientific methods and instruments had been used. Besides archaeologists from the Metropolitan Museum in New York and restorers, artists and photographers, James H. Breasted and Alan H. Gardiner were also present as acknowledged experts, together with a chemist and a radiologist. All the finds were photographed, drawn and then released for conservation. A laboratory was set up.[25] The excavators wanted the utmost secrecy to be preserved; there were constant patrols around the tomb checking up on each other. *The Times* of 5 March 1923 published an account of ancient and modern robbery and stressed the necessity of taking precautions. Many visitors would have liked to get their hands on a souvenir, and even touching the archaeological finds aroused the ire of the scientific staff.[26]

The regular accounts of Carter and Carnarvon's discovery published in *The Times* in 1922 and 1923, describing the opening of the tomb and the subsequent study of the finds, dwell on the atmosphere of controlled scientific rationality that prevailed, although subliminally emphasizing that this was one of the greatest discoveries of all time. We are told that the journalists present lay in wait by the tomb and felt like detectives themselves, captivated as they were

ROYALTY PAYS TRIBUTE TO ROYALTY

Queen Elizabeth of the Belgians entering King Tutankhamen's tomb with Lord Carnarvon, Mr. Howard Carter leading the way. Behind Her Majesty is Lady Evelyn Herbert, the daughter of Lord Carnarvon. The man with the white flower in his buttonhole (behind Lady Evelyn) is Lord Allenby, the British High Commissioner for Egypt and the Sudan.

Photographs by Maynard Owen Williams

PEEPING OVER THE RIM AT HISTORY OF THREE THOUSAND YEARS AGO

These spectators are looking down upon the entrance to the tomb of Tutankhamen on the day of the official opening, February 18, 1923.

THE LUNCHEON CARAVAN ARRIVES

The rising tide of sightseers to the Valley of the Kings became such a flood upon the opening of the tomb of Tutankhamen that practically every available transport facility within a large area had to be commandeered to take care of the visitors.

Photographs from Ledger Photo Service

HAMPERS OF FOOD FOR THE VISITORS TO THE TOMB

by the atmosphere of the mysterious past, the excavations and the surrounding desert: 'Mystery hung as heavy on the place as mystery ever can in the full light of day.'[27] The Times carried almost daily reports on individual new finds and the techniques of excavation and conservation, assessing the significance of the objects in general for historical reconstruction. Particular attention was paid to the furnishings and grave goods in the tomb, everyday objects providing an insight into the material lives of the Pharaohs.[28] Every glove and every sandal was hailed as a sensation.

An account of what might be called an atmospheric nature in The Times of 31 January 1923 spoke of the rumours circulating in Cairo after the discovery of the tomb by Carnarvon and Carter, but before its official opening, and mentioned another aspect: the supposed typically Egyptian tendency to be superstitious about the discoveries. There were local rumours to the effect that supernatural powers had led Carnarvon to the royal tomb. Another rumour, said The Times, concerned Lord Carnarvon's canary, which he always carried with him in a cage. At the time when the tomb was discovered a cobra had apparently made its way into the expedition house, got into the bird-cage and killed the canary; it was later found still lying in the cage by the archaeologists and killed in its own turn. This story, according to The Times, arose from the embellishment of a legend in which the cobra, symbol of the kingdom of ancient Egypt, had killed the clever little bird symbolizing the spirit of modern civilization. After the opening of the tomb some voices were raised protesting against the disturbance of the Pharaoh's last repose, and accusing the excavators and The Times of exploiting the event for commercial ends. The Times published a rebuttal on 14 March 1923, claiming that the Pharaoh had achieved the international fame he deserved only through the excavation of his tomb and the publication of its details.

Other journals, however, learning only as much about the excavators as the policy of The Times saw fit, fell upon these rumours, looking for weak spots in the façade of what they considered arrogant mystification. An ostrakon (sherd) found by Carter in an ante-room to the tomb, and said to have incised upon it an ancient curse on any tomb robber who entered, had vanished without trace. The find had apparently been erased from the records of the excavation, The Times remained silent on the subject, and the rumour lived and flourished.[29] Finally, within a few days Carnarvon died of an unidentified illness in Cairo. What The Times presented as a sober succession of reports running from 20 March to the announcement of his death on 6 April 1923 became a

The luncheon tent and camels bringing provisions for visitors to the tomb of Tutankhamun, *National Geographic Magazine*, February 1923

DEATH OF LORD CARNARVON.

EGYPTOLOGIST AND SPORTSMAN.—A recent studio portrait of Lord Carnarvon. His many interests included, besides Egyptological research, in which he met his death, travel, hunting, motoring, flying, and horse-racing. He was famous as an amateur photographer.

THE DISCOVERER OF TUTANKHAMEN'S TOMB.—Lord Carnarvon outside Tutankhamen's tomb in the Valley of the Kings. With him is Mr. Howard Carter, who worked with him during the sixteen years' search. Lady Evelyn Herbert, Lord Carnarvon's daughter, who was present at the discovery, can also be seen.

IN THE PHARAOH'S TOMB.—The historic photograph taken at the opening of the inner chamber. The tomb was re-sealed at the end of February and Lord Carnarvon intended to open it again in the autumn in the expectation of finding the mummy of Tutankhamen in the inner shrine.

Above The death of Lord Carnarvon, excavator of the tomb of Tutankhamun, *The Times*, 6 April 1923

Left Bust of Tutankhamun being removed from the tomb, *National Geographic Magazine*, February 1923

tense thriller in other publications. Various observations were connected with the event: Lord Carnarvon seemed to have died at the age of fifty-seven of nothing worse than an inflamed insect bite, the electricity had failed all over Cairo at the moment of his death, and far away in England the dead man's favourite dog howled and then died. All this led to the circulation of the well-known tale of the curse of Pharaoh, a story still current today.

In itself, that story contains a number of elements leading us back to the subject of detective fiction and archaeology. Interpretation of the facts and empirical science prove to be selective, and what they select can depend on impressions. Deeply felt impressions with a particularly strong influence on the selection process are linked to the uncovering of the past. The disputes among those involved were very similar to the disputes of the criminological parlour game. On the one hand there were rationalists who either totally rejected superstition or alternatively tried to explain it by scientific means; on the other there were the superstitious claiming to have found definite proof at last of the existence of supernatural forces. Furthermore, the enlightened Europeans and European science appeared to be on one side, and the traditionally superstitious Egyptians on the other. Newspapers and journals made use of these disputes to fill their pages. The whole situation seemed to cry out for the talents of the detective or archaeologist who could disentangle the network of deceptive facts and motives by bringing to bear an outsider's fresh viewpoint, along with the detailed and esoteric knowledge of an expert.

NOTES

1   Robert Barnard, *A Talent to Deceive: An Appreciation of Agatha Christie*, London 1979, p.5.
2   E. Crispin, 'The Mistress of Simplicity', in H.R.F. Keating (ed.), *Agatha Christie: First Lady of Crime*, London 1977, pp. 39–48.
3   H.R.F. Keating, 'Hercule Poirot – A Companion Portrait', in Keating, *Christie* (n. 1), pp. 205–16.
4   For instance Richard Baker in A. Christie, *They Came to Baghdad*, London 1951.
5   Agatha Christie, *Death in the Air*, New York 1984, p. 69.
6   Cf. the sober tone of M. Mallowan, *Mallowan's Memoirs*, London 1977.
7   Charles L. Woolley, *The Sumerians*, London 1928, and *Ur of the Chaldees*, London 1929. On the Mallowans' view of Woolley's journalistic approach and 'sales policy', cf. J. Morgan, *Agatha Christie: A Biography*, London 1984, pp. 171ff.
8   C. L. Woolley, *Digging up the Past*, London 1930; Mallowan, *Memoirs* (n. 4), pp. 46ff.
9   Agatha Christie, *Death on the Nile*, London 1972, p. 204.
10 Agatha Christie, *They Came to Baghdad*, London 1988, p. 201.
11 Mallowan, *Memoirs* (n. 4), p. 57, described Woolley giving a guided tour of this kind through the former city: 'Now look at the roof ... I know you cannot see it, but we know everything about it that matters. The evidence is mostly on the floor in front of you.'
12 Cf., for instance, the role of historical objects in T. Mann, *Joseph und seine Brüder*, 2nd edn,

Stuttgart 1960. On the symbolism of myths and objects cf. K. Hamburger, *Thomas Manns biblisches Werk*, Munich 1981, pp. 49ff.; A. Grimm, *Joseph und Echnaton. Thomas Mann und Ägypten*, exh. cat., Munich 1992.

13   'Die Erlebnisse des Seton Chamwese mit den Seelen des Noferka-Ptah und der Ahwere' in *Altägyptische Erzählungen und Märchen*, trans. (into German) G. Röder, Leipzig 1927, pp. 136–57; cf. E. Brunner-Traut, *Altägyptische Märchen und Erzählungen*, 11th edn, Munich 1997, pp. 221–40, also pp. 209–12 ('Das Gespenst').

14   Accounts of the background and personal interpretations of the story of the curse are given by P. Vandenberg, *Der Fluch der Pharaonen*, Berne 1973, pp. 9–29; T. Hoving, *Tutankhamun: The Untold Story*, New York 1978.

15   A. Christie, *An Autobiography*, London 1977, pp. 321–9; E. Walter, 'The Case of Escalating Sales', in Keating, *Christie* (n. 1), pp. 13ff.

16   Morgan, *Christie* (n. 5), p. 41.

17   Cf. the guest list published in *The Times* of 25 September 1923.

18   G. Brunold, 'Die Geburt des Detektivs und die Zeichen. Die literarische Avantgarde der Kriminalistik', in *Neue Zürcher Zeitung*, Fernausgabe no. 22, 28 January 1994, p. 41.

19   'The Hound of the Baskervilles' and 'The New Catacomb'.

20   Agatha Christie, *Poirot Investigates*, London 1993, p. 92.

21   Barnard, *A Talent* (n. 1).

22   Christie, *Poirot Investigates* (n. 20), p. 105.

23   Ibid., p. 106.

24   M.O. Williams in the *National Geographic* of February 1923.

25   H. Carter and A.C. Mace, *The Tomb of Tut.ankh.Amen Discovered by the Late Earl of Carnarvon and Howard Carter*, 3 vols, London 1923–33.

26   Williams, *National Geographic* (n. 17).

27   Ibid.

28   Cf. the assessment of the finds by Flinders Petrie in *The Times* of 29 November 1923.

29   Hoving, *Tutankhamun* (n. 10), pp. 234f.

Agatha Christie at home in Winterbrook House, Wallingford, in 1950

Rules of the Game: Agatha Christie's Construction of the Detective Story

Ulrich Suerbaum

I t is decades now since Agatha Christie was active and writing as the acknowledged queen of crime, but she still holds that position among readers of the genre, and her publishers can proudly boast, on the blurbs of the latest editions of her novels, that she is 'quite simply, the best-selling author in history ... translated into more languages than Shakespeare.' Literary critics have always had some difficulty in accounting for her enduring fascination and her incontestable position as the great mistress of the classic detective story, for she lacks most of the qualities usually praised in a top-ranking writer of crime novels. Her characterization has no psychological depth; her cases are unrealistic; her style is simple and often cliché-ridden. None the less, her books are masterpieces of detective fiction. They have qualities of construction never surpassed in the works of her more ambitious rivals and successors who win higher praise from the critics.

Basically, the Agatha Christie novel of detection that became the model for crime writing in general is like a Sherlock Holmes story on a larger scale. The same clearly marked structural components are present – an exposition setting out the case, then its investigation, and finally the solution, elucidating all the relevant questions – but at ten times the length of one of Conan Doyle's stories. While the pattern remains the same, however, certain aspects of the structure have changed, in particular the cast of characters. Instead of a small group of people we now have a company large enough for a whole novel, with some ten leading parts. The novel usually begins not with an exposition of the case as such – for the murder victim is still alive – but with a lengthy introduction of the separate characters and the social connections between them. Usually (for instance in Christie's prototypical first novel *The Mysterious Affair at Styles*, 1920) theirs is a society of the kind found in hundreds of classic crime novels: a large extended family of landed gentry comprising several branches

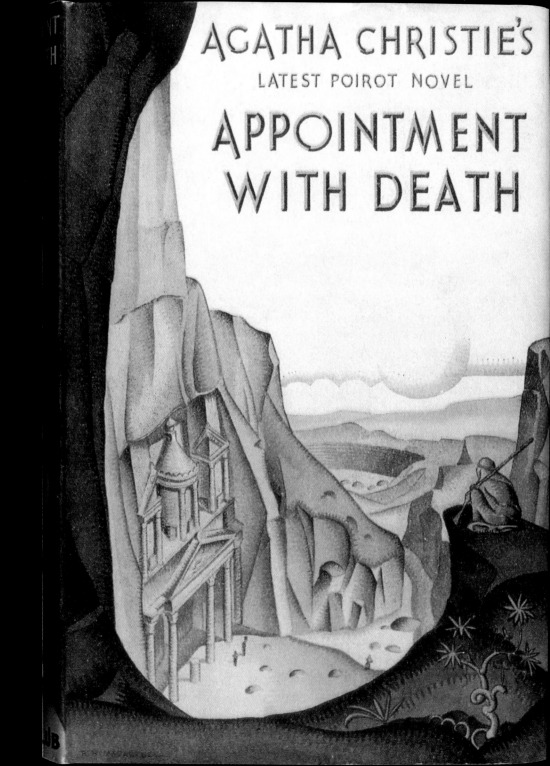

Above Manuscript notes for *Appointment with Death*

Left Jacket by Robin Macartney for the first edition of *Appointment with Death*, the Crime Club, Collins 1938

and several generations living together, and visited by a series of guests and protégés. It is a leisured society, self-contained in every way: all the characters belong to the same social class and they are living in the same place, at least at the time of the crime. The casts of characters that do not make up a family, but are travelling companions, or people living and working together during a season of archaeological excavations (for instance in *Murder in Mesopotamia*, 1936), are constructed on the same pattern.

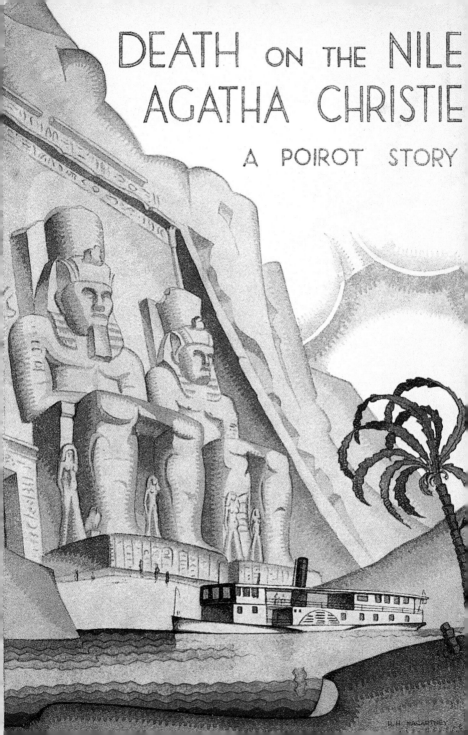

DEATH ON THE NILE
AGATHA CHRISTIE
A POIROT STORY

The society presented in the novel is structured in three ways. Each character has his or her own place and status in the family; each has a social and moral position – being for instance fully accepted and respected, or alternatively regarded as suspect and difficult; and finally – although initially this is not obvious – each character is destined to play a certain part in the mystery, becoming the victim or perpetrator of the crime, a source of information or someone who is either seeking the truth or anxious to cover it up. In the first part of the novel, where there is little action apart from conversation, mealtimes and an occasional outing, the reader is fully occupied in getting acquainted with the characters, distinguishing between them and classifying them.

Christie's fictional communities are the embodiment of a world known to every English-speaking reader, and not just readers of detective stories. For centuries the landed gentry, together with the aristocracy, have constituted the English upper class, a class into which successful newcomers strove to be accepted in every period, and whose attitudes and way of life were admired and imitated by wider social strata. From the eighteenth century novelists, too, such as Henry Fielding and Jane Austen, have preferred to draw their characters from this class. From the nineteenth century onwards its world was increasingly idealized in fiction, while in fact it was in steady decline. When Agatha Christie began writing, the golden age of the English gentry was long since over. The world of stately homes existed mainly in the mind – a modern Arcadia, the myth, still current, of a highly civilized society leading the country not because of anything it actually did, merely by setting the tone.

In the detective novel this social world always attracts considerable interest for its own sake, but a crime story cannot rely on that alone. Where its cast of characters is concerned, the classic work of detective fiction draws on the tension between the social status of the characters and their objective human and moral substance, between their ostensible social connections and their true relationships with each other. It owes its high potential for suspense and entertainment to the fact that it is not just a mystery about the identity of the criminal (whodunnit?) or a game played with the clues (how was it done?), but a question of exposure (what lay behind the façade?). Its motto is that appearances are deceptive. People are not what they seem. The whole of this society is not what it makes itself out to be.

Such casts of characters are very well suited to a game of deduction of this nature. Almost all the contact between them is relatively superficial. They know each other socially, but they do not know one another's true natures, nor

Jacket by Robin Macartney for the first edition of *Death on the Nile*, the Crime Club, Collins 1937

do they want to. Social classification and personal assessment of the characters depend on surface criteria. In such circumstances there is always the possibility of deception, and deception does not really surprise any of them. They trust each other, they do not like to attribute bad motives to anyone else, but of course they are aware that they see only the veneer. When a crime really is committed, the perpetrator could be anyone.

Another reason why it could be anyone is that almost all of them, without being in any way abnormal, have compelling motives for murder. It is one of the basic assumptions of these novels that everyone regards membership of a society such as theirs as the highest good, and would do anything not to forfeit it. That social membership depends on money – usually in the form of inherited property – and good reputation. Anyone threatened by impoverishment or the loss of reputation is thus a potential murderer. In *Appointment with Death* (1938) the tyrannical and bad-tempered Mrs Boynton is murdered not by a member of her family, although they all have their reasons for hating her, but by the ambitious politician and Member of Parliament Lady Westholme, of whose past she knows something disreputable. That is enough of a motive: 'You see the terrible dilemma she was in? Her career, her ambitions, her social position – all at stake!'[1]

In a guessing game occupying a whole novel it is not usually enough for the murderers alone to have something to hide, while other characters could have committed a crime only in theory. Those other characters must have secrets that have nothing to do with the murder, but cast suspicion on them because they have lied or behaved in some unusual way. A social community of the kind found in Agatha Christie is particularly suitable for such secondary mysteries; it is a society of people with something to hush up. Almost all the passengers on board the SS *Karnak* in *Death on the Nile* (1937), for instance, not only murderers and victims, have secrets to hide: they include a woman who is an alcoholic, a jewel thief, two lawyers surreptitiously keeping an eye on their clients, a terrorist 'with five or six cold-blooded murders to his credit',[2] and a secret service man who is on his trail.

In their construction Christie's detective novels are among the most complex in the entire field of crime fiction. This complexity arises principally from the fact that Agatha Christie pursues the game of unravelling the mystery with the utmost industry on all three levels of her story: who committed the crime, how was it done and how will the solution be revealed? The question of how the crime was committed is in the foreground – elucidation of the mechanics of the murder, the course of events and the functional part played

Plan of the cabins on the Nile steamer SS *Karnak* in *Death on the Nile*

S.S. KARNAK
PROMENADE DECK

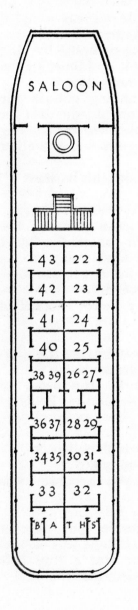

43	22 JAMES FANTHORP
42	23 TIM ALLERTON
41 CORNELIA ROBSON.	24 MRS ALLERTON
40 JACQUELINE DE BELLEFORT	25 SIMON DOYLE
38 39 ANDREW PENNINGTON	26 27 LINNET DOYLE
36 37 DR BESSNER	28 29 MISS VAN SCHUYLER
34 35 MRS AND MISS OTTERBOURNE	30 31 HERCULE POIROT
33 MISS BOWERS	32 COLONEL RACE

PLAN   CABINS

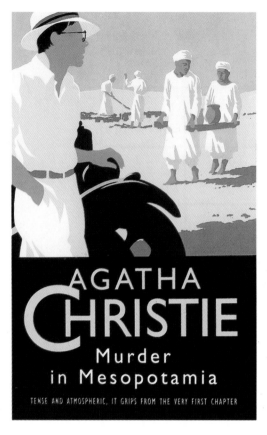

Above Paperback edition of *Murder in Mesopotamia*, HarperCollins Publishers 1994

Above right *The Mysterious Affair at Styles*, Triad/Grafton Books 1986

by such clues as stray threads or small pieces of paper. No other crime writer offers jigsaw puzzles with so many parts. Even the scene of the crime is complex; it is usually not just a room in which the crime has been committed, but a whole property. In *Murder in Mesopotamia*, for instance, the house where the participants in an archaeological excavation are living and where the wife of the leader of the expedition is murdered has over twenty rooms, all recorded on a plan and described, along with much of their contents, in the course of the novel. There are always dozens of objects and incidents obviously requiring explanation, and in order to solve the crime it is usually necessary to carry out a meticulous reconstruction of what every member of cast was doing throughout the day of the murder, often with the aid of lists and tables.

The question of the murderer's identity is similarly complex. Not only are all the characters potential suspects, but almost every one of the major protagonists is hypothetically identified as the murderer by someone else, at least once in the course of the novel. The game of social exposure is pursued equally comprehensively: all the characters must reveal their personal secrets at some point in the story.

The multiplicity of levels on which the story is told, with the many different pieces of the puzzle, make the text as a whole into a tangle of extraordinary density. Several chapters are usually required to set out the solution alone, since it answers dozens of separate questions that were asked earlier. And as the great majority of the answers relate not just to a single question but to a sequence of earlier problems, almost the whole of the long part of the book covering the investigation of the crime consists of passages relevant to its solution. Objects or situations which will play some part in the final revelation are brought up in every sentence. There is no padding, nothing that does not have its function in the narrative. The reader, although always given 'genuine' clues and hints pointing to the solution, has not the faintest chance of guessing it in advance, either in whole or in part, for Agatha Christie is a mistress of the art of misleading contextualization. Clues that will later play a part in the solution are set in context in such a way that they are striking and memorable, but the reader cannot make the correct associations.

Amy Leatheran, the narrator of *Murder in Mesopotamia*, sees the director of the expedition busy with some of the finds from the dig on the flat roof of the team's quarters: 'Dr Leidner was bending over looking at a lot of stones and broken pottery that were laid in rows. There were big things he called querns, and pestles and celts and stone axes, and more broken bits of pottery with queer patterns on them than I've ever seen all at once.'[3] Out of this medley of items, narrator and reader alike are struck by the mention of querns because of their unusual name. However, we do not guess that one of these heavy stones may become a murder weapon, as it later does. Next moment the narrator turns to the contemplation of a beautiful sunset, thus distracting the reader's attention too.

The excavations have brought to light valuable golden objects, including an early Akkadian drinking-cup. When Mrs Leidner shows it to the narrator she discovers a spot of wax: 'How extraordinary! There's actually wax on it. Someone must have been here with a candle.'[4] In fact the spot of wax is a clue to a crime. Thieves have taken wax impressions of the treasures, made copies from them and exchanged these copies for the originals. Once again the reader's attention is drawn to the clue and subsequently diverted from it, first by Mrs Leidner's superficially reasonable explanation, then by the narrator's switch of interest to some 'little terracotta figurines', most of which, she comments, were 'just rude'. Christie's clues are not only ambivalent in themselves, but are constructed so that whole groups of the pieces of the puzzle can be put

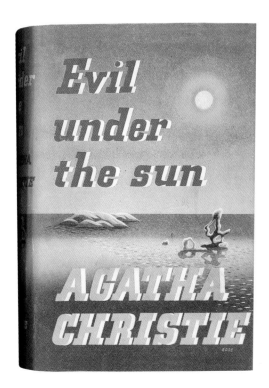

Left Agatha Christie in her house at Wallingford, 1950

Above left First edition of *At Bertram's Hotel*, The Crime Club, Collins 1965

Above right First edition of *Evil under the Sun*, The Crime Club, Collins 1941

together in different ways, for instance forming plausible hypothetical solutions which none the less turn out to be wrong.

The detective is the trademark and central character of a Christie novel, but his functions are not as important as they may at first seem. He does not usually appear until after the murder has been committed, and is thus the last of the major characters to be introduced. He is extremely active in the long central part of the story, but the reader is not yet allowed to guess what he is making of events. He is seen only from the outside.

In her early novels Agatha Christie gives her detective, who at this time was always Poirot, the function of master of ceremonies and solo entertainer in the central phase of the investigations, which is otherwise lacking in events. In her later stories Poirot is depicted as less omnipresent and flamboyant. Miss Marple was designed from the first to be a reserved and unobtrusive character. Only in the closing part of the novel does the detective's finest hour come, when he or she sets out the solution, providing complete answers to all the

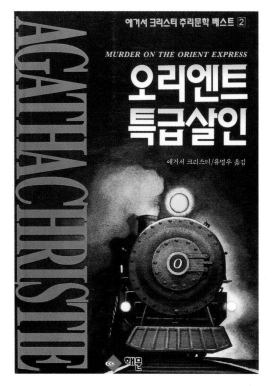

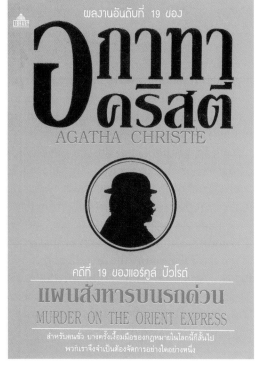

questions asked in the opening and central sections: how the crime was committed, who committed it, how the detective tracked the murderer down, what are the other secrets which had nothing to do with the crime.

Agatha Christie's detective stories are variations on a theme: a basic structure is repeated over and over again in different forms. Readers who know the theme will expect it to recur and enjoy the pleasure of recognition. They will also, however, expect something new, a deviation from familiar elements and the satisfaction of surprise. It is characteristic of Christie's variations that all the details encountered by the reader on the surface of her narrative discourse, for instance names, dialogue, personal descriptions or details of the scene of the crime, can be changed, while underlying structures such as the composition of the cast of characters, the construction of the puzzle and its solution remain practically invariable.

The main area of Christie's variations is in the background of the story, first and foremost the place where the characters are living or staying at the time of the crime. Although the country houses of the gentry are regarded as the standard setting of a Christie detective story, she did not rely entirely on them. The novels may be set in any place where the characters of the social circle concerned are together in a group. Agatha Christie plays with two versions in which they are away from home, meeting each other either in a hotel or as travelling companions. These variations have similar advantages. The community in the novel can still be socially exclusive, but at the same time it is open to access by intruders and exceptional cases of all kinds. In the criminological sense it is a self-contained society, and the places available to it – hotel rooms, lobbies, cabins, train compartments – are suitable as the scene of a crime of the 'locked room' variety. For most readers the luxury hotel and the exotic foreign journey – like life in a country house – are particularly attractive: far enough from the reality of their own lives to be interesting, but easily imagined and associated with their personal experiences.

Hotels as the setting for a crime in Christie's novels range from the old-fashioned seaside resort grand hotel, with its 'dance hosts', millionaires and people in the film industry (*The Body in the Library*, 1942), to a luxury hotel on a holiday island (*Evil under the Sun*, 1941) and a family hotel with guests permanently living in (*At Bertram's Hotel*, 1965). When her characters meet as travelling companions they are generally abroad and using various means of transport: long-distance trains (*The Mystery of the Blue Train*, 1928; *Murder on the Orient Express*, 1934); local trains (*4.50 from Paddington*, 1957); an aeroplane

Various translations of *Murder on the Orient Express*: Japanese (above left), Arabic (above right), Korean (below left) and Thai (below right)

(*Death in the Clouds*, 1935); a river steamer (*Death on the Nile*, 1937); a large cruise ship (*A Caribbean Mystery*, 1964); even an ordinary coach (*Nemesis*, 1971).

The novels set in the Near East, in particular *Death on the Nile*, *Murder in Mesopotamia* and *Appointment with Death*, fit smoothly into Agatha Christie's sets of variations. They are special cases in so far as the author worked her own experience of oriental travels and archaeological digs into the story. As detective fiction, however, they are of the same kind and constructed in the same way as the books set in England. The guessing game takes pre-eminence, as usual, over all other elements in the story. No topographical, ethnographic or archaeological descriptions are included for their own sake. Agatha Christie's Orient is presented as part of a jigsaw puzzle. Her characteristic qualities, and indeed her strength, lie in this uncompromising commitment to the crime novel as a detective story pure and simple.

NOTES

1   A. Christie, *Appointment with Death*, London 1993, p. 213.
2   A. Christie, *Death on the Nile*, London 1981, p. 90.
3   A. Christie, *Murder in Mesopotamia*, London 1978, p. 30.
4   Ibid., p. 40.

BIBLIOGRAPHY

R. Barnard, *A Talent to Deceive: An Appreciation of Agatha Christie*, London 1980
H.R.F Keating (ed.), *Agatha Christie: First Lady of Crime*, London 1977
U. Suerbaum, *Krimi. Eine Analyse der Gattung*, Stuttgart 1984

The Archaeology of Murder

Volker Neuhaus

'Between them lay the archaeology of murder. Detail photographs of the victims, full and side views. General views of the scenes of the crimes, interiors, exteriors, closeups, from various angles. Cross-sketchings, neatly compass-directed and drawn to specific scale. The file of appurtenant fingerprints. A whole library of reports, records, assignments, details of work complete with notations of time, place, names, addresses, findings, questions and answers and statements and technical information. And, on a separate table, *res gestae* evidence, the originals.'[1]

Ernst Bloch, the Marxist philosopher and a passionate devotee of all that his contemporaries and intellectual equals dismissed as lightweight literature or culture, was one of the first to define the distinctive formal features and narrative techniques of detective fiction, stressing the scope of its manifestations in the title of his essay: 'Die Form der Detektivgeschichte und die Philosophie' (The Form of the Detective Story and Philosophy).[2] It is interesting that the term chosen for the German title of this essay by Bloch, who had lived in the USA from 1939 to 1949, obviously derives from the neutral English 'detective story'; implicitly, he is distancing himself from the German habit of describing all works 'which present cases of murder and other crimes in an exciting and entertaining manner'[3] by the rather woolly and all-embracing term of *Kriminalroman* (crime novel), *Krimi* for short. Bloch is anticipating the clear distinction proposed in 1968 by Richard Alewyn, although it has not, unfortunately, been adopted in German-speaking countries: 'The crime novel [*Kriminalroman*] tells the story of a crime, the detective novel [*Detektivroman*] tells the story of the solution of a crime.'[4] Bloch is interested only in the latter, the explanation of a mystery, the solving of a puzzle; in short, his interest is in the 'form of the detective story', as it was exhaustively described by Dietrich Weber in his *Theorie der analytischen Erzählung* (Theory of analytical narrative).[5]

Ernst Bloch derives his description and definition of the form, together with its philosophical implications, from a paraphrase of the word 'detective', first coined in the nineteenth century and used both as a noun and an adjective. Fundamentally, his essay is a set of interpretations of the metaphorical connotations of the term, and he never explicitly offers its etymological derivation, from *detegere* (Latin: 'uncover'). Instead, he writes of the

uncovering of a crime, with the detective in the foreground ... clues of every kind, tracks on the ground ... The old curiosity urging us to lift the lid from our neighbour's pot, take the roof off the house next door as far as possible and cast an inquisitive glance inside, still persists ... the element of exposure and uncovering ... with particular emphasis on the esoteric ... the element of discovery derives from processes which are brought out only from what we are not told about them, from what has gone on before the narrative begins ... the theme consists entirely in bringing out that solution. The dark deeds that preceded the crime are not described either, partly because they can be identified only by digging deep, finding clues that allow reconstruction.

Below Cover of the exhibition catalogue, *Freud as Collector*, Japan 1996

Below right Cover of C.W. Ceram, *Götter, Gräber und Gelehrte*, Rowohlt Verlag 1972

収集家としてのフロイト
FREUD AS COLLECTOR

C·W·CERAM
Götter
Gräber und
Gelehrte
Roman der Archæologie

Bloch's terminology includes mention of 'excavating with a view to reconstruction', 'making enquiries, uncovering facts', 'finding what happened in the past'.[6] It is very clear that archaeology, as the science of 'finding, digging deep, uncovering', provided Bloch with his metaphors, even if he does not explicitly dwell on this comparison any more than he does on the etymology of the word 'detective'. Instead, he mentions other branches of science that share with the detective story the exposing, uncovering, excavating and reconstructing of past events and the interpretation of traces as clues – Freud's psychoanalysis, Marx's political theory in which the economy becomes the mainspring of history, and the Romantic philosophical speculations of those 'nocturnal archaeologists Baader and Schelling'[7], 'the suspicion of some dark secret *ante rem, ante lucem, ante historiam,* of a *casus ante mundum*'.[8]

In common to all these, in Bloch's analysis, is the fact that they run backwards against the flow of time, exploring factors hitherto 'untold and in the nature of prehistory', the 'excavation' of 'tracks on the ground', which become 'signs' and 'clues'. If these factors are methodically studied and interpreted it is possible to 'reconstruct' something buried, 'find' something that once existed in the past, whether a childhood trauma as in Freud, 'the true and secret history of Rome, the history of landed property' in Marx,[9] the discovery of Troy under the mound of Hissarlik, or the reconstruction of a series of murders in Paris and the exposure of the perpetrator by E.T.A. Hoffmann's elderly Mademoiselle de Scudéry. Sigmund Freud, aware that he himself was conducting, so to speak, intangible archaeological excavations, deliberately collected Greek and Roman archaeological finds as ornaments for his consulting room.

The parallels can be taken still further: scientific archaeology, aiming to be more than the eighteenth-century classicist Winckelmann's science of *antiquitas figurata* (focusing on the classic masterpieces of sculpture, architecture and painting), has abandoned the practice of mere treasure-hunting and turned to the systematic excavation of whole cultures just at the moment when the last blank areas on the map have been explored, and new discoveries of foreign ethnic groups are no longer possible in the three dimensions of space, only in the fourth dimension of time. Similarly, the detective story began to flourish as a leading genre of light literature just when even the most distant continents lost their mystery and allure as the setting for exotic adventures. The detective story needs no exoticism but makes ordinary life seem strange, and the more ordinary that life is the stranger it can seem. As G.K. Chesterton, himself a practitioner of the genre, once said, the detective story is the only fairy-tale to have come out of the modern city.

The parallels between the archaeological journey through time, studying a period of millennia, and the detective story which covers at most a single

A FRIGHTFUL LITTLE SKELETON OF A WOMAN HUNG IN A CUPBOARD.
—The Law and the Lady, Vol. Five, page 332.

generation, those parallels which have left their mark on Bloch's essay, are in fact so obvious that they have become almost commonplaces. Just as Ellery Queen in the passage taken as epigraph for the present article speaks quite naturally of the 'archaeology of murder', meaning the potential of clues in the form, for instance, of material traces left at the scene of the crime, C.W. Ceram's book *Götter, Gräber und Gelehrte* (Gods, Tombs and Scholars) holds that: 'Archaeologists are seeking trails. With the acumen of a detective, one might say, they place one stone on another (often literally) until the logically compelling conclusion becomes obvious.'[10] The proximity of the detective story to the related disciplines of 'archaeology, ethnology, prehistory', as they were enumerated in one detective story,[11] and as the doctor Rudolf Virchow represented them in their full breadth in the early days of those sciences, is methodical as well as metaphorical. In the very first detective story in literary history, written by the French author Emile Gaboriau in 1863 when he combined the figure of Poe's detective Auguste Dupin with the specific subjects and forms of the French *roman feuilleton*, the central character Tabaret is identified from the start as a private detective: 'Given a single clue from which to work, he claims to be able to reconstruct the course of events in a murder, like the scholar who can revive an extinct creature by studying a single bone.'[12] Here the detective is compared to a palaeontologist; a little later, in the work of Wilkie Collins, friend of Dickens and perhaps the major pioneer of what would later become the detective story, archaeology is the model for criminal investigation. Collins includes a compromising letter in his *The Law and the Lady*, just as Poe did in *The Purloined Letter*. None of the investigations get any- .where, however, until someone recollects that the systematic excavations in Pompeii went so far as to study the city's cesspools. The characters of the story then search through piles of domestic refuse, following archaeological procedure even to the extent of finally dispensing with tools and working only with their hands, as if carrying out a delicate process of excavation.

Sir Arthur Conan Doyle also paid tribute to archaeology and palaeontology. In his longest Sherlock Holmes novel, *The Hound of the Baskervilles*, and in the opinion of most Holmes devotees also his best, Dr Mortimer (a medical colleague of the author, since Conan Doyle was a qualified doctor too) not only possesses an anthropological collection of his own – for which he would dearly like to have the skull of Holmes himself, as he has no hesitation in telling its owner – but also successfully carries out excavations of the New Stone Age settlement at Baskerville Hall. Holmes takes up residence in the best preserved of the Neolithic stone buildings to pursue his detective enquiries on the spot incognito. Dr Mortimer also sets the process of detection on foot in the first

Page from Wilkie Collins, *The Law and the Lady*, Fenelon Collier 1875

place, which suggests that Conan Doyle may have been intentionally linking the fields of detection and archaeology. The author himself came under posthumous suspicion of responsibility for a palaeontological hoax: the English answer to the 1907 discovery of *Homo heidelbergensis* was the find in 1912 of a skull apparently older than Heidelberg Man in a gravel pit at Piltdown, very close to Conan Doyle's home. With its humanoid brow and ape-like jaw, it was thought to represent the famous 'missing link', and was not proved to be a relatively crude fake until 1953. In the September 1983 issue of the American scholarly journal *Science*, J.H. Winslow proposed the theory that Conan Doyle had perpetrated the fraud as an act of revenge on the allegedly exact science of his time, one of the grounds adduced by Winslow being that a few months before the discovery of Piltdown Man Conan Doyle had discussed the possibility of faking fossils in his novel *The Lost World*.

With such close connections between archaeology and the detective story evident from the early days of that genre, and with the methodical approach shared by both disciplines, it is rather surprising 'that there are not more stories' in which 'archaeological matters crop up', as the introduction to the only bibliographical study known to me puts it.[13] But the reason is probably obvious: it takes detailed specialist knowledge to write a convincing detective story in which the riddles of prehistory can be successfully combined with those of the recent past. In the case of a scientific discipline the usual research into a particular background that is the mark of any good detective story is not really enough. Two novels by John Trench, a professional army officer and later an advertising copywriter, illustrate the point. Their detective hero is an archaeologist called Martin Cotterell, a pleasant, amusing, educated and well-read young man, who solves his very difficult cases astutely and ingeniously. However, archaeology takes a back seat for most of the time. Its function is first to suggest that as curator of a provincial museum Cotterell pursues no regular activity of his own, and so has plenty of leisure time for his detective work, and second to bring him into contact with his cases. In *Docken Dead* (1953) he has to give an expert opinion on a private collection of antiquities potentially on offer as a donation to his museum; in *Dishonoured Bones* (1954) he is involved in the excavations of a prehistoric grave mound which soon come to an end when a new corpse is found instead of any ancient skeletons, and this and another murder call for all Cotterell's attention thenceforth – which is fortunate for him as an archaeologist, since on the last page of the book he discovers, quite by chance, that the tumulus owes its unique structure to work carried out on it in the nineteenth century.

Some rather more successful links between archaeological and criminal detection are the outcome of an impressive and very British phenomenon in the history of the genre: during the 'Golden Age' of the detective story in the

1930s and 1940s it was obviously a point of honour for an Oxbridge don to write both witty limericks and at least one detective story, naturally enough usually set in an Oxford or Cambridge college. This was the genesis of the 'donnish mystery' genre. An early example is *Gaudy Night* (1935) by Dorothy L. Sayers, born in Oxford and herself an Oxford graduate. Archaeology, archaeologists and a prehistoric skeleton play an important part in another such story, *Death at the President's Lodging*, the first novel by Michael Innes, pseudonym of the Oxford literary critic J.I.M. Stewart. Two famous archaeologists were soon to join the game: Stanley Casson (1889–1944), a fellow of New College, Oxford, and among other things a specialist in Byzantine archaeology, published his archaeological detective story *Murder by Burial* in 1938. There is a certain piquancy in the fact that Casson had been Max Mallowan's tutor at New College, and it was to his warm recommendation that Mallowan owed his first post as assistant to Leonard Woolley on the excavations at Ur, where he met his future wife Agatha Christie.

Cambridge soon followed the lead of its traditional rival – the Cambridge archaeologist Glyn Daniel, fellow of St John's, published his story

Sherlock Holmes and Dr Watson in the film of *The Hound of the Baskervilles*

The Cambridge Murders under the pseudonym of Dilwyn Rees in 1945. In this book and a second novel, *Welcome Death* (1954), his detective is the archaeologist Sir Richard Cherrington, Vice-President of the fictional Fisher College. Archaeology features in his detection only in serving as a methodological model, very much in the spirit of Ernst Bloch. He is motivated by a desire not so much for justice as to discover the truth – his scholarly ethos, so to speak – as indeed is usually the case with scholars portrayed as amateur detectives. The riddle of the murder fascinates him more than the problems in his professional field on which he is working at the time. He regards the police carrying out their parallel – and very successful – enquiries as if they were a rival team of archaeologists whom his superior method will defeat. A clue at the scene of the crime is like a find on a dig – did it originally belong to the level where it was found, or did it somehow get there earlier or later? His well-trained visual memory and his ability to draw deductions about entire cultures – or in this case backgrounds – from the evidence left behind help him in his investigations.

Far left German translation of Sir Arthur Conan Doyle, *The Hound of the Baskervilles*, Scherz Verlag 1996

Left Paperback edition of a German translation of *Murder in Mesopotamia*, Scherz Verlag, first edition, 1954

Right Gisbert Haefs, *Hamilkars Garten*, Heyne Verlag 1999

But ultimately it is Agatha Christie who can claim to have achieved the best marriage between archaeology and detection, although in the title most relevant to this subject, *Murder in Mesopotamia*, it is interesting to note the indirect restraint with which she brings out the formal parallels found so compelling by Bloch. Poirot points to those parallels only once, surprisingly cautiously and as if in passing, when a female skeleton is uncovered on the dig:

> 'Who was she?' asked Poirot.
> 'First millennium. A lady of some consequence perhaps. Skull looks rather odd – I must get Mercado to look at it. It suggests death by foul play.'
> 'A Mrs Leidner of two thousand odd years ago?' said Poirot.
> 'Perhaps,' said Mr Emmott.[14]

Directly afterwards, Poirot repeats his question in relation to 'his' case, the modern corpse: 'I want to know about Mrs Leidner ... I mean her – herself.'[15]

Agatha Christie provides a reason for this unusual restraint on Poirot's part when she is looking back on her own and her husband's work at the end of her autobiography: 'It seems a kind of miracle that both he and I should have succeeded in the work we wanted to do. Nothing could be further apart than our work. I am a lowbrow and he a highbrow ...'[16] It would obviously have seemed to her presumptuous for Poirot to compare himself with an archaeologist. She leaves it to the archaeologist in her story to point out the parallel at the end: 'You would have made a good archaeologist, M. Poirot. You have the gift of re-creating the past.'[17]

Finally, to cite a modern German example of the genre: Gisbert Haefs began his Carthage trilogy in 1984 with an archaeological crime story. In *Das Doppelgrab in der Provence* (The Double Grave in Provence) his detective Balthasar Matzbach succeeds in deciphering the Latin will of a Carthaginian merchant, complete with a plan indicating the whereabouts of his treasure, documents that have come by chance into the hands of a French archaeologist. However, the sites in question have all been destroyed long since by the buildings of 'civilization', except for one, and the tubular pottery vessel in which the Carthaginian placed his writings over 2,000 years ago has sprung a leak and the priceless literary documents have been destroyed: 'There could be a fortune in ancient coins lying in the ground, just waiting for someone eager and willing to dig it up – but the Carthaginian's papyri had not survived storage in the damp earth.'[18]

Haefs became fascinated by his archaeological interest in the trade empire of Carthage; his historical novel *Hannibal. Der Roman Karthago* (Hannibal: The Novel of Carthage) appeared in 1989. Much as Agatha Christie used the antiquarian studies she had pursued at her second husband's side in *Death Comes as the End*, a detective story set in ancient Egypt, Haefs concluded his studies of the Carthaginian period in 1999 with a historical and archaeological detective story, *Hamilkars Garten* (Hamilcar's Garden') – set, of course, in ancient Carthage.[19]

NOTES

1   E. Queen, *Cat of Many Tails*, Boston 1949, p. 36.

2   *Neue Rundschau*, vol. 71, 1960, pp. 665–83, quoted here from the later reprint with the title of E. Bloch, 'Philosophische Ansicht des Detektivromans', in V. Zmegac (ed.), *Der wohltemporierte Mord*, Frankfurt am Main 1971, pp. 111–31.

3   U. Suerbaum, *Krimi. Eine Analyse der Gattung*, Stuttgart 1984, p. 14.

4   'Anatomie des Detektivromans', in R. Alewyn, *Probleme und Gestalten*, Frankfurt am Main, p. 364. For an extensive discussion of terminology, see V. Neuhaus, 'Mysterion tes anomias – Das Geheimnis des Bösen. Der Detektivroman als regelgeleitete Gattung', in D. Schier

and M. Giersch (eds), *CID - Computergestützte Interpretation von Detektivromanen*, Frankfurt am Main 1995, pp. 11–45, 11–18.

5   D. Weber, *Theorie der analytischen Erzählung*, Munich 1975.

6   Bloch, *Ansicht* (n. 2), pp. 112, 113, 115, 116, 123, 129.

7   Ibid., p. 127.

8   Ibid., p. 125.

9   Ibid., p. 122.

10   C.W. Ceram, *Götter, Gräber und Gelehrte*, Hamburg 1949, p. 38.

11   D. Rees, *The Cambridge Murders*, London 1952, p. 39.

12   E. Gaboriau, *L'affaire Lerouge*, Paris 1961, p. 27.

13   P.L. Scowcroft, 'Digging up Murder: Archaeology in British Detective Fiction', in *CADS – Crime and Detective Stories* no. 7, December 1987.

14   A. Christie, *Murder in Mesopotamia*, London 1994, pp.149–50.

15   Ibid., p. 150.

16   A. Christie, *An Autobiography*, London 1981, p. 541.

17   Christie, *Mesopotamia* (n. 14), p. 215.

18   G. Haefs, *Das Doppelgrab in der Provence*, 2nd edn, Zurich 1988, p. 196.

19   G. Haefs, *Hamilkars Garten*, Munich 1999.

Albert Finney as Hercule Poirot in the film *Murder on the Orient Express* (photo: Lord Snowdon)

Films

The West Films the East: Agatha Christie, the Cinema and Archaeology

Tom Stern

A gatha Christie takes archaeology and the Orient as the subjects of many of her detective stories. The first part of this essay is a critical study of these themes as they appear transferred to the screen. But Agatha Christie also made films in the Orient herself, and the second part of the chapter is an attempt to place her work in the general context of films dealing with the archaeology of the Near East and Egypt.

Archaeology and the Orient in film versions of books by Agatha Christie
To begin with a superlative: if the books of Agatha Christie have gone into more editions than the Bible, then the films made from them have probably drawn larger cinema audiences than any of the biblical movies. A monograph devoted entirely to this subject lists 116 films over 65 years.[1] Chronologically, this survey brings to light two oddities: surprisingly enough, the very first film ever made of one of her novels, *Die Abenteuer-GmbH* (1928),[2] based on *The Secret Adversary*, was a German production, and over 80 per cent of the film versions were made after her death in 1976. It is clear that on the whole Agatha Christie kept her distance from any filming of her books.

To date, in fact, only four of her archaeological or oriental detective stories have been made into films: *Murder on the Orient Express, Death on the Nile, Appointment with Death*, and *The Adventure of the Egyptian Tomb*, all for cinema except the last, which was a TV production.

Murder on the Orient Express
UK 1974; directed by Sidney Lumet, starring Albert Finney (as Hercule Poirot), Lauren Bacall, Martin Balsam, Ingrid Bergman, Jacqueline Bisset, Jean Pierre Cassel, Sean Connery, John Gielgud, Anthony Perkins, Vanessa Redgrave, Richard Widmark

Wendy Hiller and Rachel Roberts on the set of the film *Murder on the Orient Express*
(photo: Lord Snowdon)

Sean Connery on the set of the film *Murder on the Orient Express* (photo: Lord Snowdon)

Perhaps the best-known film version of a Christie book, this movie was the first to pick up the theme of the Orient as it features in her work. Agatha Christie became a seasoned traveller in the East, and the novel was inspired by her observations and experiences on the Orient Express,[3] that legendary and luxurious means of travel, as well as by the well-known Lindbergh kidnapping of the time.

The book begins in Aleppo, but the opening scenes of the film are set in Istanbul. Sidney Lumet shot them on the Bosphorus, on a ferry between the two parts of the city, Haidar Pasha and Karaköy. Oriental colour was provided by fez-wearing extras and sheep, and a muezzin can be heard in the background. The audience's expectations of the Orient, however, are met only when the domes and minarets of the Sultan Ahmed Mosque and Hagia Sophia come into sight; this is a view of the city familiar from travel brochures.

The station scenes – the Orient Express starts from Sirkeci – were shot in Paris. The factory railway station at Landy, which was converted for the purpose, with its colour-enhanced façade, rosette windows and a portrait of Atatürk really does convey the impression of the station in Istanbul itself. The 'orientals' on the station, however, are mere exotic clichés – they must have escaped notice when the costume designer Tony Walton was nominated for an Oscar. Along with the costumes, busy scenes featuring goats, shoeshine boys and carpet vendors are intended to pile on the atmosphere: poverty as a romantic oriental setting. However, the production is faithful to other details:

The actors in *Murder on the Orient Express* during a break in filming (photo: Lord Snowdon)

excavations at Chagar Bazar,[15] but neither she nor Mallowan recorded any-thing in particular about it at the time: 'I wrote detective stories, Max wrote archaeological books, reports and articles.'[16]

The film version of *Appointment with Death* was not as successful as its two predecessors. When it was shown in Germany on 2 November 1989 it did not find favour with the critics. In spite of its many stars, they said, the film showed only 'faces photographed to death, with every feature desperately clinging to its image'.[17] The American press was even more outspoken: 'Another loser from Winner' (Michael Winner, the director).[18] There were no nominations for Oscars or any other film awards. Interestingly, Anthony Schaf-fer was again responsible for the screenplay, and he seems to have wanted to make amends in this film for his omission of the character of the archaeologist in *Death on the Nile* by creating the character of Miss Quinton, an archaeologist on her way to a dig by the Dead Sea. Consequently the scene of the crime – and the rest of the action – became not Petra but the excavations at Qumran. One can only speculate on the reasons for this deviation from the original novel:

- The author of the screenplay, by now well acquainted with Agatha Christie's biography, may have wanted to inform a wider public about her archaeological interests. But then why such lines as the remark by the archaeologist that she likes digging in the dirt, to which the lawyer replies that so does he?
- Qumran, the site where the Dead Sea Scrolls were found, was part of popular general knowledge and might pull in cinema audiences. But then why is the film set in the 1930s, when no finds had yet been made on the site?
- Then again, the reason could have been that archaeologists were the new heroes of the 1980s. Indiana Jones was proving a formidable rival to James Bond, and the inclusion of an archaeologist as a character might seem to promise excitement and action. But then why does the archaeologist Miss Quinton turn out to be no more than a credulously naïve character witness for Lady Westholme?

The Adventure of the Egyptian Tomb
UK 1993; produced by London Weekend Television, directed by Peter Barber-Fleming, starring David Suchet (as Hercule Poirot), Hugh Fraser, Pauline Moran, Rolf Saxon
The most 'archaeological' film version of an Agatha Christie story is Poirot's 'Adventure of the Egyptian Tomb'. Christie had written this story at the time

Angela Lansbury in the film *Death on the Nile* (photo: Lord Snowdon)

of the discovery of Tutankhamun's tomb and the deaths apparently connected
with it in 1923. She cited both Tutankhamun and Lord Carnarvon to provide
verisimilitude[19] – she was not to meet Howard Carter, the archaeologist who
really uncovered the tomb, until 1931 or perhaps 1933.[20]

The fifty-six-minute film, shown as a three-part serial on British television, begins with older footage from Egypt (showing pyramids and camels,
excavations and hieroglyphics), with edited black and white clips of the protagonists, the archaeologists of the Metropolitan Museum, New York, and the
British Museum, London, leading into the rest of the action. Meanwhile a narrator introduces the excavators in the style of a newsreel. Only when the seal
on the entrance to the tomb is broken does the main action of the film begin,
in colour.

The story is set in the Valley of the Kings, in London and in New York.
The 'Egyptian' scenes were shot in Spain. They required a desert valley with
palm trees; oriental clothing, vintage cars and cuts to shots of Egyptological
items create the illusion of a dig in Egypt itself. The archaeological camp, with
tents under palm trees, is depicted as very busy during the day, and a romantic
place with camp fires burning by night, although there are also electric light
bulbs at the entrances of the tents. The entrance to the actual site of the excavations, the tomb of Men-her-Ras, is underground, and is guarded by a soldier.

The clothes worn by the archaeologists in the film are not particularly
suitable for the demands of their work, but they do mirror the style of the
1920s, and indeed reflect the colonial conditions of the time. The archaeologists, for instance, sit in the communal tent in suits and white shirts, ties or
bow-ties, drinking from wine or cocktail glasses. A glance at Max Mallowan in
Agatha Christie's own film of Tell Brak, or at the list of the household utensils
brought out to the excavations at Arpachiyah,[21] suggests that this television
production conveys a very realistic idea of a dig in the 1920s. The workmen,
however, wear vaguely picturesque garments, and their head-dresses, wound
into turbans, suggest India rather than Egypt.

The film shows the burial chamber as the place where the archaeological work is being done as the contents of the tomb are carried out and the sar-
cophagus is opened. There is a wooden storeroom for the finds, the most solid
building in the camp, with shelves of Egyptological antiquities and a table for
work in progress. The only place where any actual excavations are going on is
a pit about 6 square metres in size with a cord across it, next to the entrance to
the tomb. Three workmen are shovelling soil out of it. These scenes certainly
suggest a dig to the audience, providing archaeological and technical colour.
However, the large number of workmen, supposed to illustrate the busy activity of an archaeological camp as they hurry back and forth, is rather excessive
in view of the extent of the excavations.

'Death on the Nile

In the bar.

Salomé Otterbourne

Miss Angela Lansbury.

Tarnished gold
tassels round.
bottom of jacket
perhaps?

AP.

Costume design by Anthony Powell for Angela Lansbury in the film *Death on the Nile* (Anthony Powell, London)

Costume design by Anthony Powell for Angela Lansbury in the film *Death on the Nile*
(Anthony Powell, London)

In preparation for his task in Egypt Poirot is shown visiting an exhibition; these scenes were probably shot in the British Museum. The silent conversation between the detective and Anubis, with the camera cutting between them, closes the first of the TV serial's three parts. It is a principle used to increase tension more than once, for instance in connection with the murder victims, and acts as a kind of quotation from feature films with a similar archaeological content but where the emphasis is on horror.[22] A further quotation has David Suchet paying tribute to his predecessor as Poirot, Peter Ustinov, by carrying a fly whisk.

Another point worth mentioning is the competition between the Metropolitan Museum and the British Museum – a new subject added for the film. But study of the division of the finds between the two museums, which

The costume designer Anthony Powell on the set of the film *Death on the Nile* (photo: Lord Snowdon)

Peter Ustinov, David Niven and Angela Lansbury, still from the film *Death on the Nile*
(photo: Lord Snowdon)

financed the expedition, suggests that this theme too may mirror actual conditions at the time. The filmed version of Agatha Christie's story certainly makes the excavations appear very realistic – apart, that is, from the corpses.

The production of this film by London Weekend Television is a pleasing example of British humour: neither archaeology nor criminology is taken very seriously. In the opening credits to each part – identifiable as advertising only at second glance[23] – the chalk outlines drawn at the scene of the murder turn out to be those of a washing machine, a refrigerator and a vacuum cleaner. The opening of the sealed tomb with a powerful blow from a hammer – whereupon the ancient seal shatters into hundreds of pieces – is a charming caricature of the work of archaeologists, who really go about their business with precision tools.

Finally, the end of the film, in which Poirot gives his secretary a statuette of Anubis from the burial chamber of Men-her-Ras, provides a critical comment on the way in which so many archaeological collections have begun – with tomb robbery.

Agatha Christie and the archaeology of the Near East on film
The 16-mm films made by Agatha Christie on Tell Brak and Nimrud (cf. the essay by Charlotte Trümpler, 'A dark-room has been allotted to me ...'), found

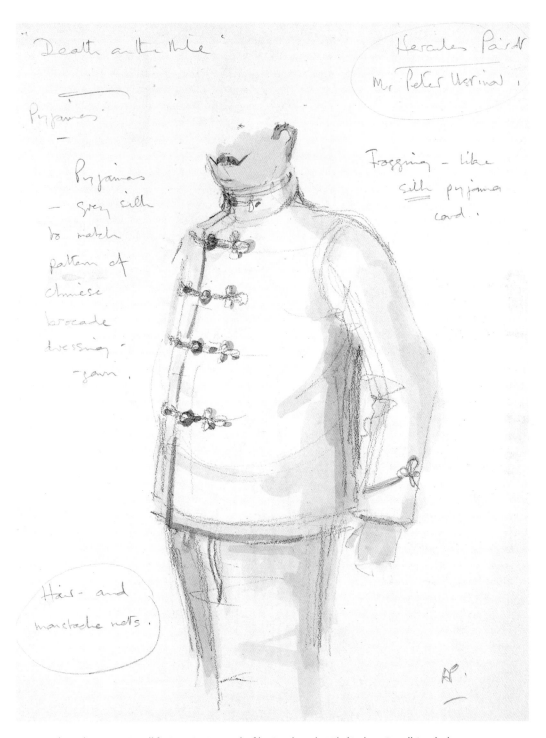

Costume design by Antony Powell for Peter Ustinov in the film *Death on the Nile* (Anthony Powell, London)

Death on the Nile.

NB – I have drawn the pyjama collar WRONG – I couldn't remember what it should look like !!!

Simon

Simon MacCorkindale

Cream silk pyjamas & dressing gown.

Add black silk scarf with cream spots.

Black silk satin piping – sash backed with black.

Costume design by Anthony Powell for Simon MacCorkindale in the film *Death on the Nile*
(Anthony Powell, London)

Costume design by Anthony Powell for Simon MacCorkindale in the film *Death on the Nile*
(Anthony Powell, London)

Costume design by Anthony Powell for Maggie Smith in the film *Death on the Nile*
(Anthony Powell, London)

Mia Farrow on the set of the film *Death on the Nile* (photo: Lord Snowdon)

after her death, are full of treasures for the historian of archaeological research. Both consist of a number of two-minute strips of film, and were shot with a Kodak camera (Magazine Cine Kodak, 237 FK, 1937).

The film of Tell Brak begins in black and white, then switches (remarkably for its time) to colour with subtitles, and more black and white material follows. Strictly speaking, it cannot be called a film, but consists of separate numbered rolls that have been edited in sequence for transfer to VHS video-tape.[24] Agatha Christie always filmed from a distance, never using a telephoto lens. She uses wide panning shots to get an overall survey, and is never tempted by detail or close-up shots. Her camera captures daily life as she saw it on the spot; her film depicts life on an archaeological dig in the Orient with loving subjectivity, but also with the distanced approach of a tourist. The Mallowans'

Above Agatha Christie on a Nile steamer, 1931 or 1933 (photo: Max Mallowan)

Above right A visit to Petra, 1930s (photo: Max Mallowan)

Right Agatha Christie at the altar in Petra, 1930s (photo: Max Mallowan)

workmen at Tell Brak who are still alive reacted to the scenes from their youth in the film by objecting that it did not show the dig as they remembered it (cf. Tom Stern's essay, 'Traces of Agatha Christie in Syria and Turkey').

The film of Nimrud is similar in structure and approach to Agatha Christie's record of Tell Brak; it too bears her individual signature. It does contain some black and white footage, but this time Agatha Christie was filming mainly in colour. Occasional subtitles give chronological references: 'The dig at Nimrud 1952' and 'Excavations at Nimrud and Balawat 1957'.

The historical importance of the films of Agatha Christie becomes clear only when one tries to sketch an outline of extant footage of archaeological material from the Near East and Egypt of the period: such films are rare or widely dispersed today, and some known to have existed must be considered lost. The following filmography makes no claim to be complete but is intended as a basic summary of the material for anyone interested in the subjects of film, archaeology and the Orient.

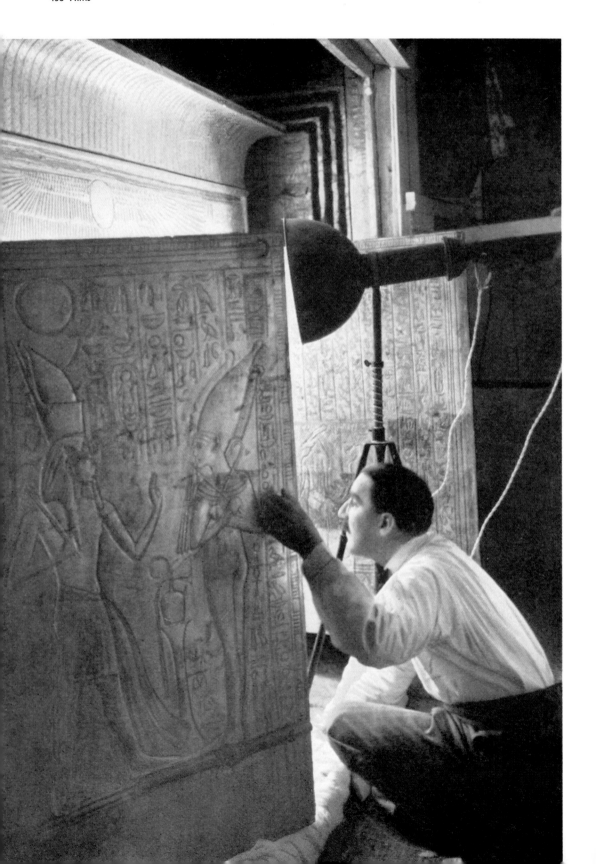

Above The sealed entrance to the tomb of Tutankhamun (Howard Carter and Arthur C. Mace, *The Tomb of Tut.ankh.Amen*, 3 vols, London 1923–33)

Previous double page Opening the doors of the innermost shrine in the tomb of Tutankhamun (Howard Carter and Arthur C. Mace, *The Tomb of Tut.ankh.Amen*, 3 vols, London 1923–33)

- *A Corner of Ancient Egypt* (1910), short film on the ruins of Luxor; British Film Institute (BFI), London
- *Babylon* (May 1912), cinematoscopic shots by Mr Dutkewich; Underwood & Underwood Agency, New York; now lost[25]
- *Ancient Temples of Egypt* (1912); George Eastman House, Rochester, New York
- *Ruins in Egypt* (1912); BFI, London
- *Monuments de l'ancienne Egypte* (1920); Cinémathèque Gaumont, Paris
- *En Syrie* (1920); Cinémathèque Gaumont, Paris
- *Egypt – Urban Movie Chats* (1921), excavation and exhibition at the Museum of Cairo; BFI, London
- *Digging into the Past* (1921–5), Valley of the Kings, Luxor, edited from the 12,000 metres of film in the archives; Metropolitan Museum, New York
- *Aerial View of the Pyramids* (4.1.1923); BFI, London
- *Tut-Ankh-Amen's Tomb* (22.2.1923), opening of the tomb; BFI, London
- *Carter and Carnarvon at Tutankhamen's Tomb* (9.4.1923); BFI, London

- *Review of the Year* (27.12.1923), scenes from the Tutankhamun excavations; BFI, London
- *Lord Allenby at the Official Opening of Tutankhamen's Tomb* (24.3.1924); BFI, London
- *Fouilles à Sahharah* (11.2.1925), excavations in Egypt; Pathé Télévision, Saint Ouen
- *En Egypte une mission américaine* (1925); Cinémathèque Gaumont, Paris
- *Ausgrabungen der alten Römerstadt Leptis Magna* (1925/27); Deulig-Wochenschau-Sujets, Bundesarchiv-Filmarchiv, Berlin
- *Les Colosses de Memnon* (1926); Pathé Télévision, Saint Ouen
- *Réparation du Sphinx de Gizeh* (1926); Cinémathèque Gaumont, Paris

Stills from the film *The Adventure of the Egyptian Tomb*: the opening of the tomb

- *Egypt* (1927), with amateur shots of archaeological sites; BFI, London
- *Les Tombeaux des Mamelouks* (1927); Pathé Télévision, Saint Ouen
- *Thèbes* (1928); Pathé Télévision, Saint Ouen
- *Die Wiege Europas* (1929); Bundesarchiv-Filmarchiv. Berlin
- *La Nécropole de Thèbes* (1930); Pathé Télévision, Saint Ouen
- *Home by Air* (1931), amateur aerial shots of archaeological sites; BFI, London
- *Egyptian Tour of an Upper Middle Class Rural Family* (1932–3), amateur shots of archaeological sites in Egypt and Jordan; BFI, London
- *Excavations at Troy* (1932), excavations carried out by Karl Blegen at Troy; Getzel Cohen, Cincinnati
- *Les Fouilles en Egypte* (1932); Pathé Télévision, Saint Ouen
- *Tell Brak* (1938); Agatha Christie
- *Petra* (1938); BFI, London
- *Fouilles en Egypte* (1940); Cinémathèque Gaumont, Paris
- *Fouilles au Pays des Pharaones* (1949); Cinémathèque Gaumont, Paris
- *Archéologie égyptienne, mission américaine* (1949); Cinémathèque Gaumont, Paris
- *The Excavations at Nimrud and Balawat* (1952/7); Agatha Christie

Still from the film *The Adventure of the Egyptian Tomb* (an advertisement for AEG)

- *Qataban and Sheba* (1949–55), excavations by Wendell Philips in the Yemen; American Foundation for the Study of Man, Merylin Philips Hodgson
- *La découverte de la Pyramide de Sakkarah* (1954); Cinémathèque Gaumont, Paris
- *Rivers of Time* (1957), archaeology on the Tigris and Euphrates; BFI, London
- *Congrès d'Archéologie des Pays Arabes* (1959); Cinémathèque Gaumont, Paris
- *La Sauvegarde des trésors de Nubie en Haute Egypte* (1959); Cinémathèque Gaumont, Paris
- *Pergamon* (1960s); Deutsches Archäologisches Institut, Berlin
- *Aus der Geschichte der Menschheit*, part 1: Iraq – Uruk-Warka (1965); FWU, Grünwald near Munich
- *Aus der Geschichte der Menschheit*, part 2: Turkey – Hattusa-Bogazköy

(1965); FWU, Grünwald near Munich
- *Aus der Geschichte der Menschheit*, part 3: Iran – Takht-I-Suleiman (1965);
  FWU, Grünwald near Munich

The geographical scope of these films ranges from Libya and Egypt by way of the Arabian peninsula to the Levant, and by way of Mesopotamia to the Aegean. The material listed above clearly shows where the centre of interest lay in shooting them: about two-thirds of them deal with the archaeology of Egypt. The reason for this polarity – and popularity – must certainly have been the discovery of the tomb of Tutankhamun and its coverage in the media (cf. Barbara Patzek's essay, 'The Detective and the Archaeologist'). Newsreel films (see above) will also have played their part, particularly on an international level. The related story of the 'curse of the Pharaohs' in the popular press inspired Agatha Christie herself, even though she did not have much interest in archaeology at the time, to write her story 'The Adventure of the Egyptian Tomb'.

Film material on the archaeology of the Near East, however, is sparse. The earliest extant film, *En Syrie* (1920), does not show archaeological work (as in *Troy*, 1932) but ruins in Syria, that is to say the remains of ancient cultures visible above ground. Agatha Christie's Tell Brak film is the first on record – the work of an amateur, but still unique – which not only shows archaeological work in progress, documenting the finds and the underground sites where they were uncovered, but also life on a dig, so that the conservation of finds is set, so to speak, in an ethnographical context. The same is true of her Nimrud and Balawat film of 1952/7; the film-maker's personal view is the same, and only the site and time of the excavations are different.

To end the filmography above at 1965 is a subjective decision, but reflects two factors. First, filmed material produced later, in view of the steadily increasing number of television viewers, is outside the scope of this essay. Second, the German film series *Aus der Geschichte der Menschheit* (From the History of Mankind) was the first to take archaeology in the Near East as the subject of educational films. The previous material can thus to some extent be said to represent the early history on film of modern archaeological clichés: the myths of exoticism and adventure.

NOTES

1   S. Palmer, *The Films of Agatha Christie*, London 1993.
2   From the first story about the detective couple Tommy Beresford and Tuppence Cowley: *The Secret Adversary* (1922); director Frederic Sauer, with Carlo Aldini, Eve Grey, Michael Rasummy, Hilda Bayley, Shayle Gardner.

3 J. Morgan, *Agatha Christie: A Biography*, London 1984, pp. 201–4.

4 M. Mallowan, *Mallowans's Memoirs*, London 1977, p. 214.

5 *Stamboul Train* (USA 1934), director Paul Martin, with Heather Angel, Norman Foster, Ralph Morgan.

The Lady Vanishes (UK 1938), director Alfred Hitchcock, with Margaret Lockwood, Michael Redgrave, Dame May Whitty, Paul Lukas.

Orientexpress (Germany 1944), director Victor Tourjansky, with Sigfried Breuer, Lisa Siebel, Paul Dahlke.

Orientexpress (Italy 1954), director Carlo Ludovico Bragaglia, with Eva Bartok, Curd Jürgens, Silvana Pampanini, Henry Vidal.

From Russia with Love (UK 1963), director Terence Young, with Sean Connery, Daniela Bianchi, Lotte Lenya.

Travels with my Aunt (1972), director George Cukor, with Maggie Smith, Alec McCowen, Louis Gossett.

6 J. des Cars, J.-P. Caracalla, *100 Jahre Orient-Express*, Paris 1984, p. 131.

7 Morgan, *Christie* (n. 3), pp. 212–13 (1933); Mallowan, *Memoirs* (n. 4), p. 310 (1931).

8 'Great blocks of pointless masonry, erected only to satisfy the egotism of vain and despotic kings.' From A. Christie, *Death on the Nile*, London 1993, p. 71.

9 *Lexikon des Internationalen Films*, Katholisches Institut für Medieninformation, Reinbek near Hamburg 1995, p. 5678.

10 Christie, *Nile* (n. 8), p. 66; all other quotations about Richetti, pp. 66, 71, 97, 152–3, 179, 234–5.

11 Mallowan, *Memoirs* (n. 4), p. 208.

12 Morgan, *Christie* (n. 3), p. 212.

13 See n. 9.

14 Parker Pyne had already solved a case here, 'The Pearl of Price', in A. Christie, *Parker Pyne Investigates*, London 1934, pp. 146–59.

15 Morgan, *Christie* (n. 3), p. 214.

16 A. Christie, *An Autobiography*, London 1981, p. 483.

17 M. Alten, *Süddeutsche Zeitung*, 28.11.1989.

18 Leonard Maltin Review, Microsoft Cinemania, 1997, p. 1.

19 A. Christie, *Poirot Investigates*, London 1992, p. 95.

20 Mallowan, *Memoirs* (n. 4), p. 221 (1931); Morgan, *Christie* (n. 3), p. 212.

21 The British Museum, Archive ANE 196.2, pp. 17–27.

22 Cf. *Die Augen der Mumie Ma* (Germany 1918), director Ernst Lubitsch; *Das Weib des Pharao* (Germany 1921), director Ernst Lubitsch; *The Mummy* (USA 1933), director Karl Freund; *The Mummy's Shroud* (UK 1966), director John Gilling; *Sphinx* (USA 1980), director Franklin S. Schaffner; *Dawn of the Mummy* (USA 1980), director Frank Agrama; *The Mummy Lives* (USA 1993), director Gerry O'Hara; and also *Al-Mumiyah* (Egypt 1970), director Shadi Abdel Salan.

23 'AEG: helping Poirot with his inquiries!'

24 According to Roger Lilley, Archive Film Productions, Plymouth.

25 I owe this information to Nadja Cholidis, Vorderasiatisches Museum Berlin. After intensive research, particularly in the USA, this film must be regarded as lost. However, the stereoscopic photographs taken by Dutkewich in Babylon are still extant.

Egypt travel brochure, 1927 (Pierre de Gigord collection, Paris)

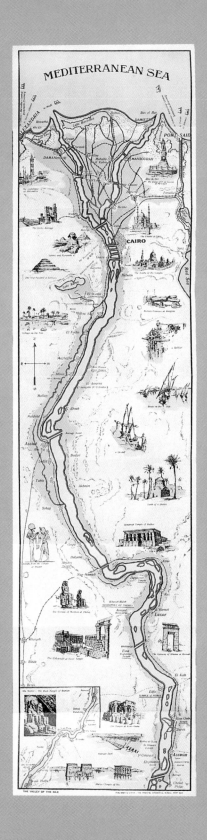

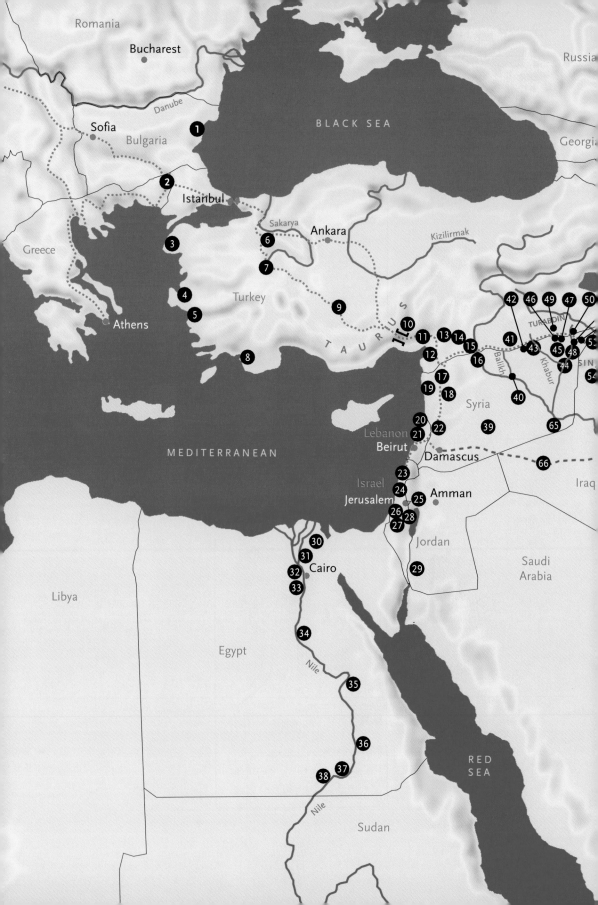

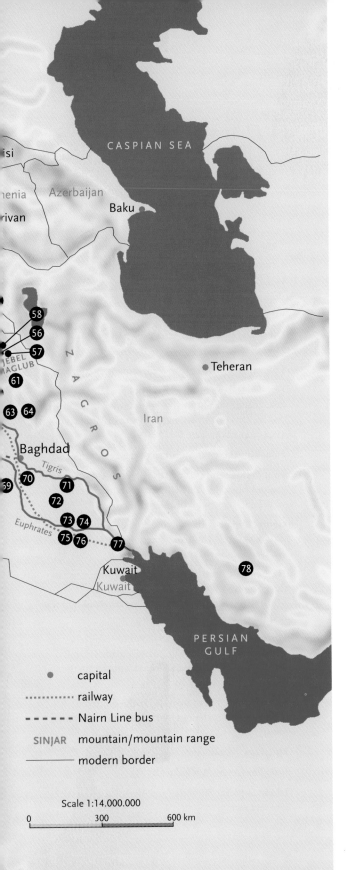

KEY

1	Varna	41	Harran
2	Pythiou	42	Tell Halaf
3	Troy	43	Ras el-Ain
4	Izmir	44	Hasseke
5	Ephesus	45	**Chagar Bazar**
6	Eskişehir	46	Tell Mozan
7	Ushak	47	Amuda
8	Xanthos	48	**Tell Brak**
9	Konya	49	Mardin
10	Cilician Gates	50	Nisibin
11	Adana	51	Kamichlie
12	Iskenderun	52	Tell Ziouane
13	Sakje Gözü	53	Tell Kotchek
14	Gaziantep	54	Tell al-Rimah
15	Carchemish	55	Tell Muhammed
16	Jerablus		Arab
17	Aleppo	56	Khorsabad
18	Ebla	57	**Tell Arpachiyah**
19	Ras Shamra	58	Tepe Gawra
20	Tripoli	59	**Nineveh** (Kuyunjik,
21	Byblos		Nebi Yunus, Tell
22	Homs		Yarimjah)
23	Haifa	60	**Nimrud**
24	Gezer	61	**Balawat**
25	Jericho	62	Mosul
26	Askalon	63	Nuzi
27	Lachish	64	Kirkuk
28	Qumran	65	Mari
29	Petra	66	Wadi Rutbah
30	Sile	67	Tell Aswad
31	Heliopolis	68	Ukhaidir
32	Gizeh	69	Kerbela
33	Memphis	70	Babylon
34	Amarna/Akhetaten	71	Kut
35	Deir el-Bahri,	72	Nippur
	Karnak, Luxor, Thebes	73	Uruk
36	Aswan	74	Nasiriyah
37	Wadi el-Sebua	75	Tell al-Ubaid
38	Abu Simbel	76	**Ur** (Tell Muqquyyar)
39	Palmyra	77	Basra
40	Raqqa	78	Shiraz

Bold type indicates Max Mallowan's
excavation sites

Glossary

Agate Mineral; microcrystalline quartz.

Akhnaton (Akhnaten) Egyptian Pharaoh (1353–1335 BC), husband of Nefertiti; lived at Tell el-Amarna.

Akkadian Semitic language of Babylonia and Assyria (ancient Iraq); found in cuneiform texts dating from before 2500 BC to the second century AD. The language of diplomacy in the Near East of the second millennium BC, also in use as a written language in Asia Minor, Syria and sometimes Egypt.

Al-magreb (Arab.) **call** The fourth of the muezzin's calls to prayer during the course of the day, before sunset.

Anubis Egyptian god of embalming, depicted as a jackal or a jackal-headed man.

Armenians People of Armenia, eastern Turkey, the north of Syria and northern Iraq. The Armenians converted to Christianity in the second century AD.

Ashurnasirpal II Assyrian king, 883–859 BC; Nimrud was his capital.

Assyria Region on the central Tigris, now part of northern Iraq; in antiquity, originally the area ruled by the kings of Assur. A powerful empire in the Near East from the thirteenth century BC onwards.

Aten The Aten was the Egyptian word for the disc of the sun, venerated by Akhnaton as the sole god.

Babylonia Historic region now part of Iraq on the lower Tigris and Euphrates, called after its old capital of Babylon.

Bakshish (Arab.) Money offered as a tip or bribe.

Bukranion Bull's head; often used as a motif on painted pottery.

Calibrate To adjust radiocarbon dates.

Carnelian A translucent variety of microquartz in shades of orange, red and red-brown.

Çayçi (Turk.) Waiter or maker of tea in teahouse.

Crush Syrian soft drink.

Deluge pit An excavation site in Ur which uncovered a level dating, according to its excavator Leonard Woolley, from the time of the Deluge story in the Bible.

Djezirah (Arab.) Island; term used for Upper Mesopotamia.

Epigraphist Scholar who reads ancient inscriptions.

Fez Conical cap made of red wool, traditional headgear of the Ottoman administration in the Orient and Balkans in the past, but not worn in Turkey since 1926 or in Egypt since 1953.

Fidos Knocking-off time, end of the day's work.

Foundation figures Protective objects deposited in the ground when the foundations of important buildings were laid; some items bear inscriptions.

Genies Protective deities; in ancient oriental art shown as winged human figures, or hybrid creatures often with the heads of birds.

Hashemites Arab dynasty in Iraq and Jordan, tracing their origin back to Hashim, an ancestor of Muhammad. The Hashemite ruling family of Iraq was dethroned in 1958.

Hittites People speaking an Indo-European language who founded an empire in Anatolia in the second millennium BC. Their capital was Hattusha, on the site of modern Boğazköy, Turkey.

Hoard Collection of items left in the ground as religious votive offerings, or buried in time of war for safety.

Hurrians *See* Mitanni

Inshallah (Arab.) 'As God wills.'

Ishtar Supreme Sumerian and Akkadian goddess of love and war.

Khan (*Pers.*) Oriental inn, caravanserai, large house with inner courtyard.

Lamassu Protective demon, winged hybrid of man and bull or lion, often placed at doorways or gateways.

Lapis lazuli (*Lat.*) Deep blue mineral.

'Locked room' crime Crime committed in an enclosed space by one of a number of restricted people.

Medes, Medians In antiquity, inhabitants of the mountainous highlands of north-west Iran who created an empire in the seventh century BC.

Mesopotamia (*Gr.*) Land between the rivers; the region between the central and upper Tigris and Euphrates. The term is primarily used in academic literature.

Mitanni State of the Hurrians in the fifteenth and fourteenth centuries BC in northern Mesopotamia, reaching at the time of its greatest extent from the eastern Tigris around Kirkuk to the Mediterranean.

Muezzin (*Arab.*) Man who calls Muslims to prayer five times a day from the minaret.

Mukhtar (*Arab.*) Village mayor.

Nabataeans North-west Arab tribe who settled south of the Dead Sea in the fifth and fourth centuries BC. Their capital was Petra from the middle of the second century BC.

Nabu Babylonian god of writing and wisdom.

Nefertiti Wife of Akhnaton.

Neutron activation analysis A method of scientific analysis to determine the presence of trace elements in the composition of an object.

Ninurta Sumerian and Akkadian god of vegetation, characterized by his warlike nature.

Obsidian Volcanic glassy rock, black to brown, often flecked with white.

Orthostat reliefs Stone slabs decorated with reliefs as protection and facing for walls.

Ostrakon (*Gr.*) Potsherd used in Egypt instead of the expensive medium of papyrus for writing a letter or other ephemeral document.

Phoenicia The old name for the narrow land strip of Syria and the Lebanon on the Mediterranean coast, from Nahr el-Kelb in the north to Carmel in the south.

Senna kelim Rug or wall hanging that looks the same on both sides, from the town of Senna in Kurdistan.

Sirdab (*Arab.*) Cellar; cool room; basement.

Stamp seal Seal in the form of a stamp pressed into malleable material such as clay to add authenticity to a document or letter.

Stratigraphy Series of levels in an excavation, allowing the finds to be dated. As a rule the top level is the most recent and the bottom layer the oldest.

Sumerian Language of the Sumerians; unrelated to any other language, ancient or modern. Died out as a spoken language *c.*1800 BC, but continued in use for religious purposes until the Seleucid period, 312–64 BC.

Tell (*Arab.*) Mound consisting of the debris from a settled area which has built up over the course of time.

Tholos, pl. tholoi (*Gr.*) Round building.

Tutankhamun Egyptian Pharaoh, son-in-law of Akhnaton, 1333–1323 BC.

Wadi (*Arab.*) Stream-bed which may fill with water in the rainy season. Dry valley in the desert.

Yezidis Members of a religious community living in the Sinjar mountains of Iraq. Their faith re-interprets old Islamic and Christian elements. Because of their fear of uttering the name of Satan or any names with a similar sound they are called 'devil-worshippers'.

Ziggurat Stepped tower; Akkadian term for a temple built on an artificial terrace. The Tower of Babel was a ziggurat.

Works by Agatha Christie

Crime novels

The Mysterious Affair at Styles, 1920
The Secret Adversary, 1922
Murder on the Links, 1923
The Man in the Brown Suit, 1924
The Secret of Chimneys, 1925
The Murder of Roger Ackroyd, 1926
The Big Four, 1927
The Mystery of the Blue Train, 1928
The Seven Dials Mystery, 1929
The Murder at the Vicarage, 1930
The Sittaford Mystery, 1931
Peril at End House, 1932
Lord Edgware Dies, 1933
Why Didn't They Ask Evans?, 1934
Murder on the Orient Express, 1934
Three Act Tragedy, 1935
Death in the Clouds, 1935
The ABC Murders, 1936
Murder in Mesopotamia, 1936
Cards on the Table, 1936
Death on the Nile, 1937
Dumb Witness, 1937
Appointment with Death, 1938
Hercule Poirot's Christmas, 1938
Murder is Easy, 1939
Ten Little Niggers, 1939
Sad Cypress, 1940
One, Two, Buckle my Shoe, 1941
Evil under the Sun, 1941
N or M?, 1941
The Body in the Library, 1942
Five Little Pigs, 1943
The Moving Finger, 1943
Towards Zero, 1944
Death Comes as the End, 1945
Sparkling Cyanide, 1945
The Hollow, 1946
Taken at the Flood, 1948
Crooked House, 1949

A Murder is Announced, 1950
They Came to Baghdad, 1951
Mrs. McGinty's Dead, 1952
They Do it with Mirrors, 1952
After the Funeral, 1953
A Pocket full of Rye, 1953
Destination Unknown, 1954
Hickory Dickory Dock, 1955
Dead Man's Folly, 1956
4.50 from Paddington, 1957
Ordeal by Innocence, 1958
Cat among the Pigeons, 1959
The Pale Horse, 1961
The Mirror Crack'd from Side to Side, 1962
The Clocks, 1963
A Caribbean Mystery, 1964
At Bertram's Hotel, 1965
Third Girl, 1966
Endless Night, 1967
By the Pricking of my Thumbs, 1968
Hallowe'en Party, 1969
Passenger to Frankfurt: An Extravaganza, 1970
Nemesis, 1971
Elephants Can Remember, 1972
Postern of Fate, 1973
Curtain, 1975
Sleeping Murder, 1976

Short stories

Poirot Investigates, 1924
Partners in Crime, 1929
The Mysterious Mr. Quin, 1930
The Thirteen Problems, 1932
The Hound of Death and Other Stories, 1933
The Listerdale Mystery, 1934
Parker Pyne Investigates, 1934
Murder in the Mews, 1937
The Regatta Mystery and Other Stories, 1939
The Labours of Hercules, 1947
Witness for the Prosecution and Other Stories, 1948

Three Blind Mice and Other Stories, 1950
The Underdog and Other Stories, 1951
The Adventure of the Christmas Pudding and a Selection of Entrees, 1960
Double Sin and Other Stories, 1961
The Golden Ball and Other Stories, 1971
Poirot's Early Cases, 1974
Miss Marple's Final Cases and Two Other Stories, 1979
Problem at Pollensa Bay, 1991
While the Light Lasts, 1997

Titles published under the pseudonym of Mary Westmacott

Giant's Bread, 1930
Unfinished Portrait, 1934
Absent in the Spring, 1944
The Rose and the Yew Tree, 1948
A Daughter's a Daughter, 1952
The Burden, 1956

Autobiographical works

Come, Tell Me How You Live, 1946
An Autobiography, 1977

Poems

The Road of Dreams, 1924
Star over Bethlehem and Other Stories, 1965
Poems, 1973

Plays

Black Coffee, 1930
Akhnaton, 1937 (published 1973)
Ten Little Niggers, 1943
Appointment with Death, 1945
Murder on the Nile, 1946
The Hollow, 1951
The Mousetrap, 1952
Witness for the Prosecution, 1953
Spider's Web, 1954
Towards Zero, 1956
Verdict, 1958
The Unexpected Guest, 1958
Go Back for Murder, 1960
Rule of Three, 1962

Plays from works by Agatha Christie

Alibi, 1928
Love from a Stranger, 1936
Peril at the End of the House, 1940
The Murder at the Vicarage, 1949
Fiddlers Three, 1972
A Murder is Announced, 1977
Cards on the Table, 1981

Picture Credits